ROUTLEDGE LIBRARY EDITIONS:
THE LABOUR MOVEMENT

Volume 41

RECONSTRUCTION, AFFLUENCE AND LABOUR POLITICS

RECONSTRUCTION, AFFLUENCE AND LABOUR POLITICS

Coventry, 1945–1960

NICK TIRATSOO

Routledge
Taylor & Francis Group
LONDON AND NEW YORK

First published in 1990 by Routledge

This edition first published in 2019
by Routledge
2 Park Square, Milton Park, Abingdon, Oxon OX14 4RN

and by Routledge
711 Third Avenue, New York, NY 10017

Routledge is an imprint of the Taylor & Francis Group, an informa business

British Library Cataloguing in Publication Data
A catalogue record for this book is available from the British Library

ISBN: 978-1-138-32435-0 (Set)
ISBN: 978-0-429-43443-3 (Set) (ebk)
ISBN: 978-1-138-32634-7 (Volume 41) (hbk)
ISBN: 978-0-429-44987-1 (Volume 41) (ebk)

Publisher's Note
The publisher has gone to great lengths to ensure the quality of this reprint but points out that some imperfections in the original copies may be apparent.

Disclaimer
The publisher has made every effort to trace copyright holders and would welcome correspondence from those they have been unable to trace.

The Reconstruction of Coventry 1945–1960

"OH, FOR THE GOOD OLD DAYS BEFORE YOU WERE BORN...!"

Reconstruction, affluence and Labour politics: Coventry 1945–60

N. Tiratsoo

ROUTLEDGE
London and New York

First published 1990
by Routledge
11 New Fetter Lane, London EC4P 4EE

Simultaneously published in the USA and Canada
by Routledge
a division of Routledge, Chapman and Hall, Inc.
29 West 35th Street, New York, NY 10001

Typeset in 10/12pt Times by
Megaron, Cardiff, Wales
Printed in Great Britain by
Biddles Ltd, Guildford, Surrey

British Library Cataloguing in Publication Data
Tiratsoo, Nick
Reconstruction, affluence and Labour politics : Coventry, 1945–1960.
1. West Midlands (Metropolitan County). Coventry. Local government, history
I. Title II. Series
352.042498

ISBN 0-415-04877-X

Library of Congress Cataloging in Publication Data
Tiratsoo, Nick, 1952–
Reconstruction, affluence and Labour politics : Coventry, 1945–1960 / Nick Tiratsoo.
p. cm.—(Britain in the twentieth century)
ISBN 0-415-04877-X : $30.00
1. Coventry (England)—Politics and government.
2. Coventry (England)—Economic conditions.
3. Reconstruction (1939–1951)—England—Coventry.
I. Title II. Series
DA690.C75T57 1990
942.4'98—dc20

Contents

Tables

Statistical Appendix

Acknowledgements

The research on which this work is based was compiled during 1986–8 while I was Senior Research Fellow at the Centre for the Study of Social History, University of Warwick. I am indebted to the Volkswagenwerk Stiftung (which supported me financially), Professor D. Petzina and the staff of the Centre for making this opportunity possible. I would particularly like to thank Dr Tony Mason of the Centre for his kindness and intellectual advice during my years at Warwick.

Secondly, I would like to acknowledge with gratitude the considerable help I have received from various archivists, notably David Rimmer and the staff at the Coventry Record Office, Richard Storey and the staff at the Modern Records Centre, University of Warwick, and the librarians who deal with Local Studies at the Coventry City Library.

Thirdly, I am grateful to a number of organisations for permission to quote from their archives, and wish to record my particular appreciation of the privileges granted to me in this connection by, amongst others, Alvis, the British Motor Industry Heritage Trust, Coventry City Council, Coventry Labour Party, the Rolls-Royce Heritage Trust and A. H. Realisations Ltd.

Finally, I would like to thank all those individuals who have advised me on different aspects of post-war history – especially Louise Campbell, Steve Fielding, John Gold, Richard Hyman, Junichi Hasegawa, David Thoms and Jim Tomlinson. I owe a more general debt to Pat Thane who gave encouragement and good counsel during the preparation of the manuscript.

1 Introduction

Few places in Britain felt the impact of the Second World War as vividly or as consistently as Coventry. An important engineering centre, with a history of motor vehicle production, the city found itself from the first caught up in the armaments drive. Such specialisation in turn inevitably brought considerable attention from the German air force, with the raids of 1940 and 1941 destroying much of the urban area's inner core. The central aim of the chapters that follow is to describe how Coventry recovered from these experiences, and subsequently emerged in the 1950s not only as a nationally known 'boom town', but also as an exemplar of a new type of city, in tune with the demands of a modern, more democratic and equitable age. In particular, this means giving considerable attention to the plans and policies of Coventry's Labour party, since it was this body, using its continuing domination of the city Council, that was most involved in attempting to shape the various facets of reconstruction – physical, social and economic. But emphasis will also be placed on the context within which this shaping took place, and on the incentives and constraints which encouraged or retarded the achievement of the Labour party's vision. Reference will be made, for example, to the web of connections which linked the city to the variety of interested government departments in London. On the other hand, it will also be necessary to explore Labour's relationship with the local electorate, and especially the growing disenchantment with the party which began to threaten its dominance during the 1950s.

In one sense, then, this is very much a local study, which seeks to use the kind of integrated approach to urban history adopted by, for example, Waller and Whiting (where the focus is not just on one dimension of a spatial form, but rather on the inter-relationship of its particular economy, society and polity) and apply it to the, as yet, relatively unstudied post-war years.[1] But the detailed local material will also be used to evaluate some broader historical questions. Indeed, specific features of Coventry's history make it something of a test case for two controversies that are at the heart of all interpretations of contemporary British history.

The first concerns the very nature of the reconstruction process. Most historians are agreed that the war years saw an upsurge of popular radicalism across the country, a phenomenon that posed some basic questions about the future peace-time shape of British society. But there is very much less agreement about what happened subsequently to this impulse. Barnett has argued that the 'New Jerusalemists' were triumphant, and as a consequence reconstruction was skewed towards welfare provision. This he judges to have been disastrous, for while a realistic 'national corporate strategy' might have secured the country's economic future after 1945, large-scale spending on housing and hospitals could not, so that Britain has inevitably gradually slipped down the international wealth league.[2] Against this, a number of leftist critics of Labour – Miliband, and more recently Blackwell and Seabrook, and Saville[3] – paint a very different picture. Here, the popular radicalism of the war years is portrayed not as victorious, but rather as effectively neutered, a consequence both of leadership betrayals or pusillanimity, and the sponge-like, absorbent qualities of the British state. In these accounts then, the emphasis is not on reconstruction but rather on restoration – the restoration of capitalism's potency.

Clearly, the examination of a city which was a bastion of Labour progressivism and at the same time a leading engineering centre will allow some evaluation to be made of these various propositions. It will be possible to comment, first of all, on the ubiquitous assumption that there was a war-time consensus for change. How far did Labour hold sway in Coventry at this time, and on what issues and promises was its support built? Alongside these kinds of questions, a number of others will have to be asked about the subsequent pattern of local reconstruction. To what extent were the Council's ambitious plans for extending services and amenities in Coventry in fact realised between 1945 and 1960? Is there any evidence of a clash between 'welfare' and 'economic' objectives in the reconstruction process? And, finally, if there is, can government departments be shown to have leant with any consistency towards one side or the other in their dealings with the city?

The second area of historiographical controversy which will be extensively referred to concerns what has been termed the 'affluent worker question'. This controversy has its roots in the mid-1950s, when a number of social commentators started arguing that British society was undergoing a profound transition, as large numbers of people – and particularly the upper sections of the working class – began acquiring new kinds of consumer durables (televisions, fridges and washing machines) at an ever-increasing pace.[4] What made this trend so significant was not so much the pattern of spreading ownership itself, as the changing social and political climate which it was allegedly ushering in. For it was widely believed that the new goods encouraged emulation of middle-class virtues and pursuits (the home, security, self-advancement and possessions) and discouraged older, proletarian beliefs in collective activity – as Harry Hopkins put it, 'semi-detachment on the Open Plan sapped solidarity'.[5] The cumulative effect of all of this was that Britain might now be observed becoming what *The Economist* termed an 'Unproletarian Society'.[6]

This kind of theorising was not without its critics, who pointed out, amongst other things, that the changes going on were perhaps not as great as some people thought; and that, anyway, the gap between the classes was not diminishing, since middle-class norms were changing, too.[7] But the question seemed finally to have been resolved in 1959 when the Conservatives, appealing to the newly upwardly mobile with the slogan 'You've had it good. Have it better, vote Conservative', pulled off a third successive general election victory.[8] It could now widely be argued that, in the changed circumstances, Labour would be doomed to endless failure unless it ditched its traditional ideology.[9]

Over the subsequent years, this embourgeoisement thesis (as it came to be known) has undergone a chequered career. Labour victories in 1964 and 1966 seemed to cast some doubt on its empirical validity, and scepticism was further increased when the findings from Goldthorpe et al.'s Luton survey were published.[10] For what this enquiry showed was that, certainly in so far as that town's car, engineering and chemical workers were concerned, little evidence existed for any widespread adoption of middle-class concerns. What was happening, rather, involved a far more subtle change in older patterns, as workers adopted an essentially instrumental view of politics. Support for Labour amongst the 'traditional' working class, it was argued, had tended to be almost instinctive, continually encouraged by experiences at work (where 'us and them' attitudes were pervasive) and in tightly demarcated, very insular local communities. By contrast, the specific forms of working and living arrangements that were prevalent in Luton – especially the privatised natures of family life and leisure pursuits – encouraged a rather different orientation. Workers were shown to be most concerned with individualistic goals, and while this did not necessarily herald the end of collective action, it did mean that support for Labour was becoming more conditional, dependent on whether the party could deliver a range of social and economic benefits. Labour's future, therefore, hinged upon how well it could adapt to this new situation.

More recently, however, variants of the embourgeoisement theory have made something of a comeback. Thus, Blackwell and Seabrook have referred to the 'remaking' of the working class that was occurring in the 1950s, as 'capitalism was able to extend its transforming power deeper and deeper into the lives of men and women'.[11] A more scholarly study by Crewe also gives some support to the embourgeoisement thesis. Crewe's focus is on the electoral histories of affluent working-class constituencies – urban constituencies with high levels of home- and car-ownership – between 1955 and 1970, in order to discover whether there was any long-term shift to the right (as the embourgeoisement theory might predict) or whether instrumental attitudes (and thus volatile patterns of voting) are discernible. He concludes that the evidence does not provide any very clear picture, but while there is some moderate support for embourgeoisement from the data, it proved impossible to find even a minority of constituencies that conformed to a pattern of instrumentalism.[12]

Again, the Coventry case study can provide a useful vantage point for reassessing the merits of these various claims, especially since car workers (who made up a high proportion of the indigenous working class) were often cited as at the very centre of whatever changes were going on.[13] Labour did lose ground in the city over the 1950s, but can this simply be ascribed to the popular experience of prosperity? Conversely, to what extent were purely political factors, like the choice of candidate or leading issue, alone responsible for the pattern of events?

Of course, this is not the first survey of Coventry's post-war history, and so this brief overview should conclude by outlining what the existing accounts have to say, and how they fit into the wider debates on reconstruction and affluence. The first wave of studies of the city, completed during the late 1960s and early 1970s, were generally celebratory in tone, and emphasised both the degree of co-operation that was evident in the post-war years (with very different interests and personalities broadly supporting the Labour Council's overall planning perspective) and the considerable element of success that marked the translation of aims into reality.[14]

More recently interpretations have tended to be very much less favourable. Indeed, for some, Coventry is a prime example of 'what went wrong' – the eclipse, during the 1950s and the 1960s, of the idealism that had fuelled Labour's 1945 election victory, and the subsequent resurgence of iniquitous urban and economic arrangements.[15] Specific explanations as to why Coventry should have conformed so closely to this pattern vary, with stress being placed on factors like the machinations of local building and engineering employers,[16] and the penetrative and transforming power of the market.[17] More commonly, the heart of the problem is seen as lying with one or more parts of the city's labour movement. Hinton argues, for example, that a key moment came during the last eighteen months of the war, when the Communist party, which had previously maintained a strong local presence, found itself increasingly at odds with leftward moving public opinion. This mistake, which originated in the party's over-concern with Moscow rather than Coventry, meant that the radical upsurge was leaderless and therefore ultimately impotent.[18] For Lancaster and Mason, the culprits lay one step to the right, in the Labour-dominated Council. Coventry, it is suggested, was strongly behind a socialist programme for reconstruction in the post-war years, but the local authority's lack of preparedness in planning (particularly over housing) and lack of political will in execution (which meant that, perhaps because of interest group pressure, redevelopment of the central shopping area took precedence over all other kinds of building) led, once again, to a growth in popular apathy and disillusionment.[19] Thirdly, reference must be made to Thompson's recent analysis of factory culture in the Coventry car industry.[20] Thompson's major concern is with how Luddite values on the shop-floor retarded technical innovation and economic progress. However, in parenthesis, he is quite critical of the local engineering unions, and certainly implies that, had they adopted a more open perspective (as their counterparts in Turin allegedly did), Coventry might have turned out a very different place. The general thrust of these arguments will have to be given very careful attention in the course of the following pages.

It remains, then, only to provide a brief guide to how this book is organised. For ease of exposition, the text has been divided into two sets of four chapters, so as to reflect the break between the post-war Labour Governments (1945–50, 1950–1) and the Conservative administrations of the 1950s (1951–5, 1955–9). The structure of each section is broadly comparable, covering, first, ideas and plans (Chapters 2 and 6), then the economy (Chapters 3 and 7), next the built-environment (Chapters 4 and 8) and finally politics and culture (Chapters 5 and 9). Chapter 10 presents some conclusions on Coventry, and tries to set the city's experience in a wider, national context. Fairly full references are included in the hope that these will be of help to other scholars (particularly other local scholars) who wish to follow up some of the points raised.

2 The politics of reconstruction: war-time plans for a new Coventry

In comparison with many other British cities, Coventry's experience of the Second World War was unusually intense. Long an engineering centre, the city was quickly assimilated into the national drive for munitions and weapons, so that, at a peak, perhaps 70 per cent of its working population were engaged on war work.[1] Such an intense involvement could only bring pressing social problems, since an already ill-formed built-environment had now to cope with waves of immigrants drawn to the booming local factories. Superimposed on all of this were the effects of the German air-raids of 1940 and 1941 – damaged housing and amenities, and an almost destroyed city centre.

This chapter traces the evolution of war-time thinking about how to cope with this legacy, and about what kind of future the city was to have with the coming of peace. Necessarily, this will mean giving considerable attention to the activities of the Labour Council, since this body was uniquely placed, with the cessation of electoral politics from 1939, to dominate many facets of the local reconstruction debate. But it will also become apparent that Coventry's planning can hardly be considered in a vacuum, since ideas and aspirations generated in the city were often discussed, indeed encouraged or opposed, in Whitehall. Questions about Coventry's future, in fact, to some extent became entangled in a wider conflict which dogged the Coalition Government, as to how it was to reconcile the 'idealism' that had been encouraged in the early years of the war with the 'realism' that some of its leading members felt would be necessary in the peace.[2] The outcome here, it will be suggested, was a situation of ambiguity and uncertainty, with the Council, buoyed up by considerable local support, clinging to a series of planning decisions it had made in the face of mounting pressure from Whitehall.

In order to begin to unravel the pattern of war-time events, it will be necessary briefly to recapitulate certain aspects of the local scene in the last years of peace. For the specific nature of the reconstruction debate in

Coventry during the early 1940s, it seems clear, was shaped partly by a particular set of urban problems and political strategies which had originated over the previous two decades.[3]

In the 1920s and 1930s, as is well known, Coventry's population grew at an exceptional rate, so that the total in 1939 – 220,000 – was 75 per cent up on the 1921 figure. Much of this growth was due to immigration, prompted by the attractions of the city's booming motor and general engineering sectors. Yet if Coventry was thus increasingly very proletarian in terms of its class structure, it was also abnormally deficient in terms of some of the kinds of working-class organisation found elsewhere. For the specific character of local industries, the historic weakness of the left in the city, and the impact of migration, had all combined to weaken the appeal of union membership and radical politics. Instead, the city developed something of a 'Klondike' atmosphere, with low rates of overcrowding, and high rates of popular house-ownership and personal consumption. The rearmament boom after 1937 reinforced these trends, and drew more away from the insecurities of unemployment and poverty. The city became remarked-upon for its affluent and self-confident working class, both used to, and desiring more of, a widening range of comforts.[4]

But, as a number of visitors noted, if Coventry was 'a good place in which to earn a living', it was also 'a bad place to live in'.[5] In part, this was because the built-environment exhibited a multiplicity of defects stemming from the phenomenal rate of overall growth.[6] The city centre, for example, based as it was on medieval scale and plan, had now become overcongested and dangerous for pedestrians.[7] At the same time, a surrounding ring of tangled slums and small industrial developments provided unsatisfactory living and working conditions. Nor, finally, could much be said for the ribbon expansion that was taking place on the periphery, since although individual houses might be relatively well-built, the new estates lacked both coherence and facilities.[8]

On top of these problems, Coventrians also suffered from a dearth of the kind of amenities that could be found elsewhere. There were few open spaces, firstly, because land was simply too valuable to leave undeveloped. Moreover, Council expenditure on social provision remained very low, reinforcing Coventry's reputation as an educational and cultural desert.[9] Finally, a local economy skewed towards manufacturing meant that the service sector was generally underdeveloped, so that the choice of shops, for example, was narrower than could be found in various other nearby Midlands cities.[10]

These problems prompted considerable local comment and a growing concern, from the mid-1930s, with reform.[11] The Tory-Liberal Coalition, which had dominated Coventry politics for nearly a decade, attempted to answer its critics by purchasing land for possible future development and at the same time persevering with existing town planning legislation, but this approach proved inadequate in terms of both scope and speed.[12] Labour, on the other hand, as the party of opposition, was untainted by these failures, and so could credibly present itself as the agent of action and efficiency. Helped by good organisation and the lassitude of its opponents, this strategy finally paid off at the local elections of 1937.[13] If the radical content of the party's campaign was fairly modest,[14] its emphasis on the need for a more efficiently planned and run city was emphatic. Labour promised welfare reforms – key activists certainly respected Winifred Holtby's exhortation that local government should be 'the first-line defence thrown up by the community against our common enemies – poverty, sickness, ignorance, isolation, mental derangement and social maladjustment'[15] — but it also underlined its aim of using existing resources to better ends, a strategy which would allow the maintenance of a rate stabilisation policy.[16] In the event, just enough were convinced, and Labour scraped home with 51 per cent of a 47 per cent turn-out.[17]

In office, the Labour party rapidly began to construct an agenda for reform. One early innovation was the creation of a Policy Advisory Committee (PAC) to decide on priorities.[18] Here, the Council was immediately caught in something of a dilemma. For it could not ignore the simple fact that municipal outgoings were already outstripping revenue from rated properties, largely because the extensive growth of the city had required considerable expenditure on infrastructure, such as sewers.[19] Given this situation, provision for a full programme of capital works – and the PAC was flooded with 'urgent' cases from the various Council sub-committees – could only lead to a large rate rise (possibly of 4s. in the pound, or 30 per cent), and thus the abandonment of any attempt at the kind of stabilisation policy Labour had pledged itself to during the recent campaign. In the end, therefore, the PAC was forced to opt for caution, and operate within the constraint of a 6d. rate rise. Thus, the Council's Five Year Programme, ratified at the beginning of 1939, aimed only at a modest 1.5 million target, with the emphasis on new streets (24 per cent of the total projected expenditure), education (23 per cent) and town planning or land sterilisation schemes (19 per cent).[20]

In parallel with these discussions, attention was also given to the question of how municipal development work could be carried out coherently, and after some debate it was decided, during 1938, that in future all the architectural aspects of projected schemes should be handled by a new department, headed by a City Architect.[21]

The first official appointed to this post, Donald Gibson, perhaps appeared as an unlikely choice, since he was both young and relatively inexperienced.[22] Yet, in terms of outlook, Gibson's views certainly had much in common with those of his new employers. For example, his experience at the Liverpool University School of Architecture[23] had clearly led him, if not to out and out modernism, at least to a strong belief that good architecture was desirable not just in terms of aesthetic improvement but also in terms of social reform.[24] At the same time, he vigorously believed in the need for, and efficacy of, trained experts, who could operate free from bureaucratic niceties, views which again closely matched those prevalent amongst key local Labour politicians.[25]

To put these ideas into practice, Gibson was allowed to form a small department. Indicatively, he began by recruiting a number of more self-consciously radical architects, so that the Association of Architects, Surveyors and Technical Assistants soon had a strong Coventry presence.[26] With its establishment settled, the department then began to consider the skeleton of the city, and how best it could intervene in the growing debate about future development.

The outbreak of war in 1939 immediately acted to increase all Coventry's town planning and amenity problems. For the city was now swamped by a wave of immigrants – as many as 4,000 to 5,000 per month in the summer of 1940[27] – drawn to work in the eight large government-financed but privately managed 'shadow' factories that had been established round its boundary.[28] This, together with the 'exaggerated specialisation' already engendered by armaments production,[29] put almost unbearable strain on the service and transport sectors, while at the same time producing considerable overcrowding in local homes.[30]

In response, Gibson's department redoubled its efforts to spread town planning ideals. Attempts were made to involve members of the Council (e.g. by distributing amongst them, on its publication in 1940, copies of Lewis Mumford's *The Culture of Cities*)[31] and also to interest and educate the general public through lectures and an exhibition on the 'Coventry of Tomorrow'. This latter event, held over a week in May 1940, was significant, not only because of its impact (it was seen by 5,000 people, including nearly all the senior schoolchildren in the city), but also because of its decidedly innovative content (which sprang in part from the heavy involvement of the Modern Architecture Research Group).[32]

Then, quite suddenly, a new ingredient was added to the situation, as Coventry came under sustained attack from the German air force. In all, the raids of November 1940 and April 1941 damaged at least 50,000 of the city's 75,000 rated properties in some way, though most of the serious destruction was concentrated in the central core.[33] Amongst the 'destroyed or damaged beyond repair' category of buildings were 4,185 houses (or 7 per cent of the 1938 inhabitable dwellings)[34]; while the city also lost school space for over 4,000 pupils.[35] More than one observer, visiting Coventry after the raids, was reminded of Ypres in the First World War;[36] subsequently, the gutted ruins of the Cathedral became an international symbol of local suffering.

At first, the Council's response to this disaster was necessarily framed in terms of crisis control. But, as the immediate danger receded, attention was focused on the question of how the damage should be repaired. Gibson was characteristically quick to point out the potential:

> Many citizens had despaired of the possibility of having a dignified and fitting city centre. High land values, the delays involved by town planning legislation, together with a lack of plan for the central area, made it seem impossible. Now . . . all this was changed . . . like a forest fire the present evil might bring forth greater riches and beauty.[37]

Meanwhile, Sir John Reith, the recently appointed Minister of Works, let it be known that he too favoured bold measures, hinting that finance would not be a problem, since the Government was coming to the view that individual councils could not, and indeed should not, bear the burden of blitz repair. Coventry, the Minister added, would be a 'test-case' to help him frame future legislation.[38]

With these assurances in mind, any prevarication seemed pointless, and so the Council quickly turned its attention to the problem of how best to secure comprehensive reconstruction. Future intentions were marked by the creation of a special Redevelopment Committee ('to secure . . . worthy re-planning and redevelopment');[39] and by the decision, in February 1941,[40] to back Gibson's radical scheme for the central core,[41] instead of a more conservative proposal.[42] Subsequently, over the next three years, discussion shifted to the wider questions of overall zoning, communications, housing and education, with major conclusions from departmental heads being presented both formally in a series of reports to the Council[43] and more informally in various journal articles, conference papers and broadcasts.[44]

In compiling their plans for Coventry, officials drew inspiration from a number of sources. The Architect's Department had certainly been impressed, to repeat, by Mumford's *The Culture of Cities*, no doubt partly because of its apocalyptic tone and anti-fascist rhetoric, but also because of its cogent argument that future reform would have to be sweeping in character and centrally related to social need.[45] Le

Corbusier's *The City of Tomorrow* provoked interest too,[46] although the works of a number of British architects and town planners – Abercrombie,[47] Alker Tripp[48] and above all Thomas Sharp[49] – probably exerted somewhat greater overall influence. Gibson himself, more practitioner than ideologue, wished to repeat successful features of locations he was familiar with – the harmony of some English villages, and the vitality and functional good sense of Chester's historic two-level shopping rows, for example.[50]

Alongside these influences were a less clearly defined set of assumptions about the optimum sociological arrangement of a city population. It seems to have been agreed, to give one illustration, that 'community' should be (and indeed could be) a central object of planning,[51] which in turn drew attention to the burgeoning literature proposing the neighbourhood unit as the fundamental constituent of any well-organised urban society.[52]

In moving to the practical application of these ideas, the planners were particularly struck by the almost total absence of proper zoning in the city. But they also noted that recent developments – the siting of the 'shadow' factories round the perimeter, the concentration of damage in the centre – did suggest the outline of a new pattern, in which industry at least might be separated in part from the other functions.[53] A more serious problem was represented by the shape and character of the existing residential areas. The central slums would clearly need to be demolished. But ribbon development at the periphery, so pervasive in the inter-war years, was also felt to be deficient, both because of the design of the individual units (monotonous frontages, linear repetition, etc.) and because of the general layout of the estates (lack of amenity, expense of extensive development, etc.).[54]

To meet these problems, the planners recommended a broad delimitation of the urban area according to function, with different zones linked by a 'spider's web' of roads. This meant, for example, that future industrial development would be encouraged only in specific locations – e.g. in the north-east of the city and along the railway line to Birmingham – away from residential areas.

Gibson's original plan for the central core provided a focus for this pattern. For within the innermost ring road were to be grouped a range of common, servicing functions, including a civic centre (grouping together all the different local and national government operations) and a new shopping zone, constructed around a traffic-free, galleried, cruciform precinct. Gibson had begun here from the needs of the user, but he had also kept in mind aesthetic considerations, by composing the different elements so as to highlight pleasing vistas whenever possible.

On housing, the proferred solutions were both more detailed and more complicated. In broad organisational terms, it was agreed that, as the neighbourhood unit theorists suggested, residential areas should be redefined into a number of similarly-sized units, co-ordinated around natural centres and using existing boundaries like roads or canals, and provided with identical sets of welfare facilities. In the central core, it was recognised, this would inevitably mean the building of flats, since there was no other way to gain enough land for amenity provision.

But Gibson was also concerned to give the Council some idea of housing need, since it was becoming clear that this issue, above most others, was at the heart of many popular concerns about the post-war world. Here, the architect started from the assumption that the city's population would be likely to reach 250,000 by 1950. Next, he demonstrated that, on the basis of billeting survey data, the current housing stock (ignoring slum property) of 60,000 units could suitably shelter about 168,000 people. Accommodation for some 82,000 would therefore have to be provided by 1950. Using various projections of population structure, and incorporating a range of assumptions about the likely requirements for gardens and the trend of the birth-rate, this translated into a need for 4,000 bungalows (to cater for the aged); 6,500 bed units in hostels and 9,100 service flats (to cater for single people); and 15,800 houses. In all, expenditure on this programme could be expected to reach about £25 million over a six-year period.[55]

Of course, these figures were daunting, but Councillors clearly felt that, if their wider ideals were to be achieved, they had no option but to accept Gibson's advice.[56] In a significant rider, it was decided that the private sector should be encouraged to play an important role in future developments: building firms would be contracted for Corporation work, but they would also be allowed to use 50 per cent of their output for private clients.[57] The Council emphasised that, by adopting this policy, it was removing any threat of 'socialistic inroads' from the local building industry.[58]

In the four years after the Council's adoption of the Gibson scheme for the central core, a range of interests and agencies sought either to modify or confirm the thrust of the city's reconstruction planning. Local opinion remained squarely behind the Corporation's general aims, although there were some doubts as to the details. Elsewhere in Britain, the story of the city's 'martyrdom' and subsequent resolution to rebuild with vision seemed to symbolise a new hope for a better post-war society. Against these positive forces were ranged a set of less encouraging responses originating in Whitehall. For as the direct threat to British cities from the air receded, so government concern with radical solutions to the problem of reconstruction tended to diminish and be replaced by more cautious emphases on 'realism'. Coventry therefore soon found itself under considerable pressure to modify the scale of its proposals, with particular criticism being directed at what was characterised as the 'grandiose' plan for the central area. At the same time, it gradually became clear that local attempts to intervene in decision-making about certain wider aspects of Coventry's future – particularly its industrial future – would not generally be received with much sympathy by civil servants, a trend that seemed likely to jeopardise the kind of ordered process of reconstruction favoured by the Coventry planners. Each of these sets of influences will now be examined in greater detail.

Support for the Corporation's proposals came from a range of different sources. In Coventry, there was some criticism as to details – worries about the likely cost of the schemes[59] or about the 'alien' proposal for flats,[60] and outright opposition from the Chamber of Commerce to the precinct idea.[61] But there was also no doubting the high level of popular support for the general aim of bold re-planning.[62]

National (even, on occasion, international) media coverage was also mainly favourable. Ernest Benn's *Truth* might call Gibson's ideas for the city centre 'the first notable product of all the Priestley and other nonsense about the millennium after the war',[63] but coverage in other papers and on the B.B.C. was far more positive.[64] In fact the frequency and character of discussion about Coventry in the media, and also in the voluminous popular pamphlet literature of the war years,[65] created the idea that the city's example was very much one that all should follow.

More specific judgements tended to confirm this picture. There was, for example, growing agreement among architects and planners that specific ideas incorporated into the Coventry plans – the precinct and the neighbourhood units, in particular – would be key elements in all post-war reconstruction.[66] More significantly, the King himself was apparently enthusiastic about at least some of what was proposed, as he disclosed during a brief visit to Coventry in early 1942:

> he was particularly satisfied at finding incorporated in the plans for the new Coventry an idea for arranging central shopping facilities under the arcading principle . . . the King . . . expressed the opinion that in all schemes of re-planning towns and cities which had been badly bombed, the future amenities for the citizens were of supreme importance. The King expressed the hope that his visit . . . would help make such plans materialise.[67]

Finally, it is important to stress in the light of what follows that although many interventions by government officials after 1941 were of a negative character, this was not universally the case. Coventry remained a potent symbol in much official and quasi-official propaganda, for example. At the same time, though general ameliorative measures launched from the centre – special financial assistance[68] or help with rubble clearance and rebuilding[69] – had no necessary links at all with wider departmental judgements on local planning, they could be read in Coventry as covertly supporting Reith's early promises.

Yet, if the Council could draw some considerable support from these different sources, it had also to recognise that many of its key ideas were very far from being accepted in Whitehall. Officials there were sceptical about Gibson's housing estimates, for example.[70] But most displeasure was reserved for the city centre plan, especially after Reith had been dismissed from the Government in February 1942. In fact, from mid-1942 until the end of the war, pressure to modify this proposal was rarely relaxed, so that the city found itself subject to almost endless exhortation and investigation, orchestrated from the newly formed Ministry of Town and Country Planning, and using such channels as the Advisory Panel of experts on blitz reconstruction.[71]

The aspect of the problem that particularly concerned the civil servants was finance. Gibson's original formulation contained only vague references to costs,[72] while subsequent Council statements, encouraged both by the initial thrust of ministerial policy and the Uthwatt recommendations of September 1942 on purchasing and compensation arrangements, simply repeated the local conviction that the problem should be solved by national legislation.[73] Yet, when the City Treasurer was finally persuaded by Advisory Panel pressure to make a full financial evaluation, Coventry's plan was revealed as being unusually expensive, largely because of the scale of the civic facilities proposed.[74] At the same time, the amount of 'dead' land (parks and other open spaces) in the scheme seemed to undermine the possibility of adequate future return.[75]

However, in their dealings with the city, the civil servants were very conscious of a number of potential political pitfalls. There was some general public concern about the way the Government was moving on town planning legislation anyway, and the terms of the new Act proposed in early 1944 further disappointed those who had expected radical change.[76] In Coventry, this kind of unease was all the greater because of the city's predicament, and considerable antipathy towards the Government continued to lurk just beneath the surface of public opinion. The Ministry was worried that too much of the wrong sort of pressure on the Council – for instance against the civic centre *per se* – would provoke a backlash. It was advised that in any trial of strength the Council might receive backing from two-thirds of the local electorate.[77]

Given these constraints, any vaguely political criticism of the Coventry plan became unacceptably risky. The Ministry therefore decided to concentrate on a range of technical points – the need for an adequate survey of future user requirements, for example – and thereby persuade the Council that it needed the advice of expert, 'responsible' interests.[78]

However, if the Ministry initially had high hopes for this kind of approach, the period of optimism did not last long. For Coventry Council proved adept at playing the Westminster game, and the enquiries on technical points were either shrugged off or answered by counter-questions, which could on occasion embarrass the civil servants concerned.[79] At the same time, hopes of developing local pressure through the Chamber of Commerce also quickly faded, as that organisation's long-awaited alternative plan for the shopping centre turned out to be patently unsuitable.[80]

The Town and Country Planning Act of November 1944 at first seemed to promise the possibility of resolving the deadlock. Councils were now offered some guidance as to their legal powers and a possible agenda to follow in the prosecution of reconstruction schemes. But, while this degree of clarification was generally welcomed, local authorities were much less impressed by the financial provisions of the new legislation. In fact, a number clearly decided to continue a policy of prevarication on certain key issues, in the hope that a return to electoral politics at the end of the war might lead to a more benevolent set of terms.[81] In Coventry, the Council's ability to pursue this strategy was founded upon its close, continuing identification with popular reconstruction enthusiasms.

One clear implication of the 1944 Act was that progress on planning schemes would not be officially recognised until consultations with local interest groups had been adequately pursued. Consequently, over the course of 1945, the tone of negotiations between Coventry Council and the Chamber of Commerce became very much more constructive, with both sides plainly interested in compromise. Attention was once again focused on the precinct idea and its various merits and disadvantages. The Council, following Gibson, stressed safety and convenience. The Chamber, on the other hand, emphasised the importance of custom and practice in shopping patterns, and argued for the necessity of vehicular access. In the end, both views were incorporated into a modified scheme: one axis of the proposed cruciform shopping precinct would be constructed as a normal road, while the other would remain for pedestrians only.[82]

If local negotiations thus proceeded fairly smoothly, relations between city and Ministry continued much as before, with the emphasis on bluff and manoeuvre. Government officials were deeply dissatisfied with the lack of progress, since they feared bad publicity if Coventry, still in the national eye, was seen to be less advanced in its reconstruction plans than other blitzed cities.[83] And they also could not ignore the widespread local enthusiasm for reconstruction, nor the success of various organised talks, films and displays on planning.[84] In this situation, there seemed to be no other choice but to continue with the policy of technical criticism and discussion over detail. By mid-1945, then, the Ministry officials were coming to the view that no major progress would be likely until the political uncertainty accompanying the cessation of hostilities was fully resolved.[85]

Alongside this dispute over the city centre, Coventry Corporation was also drawn into a second area of controversy with Whitehall. Local planners had recognised from the first that their success in rebuilding would depend ultimately, not just on questions of finance, but also on a wider matrix of government policies, particularly relating to the distribution of industry.[86] Optimism was generated by the official recognition given to the Barlow report, but as the war drew to a close, it gradually became clear that civil servants – especially those in the Board of Trade – would not be persuaded on any decision that had long-term implications. Consequently, local initiatives on industrial location met only with indecision and prevarication, and some key questions about Coventry's future remained largely undecided.

In framing their plans for reconstruction, the Council were aware that, however the issue of finance was ultimately to be settled with the Government, little progress would be possible if Coventry was either expanding too fast or, on the other hand, gripped by industrial depression. There was no wish to return to the kind of chaotic situation that had existed in the late 1930s (and particularly 1939–40), when overstimulation of the local economy was accompanied by extensive immigration into the city and multiple social problems. But it would also be necessary to guard against an alternative scenario, in which leading firms, dissatisfied both with competing for expensive labour and an inability to quickly rebuild damaged plant, left the city for more amenable locations. For in these conditions, overall purchasing power would be decreased and, as a consequence, retailers might well be deterred from involvement in the precinct experiment.

In the early years of the war, the possibility of overstimulation continued to appear as a highly potent threat, which led Gibson, for example, to the somewhat controversial conclusion that the city ought in future not to aim for too high a rate of growth.[87] But, from mid-1943 onwards, anxiety about this outcome diminished, as it was perceived that depression rather than boom would be a far more likely consequence of the peace.[88]

This latter conclusion was reinforced by consultations with local employers. For although some – like Black of Standard Motors – were quite confident about post-war markets, others remained rather pessimistic, and predicted a degree of difficulty in changing over from military production.[89] More alarmingly, a large majority stressed their dissatisfaction with the high local wage rates that had accompanied the armaments-led expansion, so that a major confrontation with the trade unions was felt to be both necessary and inevitable.[90] With these problems in mind, a number of firms were said to be contemplating leaving the city.[91]

Detailed reports by experts connected with the Nuffield Social Reconstruction Survey tended to be both less sanguine and less pessimistic, but in the end they did little to dispel local anxieties.[92] The forecast, once again, was that employment difficulties would accompany the curtailment of armaments contracts, although these were now predicted to be of short duration. On the other hand, a new ingredient was added to the situation by an emphasis on the long-term consequences of a specialisation which had pulled nearly 70 per cent of the work-force into engineering.[93] Shenfield and Sargant Florence,for example, felt that 'the problem for Coventry after the war' would be 'how to restore . . . industrial variety while maintaining the prosperity of its major industries' but they were far from confident that this would be easily achievable: 'as the distortion caused by the war has been greater than in other comparable centres . . . this problem is not likely to be a simple one.[94]

Given this climate of opinion, the Corporation began to explore how best it could help to secure future industrial prosperity. Pressure was put on the Board of Trade, firstly, to declare how it saw Coventry's future, and whether it shared the view that problems were likely.[95] Meanwhile, negotiations were initiated to try to secure municipal control over all or at least some of the Government's 'shadow' factories, in order to give the Council some capacity with which quickly to re-establish firms that had suffered damage in the bombing.[96] Finally, it was also decided to explore the possibility of purchasing land on the edges of the city, in the hope that this might provide security for longer-term industrial growth.[97]

At first, it looked as if some progress might be possible here, especially since the Ministry of Town and Country Planning was apparently at least sympathetic to some of the Council's aims.[98] But, in the end, negotiations with the Board of Trade achieved very little, since, though officials recognised that short-term unemployment might be a problem during reconversion, they were completely against making any decision which might set a precedent of departing from the *status quo ante*.[99] The Board, then, was prepared to give motor vehicle producers early permission to begin development work; to establish an interdepartmental committee on the motor industry;[100] and to remove those controls on placing orders in Coventry that had been imposed at the beginning of the war.[101] But it was not, by contrast, willing to allow the Corporation any say in 'shadow' factory allocation, preferring instead to aid certain companies – Rootes and Standard Motors – in taking up their existing-user options.[102] Nor, it emerged after some time, would it grant the local authority permission to use purchased land for industrial purposes unless there was a specific undertaking that no *new* firms would be involved in any subsequent development.[103] By mid-1945, therefore, it looked as if the Corporation's hopes of influencing decision-making in this area were likely to yield few results.

Addressing members of the Architectural Association in early 1941, Donald Gibson forecast that the forthcoming reconstruction debate would be sharp and polarised: 'After the first Battle of Britain has been won, I think there is going to be a second battle, and it will be fought-out on the drawing-boards of the architects and planners in this country.'[104]

As the previous paragraphs have shown, this prediction proved largely correct. The Labour Council in Coventry continued to see the Blitz as an opportunity, which would allow the construction of a more functional and equal city. Whitehall, on the other hand, had become more and more concerned with 'realism' and less and less inclined to encourage any move away from the pre-war norm.

Yet, for the period of the war, the outcome of this conflict, it has also been suggested, remained surprisingly inconclusive. Coventry recognised that the successful application of its plans would be only ultimately possible if the Government was prepared to help with finance and at the same time pursue an interventionist approach on the planning of population and industry, but it had been able to secure very few assurances on any of these questions by 1945. On the other hand, the civil servants were forced to recognise that, since their views remained so unpopular with most sections of public opinion in Coventry, their unilateral imposition was simply out of the question. As the war came to an end both sides hoped that a return to electoral politics would provide a way out of this stalemate.

3 Economic reconstruction: Coventry's local economy, 1945–51

At the end of the Second World War, many people in Coventry and elsewhere, it has been suggested, felt worried about how the local economy would perform during and after reconversion to civilian production. In 1945 and early 1946, their fears seemed partly justified, as there was something of a down-turn in the city. But subsequently, developments did not at all follow the path predicted by the pessimists, and Coventry quite quickly regained much of its old pre-war reputation as a boom town. This chapter concentrates on the period 1945–51, and is particularly concerned to identify why and how growth took place, and whether it was securely based or not. It will also be necessary, in the light of arguments advanced in the last chapter, to comment on what implications the pattern of industrial expansion had for the wider reconstruction of the city. Was a secure base being laid for the kind of rationally organised, welfare-orientated society that had been envisaged by the Labour Council?

In the final months of the European war, it began to seem as if some of the more pessimistic predictions that had been made about the reconversion problem in Coventry were beginning to come true. Several companies, for example, previously given over completely to government contracts, now found themselves with empty order books and so declared quite large redundancies.[1] In other cases, where a change-over to civilian production seemed possible, smooth conversion was jeopardised by shortages and disputes with employees about pricing the new work.[2] This environment in turn gave fresh impetus – especially amongst those that had suffered damage to plant in the war[3] – to the desire for re-location, with one firm, Rover, actually deciding to transfer completely out of the city.[4]

But to the surprise of many the down-turn did not last. In part, this reflected the purely fortuitous fact that the exodus of temporary war workers was taking place at a rate that more than compensated for the return of Service personnel, so that the insured population at work locally fell from 139,000 in 1944 to 111,000 in 1946.[5] But the employment situation was also helped by the Board of Trade's refusal – under pressure from local trade unions and politicians[6] – to allow any other firms to leave the city.[7] Finally, if the change-over to civilian production in the key vehicles sector did not proceed particularly fast, the strategy of concentrating on pre-war models which most companies pursued,[8] together with some large government orders,[9] at least ensured continuity of production and laid the basis for a gradual build-up of output to significant levels during 1946.[10]

Over the following four or five years, Coventry's problems at the end of the war appeared more and more as an insignificant hiccup on an otherwise uninterrupted upward growth curve. For, as the *People* put it in September 1950, 'the city that the Luftwaffe tore the heart out of' had been rapidly transformed in the post-war world 'from Blitz Town to Boom Town'.[11] Behind the hyperbole were some impressive figures. For example, car production from the city was running at over 130,000 units per annum by 1951, a quarter of the U.K.'s gross total.[12] At the same time, there were major outputs in a number of very modern growth areas – tractors, rayon, telephones and television sets.[13] These changes had in turn promoted considerable migration into the city – the population grew by about 16 per cent between 1945 and 1951[14] – and provided the basis for unprecedented popular affluence.[15] How had this remarkable transformation taken place?

It should be noted, to begin with, that one possible source of growth – diversification through the multiplication of sectors – can be quickly discounted. For, as Coventry's peace-time economy began to spark, so the Government's will to prevent the importation of new industries strengthened. It seems likely that the city's industrial profile remained little changed between 1945 and 1951.[16]

The strait-jacket imposed on Coventry during these years was the obverse of an emerging regional policy primarily concerned with the welfare of the Development Areas.[17] As has already been indicated, the Government had initially adopted a policy designed to keep existing industry in the city. But a Board of Trade enquiry in 1945–6 led to a change of emphasis, with the accent now on keeping out new industry. Government departments charged with running the complicated machinery for vetting industrial building were consequently advised that 'any expansions in Coventry should be severely discouraged . . . and no new enterprise . . . allowed, save in the most exceptional circumstances'.[18]

Available figures (summarised in Table 3:1) are unfortunately too tangential to demonstrate the exact impact of this policy, but they do

Table 3:1 Issued Industrial Development Certificates and rejected projects (5,000 sq.ft. plus) July 1948–Dec.1953.[19]

Part A: Issued I.D.C.s, new and replacement/extension projects

Year	*No.*	*New projects Sq.ft. (total)*	*No.*	*Repl./ext. projects Sq.ft. (total)*
July–Dec. 1948	7	95,275	15	337,504
1949	5	73,230	20	654,493
1950	9	116,826	20	839,410
1951	5	67,100	24	423,607
1952	1	7,000	15	340,518
1953	3	77,200	19	502,488

Part B: I.D.C. applications

Year	*Description of project*		
July–Dec. 1948	[none]		
1949	Standard Motor Co.	Ext.	83,000 sq.ft.[a]
1950	The Car Collection Co. (auto-conveyors)	New	58,000 sq.ft.
	Haddon and Abbotts Ltd. (machine tools)	New	9,500 sq.ft.
	Veasey and Sharples Ltd. (machine tools)	New	7,000 sq.ft.
	The Car Collection Co. (auto-conveyors)	New	25,000 sq.ft.
1951	[none]		
1952	Morris Motors Ltd.	Ext.	56,800 sq.ft.
	Powderloys Ltd. (tungsten-tipped tools)	Ext.	9,100 sq.ft.
	Veasey and Sharples Ltd.	New	20,000 sq.ft.
1953	[none]		

Note: [a]later accepted

suggest, at least, a strict level of control. Licences granted for industrial building (structures of more than 5,000 sq.ft. only) involved a total of 2.8 million sq.ft. between February 1945 and December 1950, equivalent to about 14 per cent of the factory space with which Coventry finished the war.[20] But *new* projects involved only a small fraction of this total, since most of the building was to do with replacement or extension. Furthermore new projects involving new companies were virtually unheard of.[21] It seems fair to conclude, as a later review put it, that the application of this policy was 'extremely stringent'.[22]

If this interpretation is correct, attention must therefore be focused on the major sectors that were already well established in the city by 1945. The following discussion begins with a description of the operating environment firms faced after the war – the matrix of demand and supply-side constraints – and then outlines the various strategies that were used in the pursuit of growth and profitability.

The demand situation confronting Coventry entrepreneurs in peacetime was of course generally very favourable, simply because the war had acted to remove many sources of foreign competition.[23] Firms in a variety of trades recognised that this gave them a unique opportunity to prosper.[24]

But certain qualifications to this position also quickly became apparent. Firstly, companies in some sectors had to accept that demand for their goods would often be segmented or controlled by the Government. Car manufacturers, for example, were expected to meet significant export quotas – 75 per cent of output in 1948 – while home orders for vehicles could fluctuate unpredictably due to variations in purchase tax.[25] There were also numerous problems in actually reaching targeted markets: Coventry firms were troubled, at one time or another, by shipping difficulties;[26] importing countries' currency shortages;[27] variations in overseas tariff or trading arrangements;[28] and the eccentric commercial practices of distant foreign distributors.[29] Finally, there was a growing awareness of the fragility of market domination. British car manufacturers were warned more than once that their models were often selling abroad by default rather than because of good design;[30] so that, by the end of the period, the reappearance of American and German competition was beginning to represent something of a threat.[31]

On the supply side, there was also a variety of quite significant constraints. While it is true that, at least in the first instance, there was no shortage of capital funds – several local firms floated new issues after the war, while others made use of extensive overdraft facilities from the banks[32] – problems were certainly evident when attempts were made to turn money into plant and equipment. Factory construction and repair, for example, could be hampered by building labour shortage[33] or an official reluctance, on occasion, to sanction projects.[34] In fact, only a minority of building licences issued were actually ever turned into completed buildings during this period,[35] so that a few companies had to make do with war-damaged (and uneconomic) facilities well into the 1950s.[36] In parallel, there was also a general and continuing shortage of machine tools,[37]which meant that 'free-hand' or 'knife and fork' methods were not uncommon.[38]

But if firms often found their scope for new investment cramped, the use of existing capacity was sometimes not without its problems, too. Raw materials of all kinds were increasingly costly[39] and sporadically scarce, with steel (which was rationed throughout this period) the most usual headache.[40] Nor could the complexion of the local labour market offer many compensating advantages. Coventry's firms were particularly reliant on skilled labour (although to differing extents)[41] but this could be both relatively difficult to find and expensive. For although unionisation was by no means all-inclusive,[42] there was normally sufficient organisation in the tool-rooms to maintain some kind of hold over conditions of entry[43] and promotion[44] and thereby maintain differentials.[45] Perhaps surprisingly, there was also a knock-on effect relating to the supply of unskilled labour, with at least one group in the population – married women – proving difficult to entice into the factories, precisely because of the high male skilled rates.[46] Firms specialising in textiles or the assembly of electrical appliances were just as likely to suffer from labour shortages, then, as their neighbours in precision engineering, and this in spite of the migration stream into the city.[47]

The cumulative effect of these various difficulties meant, finally, that, for many companies, long periods of output at capacity might be quite unusual.[48] This could be especially damaging in sectors – like much of the engineering industry – where volume production was the essential precondition for diminished overheads.[49] In fact, it could even call into question a company's long-term viability, by compromising its ability to generate sufficient funds for the kind of 'lumpy' investment (in tools and jigs) necessary to keep up with changing market conditions.[50]

To escape from these various potential traps, local entrepreneurs adopted a range of more or less effective strategies. Reactions to prevailing demand conditions, firstly, differed considerably. Most companies involved themselves in lobbying government departments for preferential treatment, citing, for example, special reasons why they could not meet export quotas.[51] Differential pricing was also fairly common.[52] But more active attempts to respond closely to the needs of particular markets were less in evidence. The Rootes organisation had traditionally been involved in the export trade and certainly benefited post-war from an ability to offer back-up and spares overseas.[53] Jaguar took this approach further and actually tailored its cars to American consumer choice, with Lyons (the Managing Director) emphasising the importance of aggressive marketing and on-the-spot service.[54] By contrast, Standard had an ignominious export flop with the Mayflower, and began seriously to question its future involvement in the U.S. market.[55]

The scope for action over raw materials was rather limited. Again, most companies indulged in lobbying for preference.[56] Limited vertical integration was rarer, with only a few large firms seriously pursuing this option.[57] Finally, there was also some advantage to be gained from substitutions between materials (i.e. timber for steel) although gains here were certainly not open to all.[58]

Labour strategies, on the other hand, both provoked more comment and were of considerably greater overall significance. One pole was provided by Standard, which opted from 1945 for a high wage policy, thus trading inflated costs for good productivity and industrial relations.[59] By contrast, several other local firms adopted a far more abrasive approach, in which redundancy and confrontation[60] were used to peg wage rates back from their war-time peak.[61]

A final field of action involved choices about the configuration of production itself. Many companies, for example, were involved in sub-contracting work, so as to 'export' costs.[62] Another common strategy was to vary or extend the product mix so as to guard against fluctuations in any one particular area of activity. Standard thus moved into tractor production in partnership with Harry Ferguson, while Alvis added the construction of printing machines to their aero-engine and vehicle staples.[63]

An important variant involved obtaining work on defence contracts. Relations with commissioning Ministries here were not always easy – one firm complained of 'too much advice and too many committees for comfort'[64] – but returns were usually worthwhile, if only because steady and predictable.[65] Given these advantages, it is perhaps not surprising to find that probably one-third of all the city's engineering companies were involved in defence work during this period.[66]

No doubt firms chose between these different strategies partly on purely idiosyncratic grounds. But choice in some areas was also significantly influenced by the Government, through the apparatus of raw material allocation and the network of 'sponsoring' departments, regional committees and advisory quangos.[67]

Government requirements from industry at this time involved a number of elements, but two key strands running through much of its activity were the promotion of exports and the maintenance of a capacity for armaments production. Firms planning developments in these areas could therefore usually count on a high degree of official help. There was close ministerial involvement, then, over Standard's diversification into tractors, since agricultural machinery was seen as a significant dollar earner.[68] Jaguar, too, received considerable aid in its efforts to penetrate the U.S. market: it was rated 'one of our star turns' by the Ministry of Supply, worthy of all possible help.[69] Daimler, by contrast, was regarded as a 'shocking' export performer, but received extra steel, despite this, because of its armaments capacity.[70]

Of course, this kind of stimulation of production was not always in harmony with other official objectives. One frequent site of conflict was the planning process, since 'distribution of industry' and 'output' objectives could imply rather different kinds of development. Nevertheless, the evidence suggests that firms wishing to expand their Coventry operations had generally only to stress a 'production' or strategic case for the necessary permission to be granted.[71] As one Ministry of Town and Country Planning officer ruefully remarked of the overcrowded Midlands in general:

> The difficulty is that, although Departments can readily agree on a general policy to be followed . . . when this policy comes to be applied to individual cases there are always overriding reasons why the policy cannot, at the moment, be applied. . . . And those reasons are of such a character . . . that we as a Department can hardly maintain our objections without being quite unrealistic.[72]

It seems reasonable to suggest, then, that in the years after the war the Coventry economy was developing within something of a government 'forcing frame', which allowed some firms and sectors – especially those that were important in terms of exports and strategic considerations – to obtain considerable stimulation, and limited disruptive movements of capacity in and out. The advantages of this symbiotic relationship – strong growth and popular prosperity – have already been touched upon. But what of the disadvantages?

The most immediately obvious set of 'costs' associated with the growth pattern stemmed from the fact that the magnetic attractions of manufacturing expansion were continuously felt not only outside the city – encouraging immigration – but also *within* its boundaries – diverting resources and labour from other sectors. Consequently, local service, building and transport industries, in particular, were condemned to struggle at the very time when the demand for their output was increasing significantly.[73] The end product of this – as the next chapter will detail – was a shortfall in the provision of a wide range of amenities and services, most especially housing.

But if conditions on the periphery of the 'forcing frame' were precarious, the situation at its core was perhaps less favourable than it at first sight appeared. Direct work for the government was generally lucrative, as has been mentioned, yet this was not always the case, and there were examples of large quantities of private development money being lost because of Whitehall capriciousness.[74] Moreover, in a very few cases, official attention was actually unwelcome, since the firms in question already had booming civilian markets, and did not relish government requests to set aside a proportion of their capacity for armaments work.[75] But the biggest problem here was that since government policies and inputs were largely unplanned and unco-ordinated[76] – the responsibility often of competing departments – they tended in combination to produce symptoms of 'overheating', and thereby magnified the latent production difficulties that were experienced by many less resilient or less favoured Coventry firms.

This phenomenon was evident to a greater or lesser extent throughout the period, but it became particularly pronounced after the government announcement of August 1950 that military expenditure was to be sharply increased in response to the Korean crisis.[77] The initial symptoms at this time, as before, were a scramble for labour[78] and a shortage of steel;[79] but from early 1951 the situation became rather more damaging, with small firms in particular unable to compete in the bidding for resources,[80] and short-time work growing as a result.[81] Anxiety increased further when rumours began to spread that Standard was about to land a massive contract to manufacture Avon engines for Canberra bombers – a development that Alvis directors, amongst others, predicted would lead to an 'unsettlement' of labour conditions.[82] In fact, some manufacturers had become worried enough to start lobbying for an end to military spending in the city altogether, a theme later taken up by the Mayor in the national press ('Boom City Asks: Stop Orders').[83]

A measure of the seriousness of the city's predicament was that various government departments now finally began to question the efficacy of the 'free-for-all' approach. Attention was focused initially on the Avon contract, and in the end it was agreed that Standard should only be allowed to proceed provided it engaged no more than 2,000 extra workers on the project.[84] This recommendation did not, however, end unease about the city's problems,[85] and officials therefore continued to deliberate over possible palliatives. A comprehensive survey by regional administrators was undertaken, and this concluded that because some essential services were 'strained to breaking point' no further military contracts should be given to Coventry firms unless civil work could be diverted elsewhere.[86] Further investigation led to the prediction that, unless checked, arms orders already placed would demand 11,000 extra workers by 1954, a total that could not possibly be provided within the existing framework.[87] In the light of this 'serious labour problem', the incoming Conservative Government was forced to recognise that more comprehensive intervention could simply not be avoided any longer, and a ban was placed on further armaments spending in the city, to take effect from December 1951.[88]

The events of 1950–1 – and some of the information about them that was contained in the various reports – rekindled the kind of fears that had been expressed at the end of the war about the city's future prosperity. An official enquiry, it is true, which ranked areas in terms of vulnerability to trade depression, argued that Coventry was no worse off than many other places.[89] But this did not alleviate feelings that there were, nevertheless, several disturbing features in the local situation.

In terms of the structural level, concern focused once again on the lack of diversity in the city's economy. Too much capacity, it seemed, was massed in too few sectors – vehicles, aircraft, engineering and electrical goods. What made this situation more disturbing was the high degree of interdependence existing within each sector (with, for example, 26,000 being employed by the four biggest motor vehicle firms, and a further 19,500 working for vital sub-contractors)[90] and the large average size of the firms involved.[91]

But, even accepting this structural configuration, it could not be denied that growth and profitability were hardly securely based. Thus, the various production problems outlined above had meant that much of the output of cars remained financially problematic throughout this period,[92] so that by the early 1950s there were rumours about the viability of such well-known firms as Standard, Daimler and Singer.[93] On the other hand, although defence work could be lucrative, questions were certainly in order about its suitability as a future source of stable income. For, as the events of 1950–1 had shown, if the Government could turn the tap of military spending on, it could equally well turn it off. The spectre of these problems, as a later chapter will show, was to return with some frequency throughout the 1950s.

4 City reconstruction: building a new Coventry, 1945–51

As has been outlined in Chapter 2, Coventry ended the war with some ambitious plans for rebuilding, which encompassed, amongst other things, a new city centre and a re-styled network of urban neighbourhoods. The aim was to create no less than the physical basis of a vision – 'a vision not of a dream city, but of practical accomplishment and operational usefulness, catering for the needs of a new rising democratic and progressive generation'.[1] The following paragraphs look at whether Coventry's goals were achieved up to 1951. In particular, emphasis will be placed on trying to find out how far local initiatives were either sustained or undermined by various features of the post-war situation. Was the newly elected Labour Government, for example, more sympathetic than the Coalition had been? Equally, how did the Council cope with the concomitants of a booming local economy – immigration into the city, and a consistently over-stretched construction sector?

As the battle for Europe reached its climax in 1945, there was a growing recognition in Coventry that the period of planning for reconstruction was now drawing to a close and that in the immediate future the key questions would be to do with practicalities. Where, most important of all, should the priority in rebuilding lie?

In considering this question, the Council rapidly came to agree that, very much as Gibson had forecast, housing would be the major local issue. Prices for dwellings in the city were beginning to rise spectacularly.[2] At the same time there was a sharp upward trend in applications for Council accommodation – from 2,900 in 1944 to 5,307 in 1945 – which pushed the waiting list from 7,141 in March 1945 to well over 10,000 by the end of the year.[3] Furthermore, in the knowledge that the major impact of demobilisation lay as yet in the future, a variety of citizens' groups had started to express grave fears about the scale of the city's problems.[4]

However, some practical details about how exactly the housing programme was to be started still remained unclear. A number of official and semi-official reports seemed to confirm that the kind of approach Coventry had planned was indeed within mainstream thinking about the housing question.[5] And Ministries in London certainly appeared to recognise the scale of the local predicament, offering to erect, for example, 1,000 temporary prefabricated bungalows, as long as the Corporation could provide the sites.[6] But there was still the problem of finance: who exactly would pay, once the full programme got underway? In this situation – especially given the scale of all the other Council plans – speculation and rumour were rife, with talk of 'devastating' rate rises sweeping the city.[7]

To quell such fears, the Council agreed, at least for the immediate future, to move cautiously. It opted, first, for only a small rise in the rates, and reaffirmed its general intention to maintain a policy of financial orthodoxy.[8] On housing specifically, the first priority was the preparation of sites for the bungalows, and this allowed a fairly quick start to actual construction, in May 1945.[9] At the same time, the Council agreed to survey what other land it had available, a move that led to the purchase of 1,330 extra acres on the city's periphery.[10] Finally, under pressure from the Ministry of Health in London, which was in charge of housing, the targets for a possible six-month house building programme were announced: the Council hoped that by March 1946 it would have finished all of the bungalow 'prefabs', erected 216 ordinary houses, and rebuilt 140 Corporation-owned units damaged by enemy action. Additionally, private enterprise was set the task of producing 300 dwellings. However, it was clearly recognised (and emphasised to the Minister) that swift progress would be unlikely unless Coventry received some extra aid, particularly with the size of its labour force.[11]

In the second half of 1945, a number of events interacted to confirm the Council's belief in its overall strategy and objectives. The election of a Labour Government at Westminster, firstly, seemed to auger well for housing and town planning in general, since Labour was ostensibly more committed to an interventionist approach than its adversaries.[12] Hopes were raised further by some early pronouncements of key Ministers, with Silkin, at Town and Country Planning, letting it be known widely that he wished to expedite the rebuilding of blitzed cities, even before the introduction of promised new legislation, and Bevan, at Health, emphasising that local authorities would be expected to play a crucial role over housing.[13] In Coventry, meanwhile, reconstruction enthusiasms had reached new levels, with 57,500 visitors attending a municipally organised 'Coventry of the Future' exhibition over a two-week period during October.[14] The results of the first peace-time local elections, finally, reinforced the mood of confidence. For Labour's victory, despite a low turn-out,[15] suggested that many in the electorate broadly shared the kind of ideas for local development – and the emphases on housing and welfare provision – which had been at the heart of its campaign.[16]

At any rate, the prospects looked sufficiently promising for there to be a move towards some fairly detailed clarification of immediately achievable objectives. One result here was the three-year investment programme adopted in early 1946. Overall the Council intended to spend nearly £13 million by 1949. A number of big projects were specified, including a new general hospital, though once again housing was featured as the main priority area (it was to absorb 38 per cent of all spending).[17]

Alongside this work, the Council and its officers also began a more serious consideration of how best to use the 1944 Act's machinery for initiating progress on the city centre plan. The objective was to move along a prescribed path, involving official scrutiny and a public enquiry, to obtain a Ministerial Declaratory Order – the measure which would allow the Council the right of compulsory purchase within a given area. Nevertheless, on close examination, it was by no means clear in the statute what kind of land could or could not be permissively included in any specific proposal, and so local opinion was somewhat divided about optimum boundaries. Should the Council endorse the 1941 scheme (basically the city centre and the run-down Spon Street neighbourhood) or should it press for a much larger area, including further central slums, as some radicals suggested?[18]

A number of factors counselled caution here. The first, perhaps surprisingly, was the complexion of the local political situation. Labour was of course gratified by the 1945 result, but it also recognised that its espousal of the city centre scheme had not been the major reason behind the victory. For while the Gibson plan no doubt did have a strong degree of bi-partisan support, there were also continuing undercurrents of scepticism about its real viability.[19] Central redevelopment could certainly not, therefore, be regarded any longer simply as a popular talisman, in the way it had been in 1940–1.

The Council had also to take account of a whole number of procedural and logistical uncertainties about its precise role in the scheme. There was, for example, the problem of the 40 manufacturing enterprises owning sites within the central area.[20] Some of these would have to be moved if the plan was to be adhered to, but it was by no means clear how this process would be financed, nor was it even certain that the Government would sanction industrial re-location on surrounding 'greenfield' sites, given the increasing stringency of Board of Trade policy towards the city.[21]

A related problem concerned the fate of the 150-odd firms that had owned shops in the central area before the blitz:[22] while the Council publicly recognised its moral responsibility to include these retailers in any new development, few were confident about how easily this pledge could be realised. Given the tangle of leaseholds and the very different sizes of undertaking that were involved, it was legitimate to suppose, certainly, that hardly any firms would be able to consider simply rebuilding their own premises.

In fact, this latter problem represented a considerable difficulty for the authority. The Council had never really explicitly decided who would be responsible for central redevelopment, but an implicit assumption, encouraged by Gibson, was that overall control could not be left to market forces, since private developers appeared unlikely to be able to guarantee aesthetic co-ordination.[23] Yet the 1944 Act was, once again, ultimately rather unclear as to how much redevelopment a Council could undertake itself.[24] Furthermore, even if a local authority was allowed to play a major role, it would still have to traverse the so-called 'dead period' – the years of rebuilding when considerable outgoings (on servicing reconstruction loans) might substantially exceed income from a fairly restricted revenue base. What made this situation particularly discouraging was that the legislation implied that central government grants (equal to charges on the cost of purchase and clearance) would only normally run for two years.[25] The Council began, therefore, to glimpse the terms of a rather unwelcome choice: they might either have to opt for a smaller, cheaper, more revenue-orientated scheme or call in private capital and thereby jeopardise the aesthetic and co-ordinated nature of the development.

In the end, the authority concluded that, given these conditions, it would be unwise to move too fast, too quickly, and more prudent to stick with existing plans, in the hope that lobbying from all the blitzed authorities would eventually persuade the Labour Government quickly to change the overall legislative framework. The 452 acre 'Area of Extensive War Damage No.1', submitted for the Minister's scrutiny in the application of April 1946, therefore largely followed the original configuration outlined by Gibson five years earlier.[26]

If the final aim of a planned city had necessarily to be a long-term project, the Council was determined that, from the first, its policies should reflect the direction in which it meant to progress. Strong and successful resistance was thus mounted against a government campaign to curtail nursery provision.[27] At the same time, the local medical services were encouraged to launch a drive which was quickly to eradicate diphtheria.[28] A start was made, too, on the neighbourhood unit scheme, with the construction of three community centres in residential areas, financed by money provided as a gift from the U.S.A.[29] Nor was cultural provision forgotten, as the Council entered negotiations for the creation of a municipal orchestra.[30]

Progress with housing was somewhat disappointing, as the figures in Table 4:1 demonstrate. But, even here, the picture was by no means all bleak. In a relative perspective, for example, Coventry's performance was very good.[31] Moreover, local perceptions of the Council's initiatives were quite positive, with the bungalows in particular attracting favourable responses.[32] Grounds for optimism were further strengthened with the news that the Government had offered Coventry 2,000 prefabricated permanent British Iron and Steel Federation (B.I.S.F.) houses.[33] The point here was that, though these units were by no means cheap, they could be assembled with far less labour (notably, far less skilled labour) than normal brick units.[34] This gave reasons for believing that the emerging threat of a local building labour shortage[35] – which could only grow worse once the engineering sector fully reconverted – might be successfully side-stepped, and housing provision thereby substantially increased.

Table 4:1 Housing targets and construction in Coventry, 1945–6.[36]

	Corporation		*Private*
	permanent houses	*temporary houses*	*enterprise houses*
Six-month target set Aug. 1945	216	1,000	300
Completions by:			
March 1946	82	392	44
Sept. 1946	110	844	315
Dec. 1946	128	881	492

Progress with the city centre scheme, finally, also seemed to be assured. The Minister, for example, specifically underlined his desire for progress in the city, and informed Council representatives that his interpretation of the 1944 Act's rather confusing statutes would be as liberal as possible.[37] The public inquiry, held in Coventry during the summer of 1946, also went well. All told, 259 objections were raised to the scheme, representing 1,000 of the probable 10,000 interests in the area. The great majority of objections (177) were in 'common form' and dealt with precise legal interpretations of the 1944 Act. The substantive criticism of the planning scheme as such (limited to six objections) tended to be based on more conservative aesthetic sensibilities.[38] Anti-modernism was given a clever ideological twist by one 'planning expert', who argued that Gibson's scheme was '"diabolically German and Fascist in character"'. But, the prescription he offered instead turned out to be rather vague:

> If the matter were put to someone like Sir Giles Scott, he would take up the atmosphere of Coventry itself and while he would interpret it on modern lines, it would be very different from what you have there [i.e. Gibson's scheme].[39]

In fact, the opposition markedly faded as the inquiry proceeded, partly because of the convincing performances of the Council's officials, and partly because of the strong degree of overall public support for the scheme. The *Standard*, indeed, noted a definite change of heart amongst some erstwhile objectors:

> However aggrieved some of the businessmen in the centre of the city feel, they realise that the bombing of the city has made new planning inevitable. Moreover, many of them know that in a problem of such magnitude, private interests are bound to be affected.[40]

The inquiry therefore ended on a high note for the Council, in that public acceptance of its plan, 'uninformed as to detail . . . but nevertheless weighty', was now incontrovertible.[41]

Yet, as the months of 1946 passed, the Council was more and more drawn into a multi-dimensional crisis. One aspect of this was a growing sense of unease in Coventry about the pace of reconstruction, made manifest, for example, in the Labour party's somewhat disappointing showing at the end-of-year local elections.[42] Nor could all the criticism simply be deflected. Thus, at other times, Professor Joad's public indictment of Coventry's alleged philistinism – published in the *Telegraph* during November[43] – might easily have been shrugged off as the outpourings of a prejudiced eccentric. But now it gave rise to some heart-searching amongst the Labour group,[44] particularly since it almost coincided with a decision to abandon the idea of a municipal orchestra on grounds of cost.[45]

But the biggest practical problem revolved, predictably, around the housing situation. On the one hand, demand showed no signs of abating, with the municipal housing department besieged almost all the hours it was open.[46] In total, there were 6,238 new applications over the year, so that the April waiting list had already reached a record 11,674 (including 4,950 current or ex-Servicemen).[47] But, against this, there were growing problems over completions. Many materials and fittings were in short supply.[48] More seriously, the building labour position appeared to be deteriorating much more quickly than expected, so that by October only one-quarter of the required numbers were at work on Corporation schemes.[49] The end product was slow site preparation, a factor which in turn persuaded the Government to unilaterally redirect half of Coventry's B.I.S.F. allocation to other, more amenable localities.[50] The whole situation was vividly dramatised in the early winter months by a wave of squatting, involving perhaps 500 to 1,000 people at a number of locations throughout the city.[51]

Yet, if each of these practical difficulties proved menacing, the local Council (in company with many other similar authorities)[52] was worried still further by doubts about its future financial viability. The Government, it is true, had pledged itself to a full review of the rates system and the support given by central exchequer grants to local administrations. But in the interim, the unsolved problem of the pre-war years – how to provide a full and expanding range of services within a strategy of budget orthodoxy – seemed to be returning with a vengeance.

The basic fact, from which the Council had to start, was that costs were steadily rising. This was partly the result of new legislation (the new school-leaving age stipulated under the 1946 Education Act), partly a reflection of general inflation (which was particularly marked in the building sector),[53] and partly a consequence of a deliberate move to ameliorate conditions and pay which the Council had agreed with its unions.[54] Against this, revenue sources seemed to be somewhat problematic. Government grants were increasingly important – making up between 35 and 40 per cent of income[55] – but were not always geared to facilitate expansion. For example, housing support, introduced under the 1946 Act, was organised on a flat-rate basis (i.e. a standard amount per unit built), a system that did not seem to be best suited to the inflationary conditions.[56] Secondly, the scope for increasing income from charges on services (e.g. rents) or trading undertakings (gas, transport, etc.) remained limited. The problem here was political rather than financial: since these accounts had not previously been used to generate surpluses, any future attempt to raise prices out of trend would be bound to meet consumer resistance.[57]

To circumvent these problems, the Council could of course freely turn to borrowing, on the strength of the credit-servicing potential of its normal rates revenue. Indeed, this was the preferred solution of the Government, which had specifically directed the Public Works Loan Board to provide funds on advantageous terms.[58] But, once again, the room for manoeuvre open to the Council was considerably less than it at first sight appeared. The problem, in a nutshell, was that rate income in Coventry appeared to be too inelastic, so that sufficient revenue would simply not be available to pay for the kind of loans the city required.

The rate base, it is true, was fairly buoyant because of the recent years of war-induced boom conditions.[59] But prospects for a further increase in total rateable value because of new building looked slim, as traders postponed investment decisions pending the Minister's final decision over the Declaratory Order application.[60] Thus, on this tack, the Council was left only with the option of reassessment (re-valuing existing properties upwards), a strategy that yielded results, but could not be pushed too far, too fast, for practical as well as political reasons.[61]

The more direct way of raising rate income – the simple variation upwards of the shilling charge in the pound – also appeared to be rather unattractive. Labour politicians were very aware that, because of the city's particular rate structure – and especially the high proportion of the overall take coming from homes valued at £25 and under – the brunt of any rise would be borne by the very constituency upon which they depended for votes.[62] Equally, a high rate in the pound would hardly appear attractive to the kind of retail traders that Coventry wished to attract to its new shopping centre.

The immediate response of the Council to this complex situation was to turn for help to the Government. In all, appeals were made about four separate issues over the course of 1946 and early 1947. Much play was made of the city's past suffering and current predicament. Yet, in the end, Coventry achieved very little: departmental policies were not homogeneous, but there seems to have been a general feeling that, in a relative perspective, Coventry was hardly deserving of priority status.

The first two approaches to the Government were both completely unsuccessful. Thus, the city was informed early on that it would not be receiving any special grant aid in lieu of destroyed rateable value, since official surveys showed that its losses had been nowhere as severe as those of several other British cities.[63] Later in 1946, a request for extra building labour to be sent to the city was similarly summarily dismissed by the Ministries of Works and Health.[64]

But Government stone-walling clearly could not continue forever, particularly since the city had so recently returned two Labour M.P.s. Consequently, a third appeal, in the winter of 1946, met with a more positive response, and it was agreed that officials in the regional building directorate should meet the Council to thrash out the problems of the local construction industry.[65]

The enquiry launched under this initiative revealed that one obvious cause of the housing crisis was the low rate of completions on

Corporation contracts (see Table 4:2).[66] At bottom this was due to the fact that builders employed by the local authority were finding other work – private sector housing, factory repairs and rebuilds – much more lucrative, and therefore tended to view Council projects only as 'hospitable jobs'.[67]

Of course, the Labour Government had to some extent anticipated that these kinds of problems might well occur in certain parts of the country, and a complex regulatory mechanism now existed to control the private sector.[68] Local authorities were supposed to be granting licences for private building at a fixed rate of one to four against their own projects, while there were also restrictions on the type of dwelling an individual client could order. Equally, regional boards, comprised of representatives of key government departments, were charged with regulating commercial and industrial development so as to harmonise them not only with the wider aspects of policy, but also with local resource flows and housing allocations. The difficulty was to see exactly why these various controls were not working in Coventry.

Table 4:2 The performance of the Coventry building industry on housing, late 1945 to January 1947

	No. of licences issued	No. of completions	No. of outstanding licences at 1/1/1947
For Corporation contracts	1,578	128	1,450
For private contracts	1,745	492	1,253

Here, the analyses proffered were quite different. To the Government's representatives, the problem was the Corporation's rather soft attitude to local builders, who had been allowed to obtain too many licences for private housing work. The Council, on the other hand, argued that housing in general had to be a priority; and that if the regional apparatus wished to sanction so much commercial and industrial work as well, then it was the clear responsibility of the Government, also, to provide an adequate inflow of building labour.

In the end, the compromise solution went only a little way to meeting the Council's objectives. For while Coventry agreed to suspend the issuing of private house building licences for six months, the Government steadfastly refused to countenance any importation of labour. The regional apparatus merely pledged itself to a future licensing policy which would attempt to ensure that 60 per cent of the available labour force would always be engaged on housing.

But if Coventry received little encouragement from this episode, the fourth approach to the Government, which followed, could only be described as disastrous.[69] Problems began in early 1947, when contractors erecting the B.I.S.F. houses, of which so much was hoped, began to experience severe labour shortages, and put in an application to import labour from outside Coventry – a move that was predicted to add £30 to the final cost of each house. The Corporation's response was to agree to this request, provided the Government accept final liability for the extra sums involved. But here lay a considerable problem, since the Ministry of Health – and eventually the Minister himself – steadfastly refused to provide any further payments. Meanwhile, as negotiations continued, B.I.S.F. sites were reduced to a virtual standstill. In the end, Coventry was forced into a damaging retreat: the order to import labour was given, but the B.I.S.F. programme would be curtailed at only 506 units so as to minimise any possible financial damage to the Corporation.

Meanwhile, the city was also running into some trouble with its Declaratory Order application. The public enquiry, to repeat, had gone very well, but opinion in the Ministry of Town and Country Planning remained very much less favourable. Officials continued to reiterate their general belief that 'Lord Reith's "plan boldly" . . . [had] been worked to death in Coventry'; and that the need over the coming years was, rather, for a major injection of 'realism'.[70] To this end, Coventry's submission was handed to a Reconstruction Area Technical Examination Committee for detailed assessment. The results were predictably damning. The Committee began by noting the application's lack of substance – it was 'little more than a description' which did not explain either the need to acquire the area or the principles upon which reconstruction was to be based. Following on from this were a series of detailed criticisms, involving the alignment of the ring road, the layout of the shopping centre (too many big units), the provision of office space (too much) and the intended industrial and residential zones in the inner area (which were judged inappropriate). The proposals for the civic centre received especially withering comment. The Committee concluded that their examination could only suggest 'a considerable reduction in the area of land enclosed by the inner ring road'. The application ought therefore to be granted, but redevelopment should be on a reduced scale.[71]

It is not clear how far this report influenced the Minister. But more pragmatic reasoning was certainly leading him in a similar direction, since his fairly liberal judgement over an application by Plymouth under the 1944 Act had been successfully challenged in the King's Bench Court.[72] In the end, the Declaratory Order for Coventry, legalised in July 1947, covered only about 280 acres of the central core. The aim, it seems, was to ensure that the first stages of reconstruction would be exclusively concerned with shops and businesses, in order to maximise possible financial returns to the local authority.[73]

In the face of this government indifference, the Council was forced into some fairly drastic measures of its own. It decided, for example, to re-examine all the cases on the housing waiting list, in order to categorise applications by need, and weed out the ineligible.[74] The spending plans of various welfare committees were also somewhat curtailed, in order to keep the rate for 1947–8 to 18s. 6d. in the pound (an increase of 2s.).[75] The optimism of the immediate post-war period was, thus, now replaced by an emphasis on austerity. As one Councillor ruefully reflected,'people were beginning to realise they could not do what they wished, but only within the limits of the rates'.[76]

The Corporation's predicament attracted some sympathy within the city, but there was also a growing mood of criticism.[77] Once again, the key issue was housing. For although completion rates had shown some improvement under the combined measures of early 1947,[78] the overall scale of achievements was disappointing, particularly in a relative perspective.[79] At the same time, immigrants continued to be attracted to the city – there were 3,272 new applications for Corporation property in 1947 – so that the end result was a considerable increase in the waiting list.[80] In addition, of course, the growing numbers of those wishing to have their own houses built[81] were hardly pleased by the virtual moratorium on private licence provision.

If little could be done in real terms to solve these problems, the Council recognised that some kind of effort should at least be made to explain publicly why this was so. Consequently, there was a move to set up a public relations apparatus, with a full-time staff, an information office in the centre of the city, and eventually a broadsheet covering civic affairs.[82] But these initiatives came too late to influence opinion in the short term, and Labour's performance in the end-of-the-year Council elections was predictably lacklustre.[83] The 'honeymoon' period was now completely over, the party recognised. Indeed future strategy would explicitly have to take account of a revitalised 'middle-class' voter, easily antagonised by national as well as local, Labour policy – 'the man buying his house in Whoberley . . . the man in Bablake who has laid up his car, and . . . the housewife in Cheylesmore who is discontented with her bacon ration'.[84]

This lesson was still further driven home in the winter of 1947–8 by events that followed a Council proposal to extend municipal trading – to provide a civic hotel, taxi service and radio-relay service, amongst other things.[85] If the implicit motive behind this move was to increase Corporation revenues, the Council's explicit justification was phrased in terms of need and efficiency. But neither line of reasoning proved popular, and after a campaign of opposition led by the Chamber of Commerce and the local papers, a town poll at the beginning of 1948 rejected any change in the *status quo*. If Labour activists could justifiably discount part of this defeat in terms of poor organisation,[86] they had also to recognise, again, that the high tide of 1945 definitely was now ebbing.

Over the following two years – 1948 and 1949 – changes introduced as a result of central government legislation substantially modified the parameters within which the Coventry Council had to work. One encouraging factor was the new Town and Country Planning Act, which allowed local authorities wider powers to initiate direct development and a more liberal grant environment than had existed previously.[87] Secondly, reforms introduced by the Local Government Act of 1948, particularly a specially formulated grant equalisation system, provided most urban county boroughs with an enhanced level of monetary support from the centre. Coventry therefore found itself, almost at a stroke, with considerably more financial leeway than it had experienced in any of the years immediately after the war.[88]

The Council's immediate reaction to this new environment was narrowly political, in that the rates were immediately pegged back to 17s. 6d. in the pound – a level that was maintained, despite rising costs, until April 1950.[89] But there was also growing recognition that an expansion of services was now very much more possible, since a portion of the extra support from the centre could be used to secure loan funds.[90] The Council therefore began to consider a fairly ambitious series of expenditures, encompassing welfare initiatives (the introduction of a 'meals on wheels' service for old people, for example),[91] cultural facilities (a municipal theatre),[92] an expanded programme of miscellaneous capital works,[93] and increased housing provision (including the creation of the first new neighbourhood unit at Tile Hill).[94] Furthermore, pressure was to be exerted on the Government to help alleviate Coventry's woefully inadequate shopping facilities.[95] Finally, to underpin the expansionist perspective, and in the light of encouraging recommendations made in the advisory West Midlands Plan,[96] an application was made to the Boundary Commission for some 13,000 acres of surrounding rural land to be added to the city.[97]

Alongside these various decisions, the Council also began to consider how best to begin rebuilding in the Declaratory Order Area.[98] Wholesale municipal reconstruction was out of the question – it would be too costly – and so the best solution available seemed to be for the Corporation to buy up all the land (thereby safeguarding the public interest) and then lease it out to private companies for development. But what kind of control could be exercised over such firms? How, for example, could aesthetic co-ordination be maintained? Furthermore, would the companies involved accept the kind of 75 year leases, with periodic revision clauses, which seemed to allow the Council the best trade-off between return and flexibility, or would they insist on the 99 year fixed agreements which had been common before the war?[99] A second set of problems concerned the overall pace of reconstruction. Certain factors, such as the need to restore a good rateable income from the shopping sector and the threatening possibility of betterment,[100] encouraged an expansionist perspective. But, the Council also had to reckon with the fact that large-scale development would require large-scale land purchase, which in turn would mean big loans and large servicing payments, a situation that might well not be politically acceptable to many voters.

In the light of the complexity of these problems, the Council once again opted to pursue a fairly cautious approach. The first phase of reconstruction was to involve five blocks in the precinct – an hotel and four large stores with inset shops. Generally, the main prospective tenants were to act as developers, on the understanding that they would then be offered ground leases by the Council. It was, in the end, conceded that these agreements should run for 99 years (with, possibly, one revision), since any other arrangement was likely to encounter strong resistance from the firms involved and at the same time place Coventry in an unfavourable position relative to what was being offered elsewhere. But, the developers were, at least, to be closely directed on the aesthetic side, with control over design, elevations and materials remaining with the City Architect. As an extra safeguard, the Council reserved the power to act as a developer in its own right, if the circumstances were held to warrant it.[101]

At first, progress with these various schemes and initiatives went reasonably well. Thus, completions on municipal housing contracts reached a record level in 1948, with four times as many units finished as a year previously, and, in all, well over one thousand families rehoused.[102] The Council was further reassured when its plan to complete the five precinct blocks over a three year period from 1 January 1949 was judged 'reasonable' by the regional representatives of the controlling Ministry.[103] There also seemed to be no shortage of possible takers for precinct sites:

according to the *Standard*, by the end of 1947, applications for shops had already exceeded the space likely to be available.[104]

However, by mid-1949, it became clear that the Council's plans were, once again, becoming ensnared in difficulties. One problem concerned the attitude of potential developers over the precinct scheme. For as negotiations proceeded, the authority was forced to recognise that its insistence on aesthetic and amenity provision was indeed acting to deter companies that otherwise might be attracted. Firms, for example, could not be interested in Block 'C' – the projected hotel at the top of the precinct – because it did not appear to be a particularly profitable proposition.[105] Considerable difficulty was also encountered over Block 'B' (opposite Block 'C'). The central issue here was that the development companies initially involved (principally Burtons) would not agree to build a connecting bridge over an adjoining street which the Council insisted was part of the overall package, because it was 'an architectural feature of the first importance to the redevelopment scheme as a whole'. In the end, the need to get reconstruction started persuaded the Council to act as a developer itself over this site, and a loan of nearly £400,000 was obtained from the Government to cover building costs.[106]

But, if these problems with developers proved quite serious, the Council's main area of worry lay elsewhere. For it could not avoid concluding that its expansion scheme was now increasingly at odds with some crucial objectives of government policy, so that further progress would be very slow without some special dispensation.

The Government had, in fact, moved to a more directive and interventionist position over Coventry in the wake of the economic crisis of 1947. In effect, it was accepted that the repair of blitz damage *per se* would henceforth have to be considered something of a luxury, which could not be allowed to interfere with the priority of improving the overall economic performance of the city's industries.[107] Specifically, this meant that the regional planning and building apparatus began concentrating more and more on engineering concerns, so that there was an increase, for example, in the licensed square footage of industrial rebuilds and additions.[108]

But the Government also recognised that positive stimulation of this kind was not enough, particularly because of the relatively small size of the city's construction sector. Consequently, departments were also concerned to discourage, and if possible curtail, any development that could be characterised as 'unnecessary'. Thus, Council pressure for additional shopping facilities to be sited in the city was simply deflected, even though there was a measure of official agreement that the existing situation had many disadvantages.[109] Similarly, the Boundary

Commission was advised against taking any positive action over Coventry's submission for more land, with civil servants emphasising their view that the city Councillors 'had opened their mouths too wide'.[110]

Of course, housing and the precinct scheme could not be treated in such an off-hand manner, because of the political ramifications involved, but even in these areas the imprint of government restriction was only thinly disguised. Control of construction in the centre was exercised through steel allocations, and though the total for 1949 (about 900 tons) appeared relatively generous, it fell far below what Coventry had requested, and would not, in fact, have satisfied the programmed demand for one block.[111] Local authority housing ostensibly remained free from such restriction, and the Ministry of Health suggested both quite generous annual ceilings for the Corporation to aim at and a new measure of control over licensing (which would ensure that the private sector received only one-fifth of any given allocation). But this policy was really somewhat disingenuous, since it left out of the account any mention of industrial building, the most lucrative and sought-after work available to local builders. Civil servants were, therefore, relying upon market forces to achieve goals that were too politically sensitive to be openly specified. The Corporation, then, simply found it more and more difficult to hold on to sufficient labour: while 749 men were employed on the 1,076 houses being built for it in December 1947, only 598 could be deployed on the 1,352 units under construction two years later.[112]

Yet if 1949 ended badly for the Corporation, things were very soon to deteriorate even further. One problem was the general inflation, which necessitated a rate rise of 2s. 6d. (14 per cent) virtually just to maintain parity: as the *Standard* put it, the Council had been 'caught like a wisp of straw in the whirlwind of rising prices'.[113] In this situation, any initiatives which might be seen as extravagant (like the municipal theatre) were quietly dropped.[114]

Nor could progress with central reconstruction provide much compensation. Activity on one of the sites where agreements with private developers had been signed was at a standstill while complicated negotiations with the existing occupiers dragged on.[115] Coventry's central area resource allocation for 1950 was also disappointing (again very much less than it had requested),[116] while a delay over making any decision about the scale of provision meant that the possibility of coherent programming was almost completely lost.[117]

Housing, however, remained the biggest problem. For the export drive (and possibly the prospect of rearmament) had convinced government departments that even any semblance of prioritisation in this area could no longer be maintained. Consequently, Coventry was told, firstly, that the 60:40 target ratio had been abandoned; and secondly, that its ceiling for house building in 1950 would be only 666 units – just over half of the 1949 figure.[118] In this situation, completions plummeted to 383, or 40 per cent of the 1948 high; and there was an appreciable increase in the size of the Council waiting list.[119]

Given these conditions, the Council began to explore some fairly drastic solutions to its main problems. There was some pressure to abandon plans to make Block 'C' a hotel, for example, and concentrate on much needed shops or use the resources to boost the housing programme.[120] But civic pride, in the end, proved more important than commercial gain, with the controlling committee of the Council concluding that:

> the loss of potential income involved in the siting of the hotel in Broadgate [at the top of the precinct] would be offset by the asset to the city in having its major hotel in the ideal position offered by the site overlooking the Broadgate garden island.[121]

On housing, some favoured the sale of Corporation properties, in order to cut costs, but this suggestion was quickly vetoed by the Ministry.[122] For others, the solution lay in a drop in building standards – especially the size of rooms – but in the end a majority on the Council decided that this could not be justified.[123] Agreement was, however, reached on the need for flats, and the City Architect began planning for a scheme involving nine-storey blocks in Hillfields.[124]

Yet, in the end, 1951 turned out to be a rather more favourable year for the Council than might have been expected. Another rise in the rates was inevitable, given the general conditions of inflation, but careful budgeting kept the increase down to 2s. (10 per cent). Meanwhile the prospects for the precinct blocks somewhat improved, because of an increased allocation,[125] even if the whole development was still dogged by difficulties over programming[126] and labour shortages.[127] Most importantly, the implementation of a contract with Wimpey[128] for over a thousand 'no fines' homes – houses built using a system that required very little skilled labour[129] – ensured a steep rise in completions. As applications for municipal property had, at last, considerably slowed down, the Council could end the year with the lowest aggregate waiting list since the end of the war.[130]

To what extent, in conclusion, had the Corporation been able to create the infrastructure for its ambitious 'welfare city' in the period to 1951? How, if at all, had the local built-environment and network of amenity and welfare facilities been modified by six years of Labour rule?

Many of the Council's achievements have already been touched upon. There were, for example, real gains for ordinary people in such measures as the continuation of the war-time nursery system, and the newly introduced 'meals on wheels' service for the elderly. Moreover, the Corporation's provision of nearly 3,000 permanent houses between 1945 and 1951 was quite impressive, particularly because many of these were of very high quality (bigger, for example, than guidelines established by the Ministry of Health recommended),[131] and on estates which won much praise for their sympathetic layouts.[132] And all this had been achieved, it could be pointed out, on rates which were, apart from two years, below the county borough average.[133]

But overall, progress was, no doubt, disappointingly slow. Certainly, the Council never came near to realising its own targets, for example, as the crude comparison of desired and actual spending in Table 4:3[134] demonstrates. In fact some priority projects – like the new general hospital[135] and the school building programme[136] – were simply shelved during this period. Elsewhere, municipal provision was wholly inadequate to meet the scale of the problem it was meant to solve. The Council could claim, therefore, to have dealt with most of the worst situated applicants on its waiting list by 1951,[137] but this still left a large residue of poorly housed families, and a blight of shanty town sites[138] and older slums.[139] The continued existence of T.B. at relatively high levels in the city was a measure of the Council's problems here.[140] Perhaps the lack of progress over the precinct scheme symbolised it all: of the five blocks, only one (the Council's Block 'B') had really been started by mid-1951.[141]

Table 4:3. Projected and actual capital expenditure by Coventry Corporation, 1945–51(s).

Capital programmes	*Projected targets*	*Actual expenditure*
1946–7	2,778,617	742,000
1947–8	4,761,200	1,463,000
1948–9	5,636,200	1,910,000
1949–50	6,254,800	1,709,000
1950–1	(no figure available)	2,140,000

More damagingly, critics could also argue that the full welfare impact of the various Council initiatives, even where they were in operation, was less than it appeared, since services were in some cases charged for at or near cost price. This was particularly true of housing, where the rent structure maintained by the Corporation in the post-war years – based as it was partly on current building prices – meant that tenants as a group were actually funding more of the total cost burden in 1951 than they had been in 1939.[142]

Why, therefore, was there such a gap between vision and reality? Lancaster and Mason's thesis, it will be recalled, puts the blame squarely on the Council itself, citing its lack of preparedness and subsequent failure of political will. However, when put in this particular way, the argument is open to criticism, because it leaves too much out of the account. The charge that the Council ignored issues like housing is certainly somewhat misleading. In fact, as has been exhaustively shown in Chapter 1, plans were relatively sophisticated and detailed on all issues of welfare and amenity provision;[143] and Councillors seem to have been fully aware of 'progressive' ideas circulating in other parts of the country.[144]

But a more serious omission by the authors is their failure to even acknowledge a whole set of external constraints within which Councillors found themselves working. Of course, all cities experienced shortages in resource allocation and limitations on their financial powers at this time. However, the argument developed over the preceding pages suggests that the interventions and restrictions of central government were especially marked in Coventry's case. The problem was not only outright opposition, but also the continuing undermining influence of disparate national policies aimed at, or influenced by, one end – the development of the city's engineering sector.

Yet, accepting these criticisms, might not the Lancaster and Mason thesis still hold good, albeit in a weaker version? For could it not be argued that, though important parameters were certainly set in Whitehall, a residual amount of leeway continued to exist for Coventry – leeway which the Corporation did not use because of its overcautious stance? To evaluate this argument, it will be necessary to turn to a more detailed analysis of the local political situation.

5 Social reconstruction? Politics and culture in Coventry, 1945–51

Commenting on the 1951 election results, George Hodgkinson, a local Labour leader, noted with some satisfaction that, in spite of all the Council's problems (and indeed Labour's predicament nationally), the people of Coventry had continued to show faith in the ideals of 1945 – 'the Welfare State and the welfare city'.[1] A superficial examination of voting data for the city over the post-war years, or a review of individual membership trends for the local Labour party, gives some support to the veracity of this observation.

Yet a close examination of the evidence on this proposition suggests that some qualifications to the picture it suggests may also be necessary. For Labour's hold on the electorate, it can be demonstrated, was at all times considerably more frail than it superficially appeared. Furthermore, certain major social developments in post-war Coventry – particularly the re-emergence of a vibrant consumer-orientated culture – certainly raised questions about the party's long-term ability to dominate locally.

Labour's appeal to the electorate in 1937, it will be remembered, was essentially about limited municipal reform. The party stressed that *all* Coventrians would benefit from certain changes – in the quality of life, welfare provision and cultural amenity particularly. The problem was that a small group of vested interests were exercising too much influence over the direction of municipal spending, so that resources were being squandered or used corruptly. Progress therefore depended ultimately on a return to business-like, efficient management, a shift that only Labour could orchestrate, since it alone was responsible to no one constituency in the community.[2]

Now, if these ideas were quite popular locally at the end of the 1930s, they became very much more so during the course of the war. In part, this change was encouraged by developing national concerns – emphases on the need for planning and a fairer society, for example.[3] But local factors, like the heightened civic consciousness generated by the bombing of 1940–1, were also important.[4] And, of course, the fact that Labour was in power throughout the period meant that it could, to some extent, guide public opinion, if only because its pronouncements and plans were very often the only ones available.

Against this background, the kind of reconstruction proposals framed by the Labour Council were bound to achieve popularity. Indeed, they matched popular perceptions and aspirations so well, that they could be presented as essentially non-political.[5] The consensus extended at least as far as the Conservative *Standard*, which noted after the 1945 election: 'our faces are set towards the same goal, and if we are to reach it we must adopt and adhere to the motto '"Pull together"'.[6]

In the first years of peace, Labour remained very concerned to uphold the terms of this consensus. It maintained a commitment to rate stability, for example. At the same time, the party was anxious not to become too identified with any particular interest group, so that pressure from trade unions[7] or others on the left (like the Family Health Club)[8] was firmly resisted. Conversely, the Council's committees spent a lot of time consulting with trade or licensed victuallers' representatives, since these groups could be regarded as expert in particular areas of reconstruction.[9] Finally, Labour emphasised on many occasions that it was not in favour of extending 'politics' any further into civil society: the suggestion that the education system should be 'socialised' could thus be greeted with horror by activists.[10]

Of course, other pressures sometimes provoked a departure from the consensus, and this was particularly true of events surrounding the proposed extension of municipal trading in 1947–8. But when Labour strayed, it was quickly reminded of what was at stake. As the *Standard* lectured on this occasion:

> The desire to establish a new Coventry worthy of the city is not confined to any section of the population, nor to any exponents of particular political creeds. Practically every citizen has a hungering after an ideal community, embracing the arts and sciences and moral virtues. Wednesday's vote [the town poll on the municipal trading proposals] constitutes a salutary warning to those who would imperil this unity of desire for the sake of doctrinaire experimentalism.[11]

Nevertheless, such polemic was somewhat unusual, and discussion normally centred only on detail rather than substance. One obvious area of public concern was over the pace of reconstruction, and this question provoked some controversy on a number of occasions. Labour argued that Coventry was in an abnormally difficult situation ('we are grafting on to an old town a new town's problems').[12] Conservative sources recognised that this was true, but suggested that the city's predicament was being exacerbated by the 'socialist' Government in London.[13] Significantly, neither the *Standard* nor the *Telegraph* extended much sustained criticism to the Council in Coventry.[14]

Quite a lot of evidence, then, does suggest that Labour had indeed achieved almost hegemonic status in Coventry over this period. The party's ideas and programme, in other words, formed the bedrock upon which discussion about reconstruction had to be founded.

Yet the analysis cannot simply be left at this point. For a closer look at the evidence reveals that this hegemony may not have been as all-embracing and stable as it at first sight appears. Labour was certainly the dominant party during these years, but even so a substantial number of the electorate remained unconvinced by its appeal. At the same time, some emphasis must be placed on the fact that the Labour ascendancy was achieved in a kind of political vacuum – a situation that was already beginning to change in the early 1950s. Furthermore, outside the immediate domain of politics, there were few signs indicating the emergence of the kind of 'responsible', community-orientated society so desired by the Council. In fact, many Coventry people remained wedded to those consumerist or 'low brow' pursuits that had been a feature of city life before the war.

The facts demonstrating Labour's domination of Coventry politics have already been discussed. The party maintained control of the council between 1945 and 1951, and also won every Parliamentary contest in the city.[15] Meanwhile, individual membership climbed by 51 per cent, to a total in 1951 of 4,557.[16] Surely this is enough to confirm the thesis of Labour's political hegemony?

The first point to make is that the Labour was perhaps less strong organisationally than these figures may suggest.[17] For example, several party ward committees were virtually non-existent at times over the period.[18] Similarly, while the party's women's sections appear to have been vibrant at all times,[19]the factory network established in the war collapsed rapidly after 1945 and was never revived.[20] Nor may all of the membership have been particularly active: an attendance of 500 was considered a good turn-out for a May Day rally, traditionally an important event in local left-wing circles.[21]

Secondly, it is important to emphasise that, even though Labour had majority control of the Council, the opposition parties together often polled more individual votes in local elections.[22] Furthermore, an examination of voting patterns ward by ward shows that Labour never came near to gaining a majority in five of the sixteen divisions.[23] Certain sections of the population therefore seem to have remained impervious to its appeal.

A final rider concerns the state of the opposition parties. For scattered evidence indicates that the Conservative and centrist progressive organisations were both weak at the beginning of this period.[24] Also, even in later years, personality clashes prevented effective opposition, so that attempts at an electoral pact continually yielded unsatisfactory results.[25] In fact, a coherent alternative to Labour only really began to emerge at the very end of the 1940s, when the opposition parties started to caucus before Council meetings,[26] and issue rather more persuasive propaganda.[27]

However, if Labour's immediate electoral strength was more precarious than it at first sight appeared, the party had also good reason to be anxious at some of the wider social trends that were emerging in post-war Coventry. Labour activists believed that their ability to stay in power depended to a certain extent on the efficacy of their own, and their Government's, political activity. But they also felt that the new housing and infrastructure arrangements in the city would be of decisive importance, not just because building would directly benefit an ever-widening circle of electors, but equally because of the indirect spin-offs that might be expected in the way of heightened civic consciousness and community identity.[28] Yet, as time passed after 1945, it became more and more obvious that the desired 'new society' was not, in fact, emerging, and that Coventrians were instead remaining wedded to their pre-war passions for consumption and popular entertainment.

It should be noted, firstly, that, for the ordinary citizen, everyday life in Coventry during the immediate post-war years was fraught with problems, but also pregnant with possibilities. Much of the work on offer in local factories was boring and monotonous, and insecurity provoked by regular bouts of short-time working was rife. On the other hand, wages were unusually high, and in the general conditions of labour shortage, it was quite easy to move from job to job in search of better money, particularly if family or social contacts could be utilised.[29] Indeed opportunities were open to many kinds of workers, with the Vice-president of the Coventry Chamber of Commerce retail section lamenting in 1950, for example, that 'we've got to be [polite] . . . if we said "boo" to what staffs we have left they would be off like a flash to the factories'.[30] Away from work, housing, as the previous chapter has documented, was in short supply, so that many individuals and families had to put up with overcrowding. But, again, the situation was not all bleak, in that the city had a large stock of reasonably priced private dwellings, and the path to owner-occupancy was by no means difficult to follow. Similarly, though Coventry had a dearth of shops,[31] which meant that obtaining even rationed goods could be a struggle, luxury items were not unknown, and, given only a little trouble, might be purchased on a burgeoning black market.[32]

Given these conditions, it is hardly surprising to find that getting and spending money were high on many people's list of priorities. Labour turn-over in the factories was considerable, as individuals sought to move up a well-known wages league table of local firms.[33] At the same time, the demand for sophisticated and expensive consumer goods – telephones or private cars, for example – consistently outpaced whatever level of supply was available.[34] Leisure activities also boomed, with enormous numbers of spectators at just about every kind of popular entertainment, from cinema[35] to speedway.[36] The local holiday industry, at first, was fairly stunted, so that the summer break in 1946 saw 'thousands of people . . . walking aimlessly through the streets or standing in queues for buses to take them a few miles away for a change from the every-day'.[37] But by the end of the decade, the general trend was observable here, too, with many families enjoying a variety of organised holidays in Britain, and a discernible number venturing abroad.[38]

The existence of this vibrant popular culture provoked frequent bouts of middle-class comment and concern. It was normally agreed that the problem was the hedonistic nature of local life. Coventrians did not seem to be interested in intellectual or artistic pursuits, as a correspondent to the *Telegraph* documented in April 1947:

> The Ice Follies, the Ballet as presented at the Hippodrome in full glory of costume and decor, the Chrysanthemum Society's lectures, an informal causerie-recital with refreshments, not forgetting the greyhound races, all drew a large and enthusiastic public; the Ballet Rambert, which had to rely purely on the excellence of its dancing, without scenic splendours, the concert for which the causerie-recital was a preliminary, were miserably attended, the latter attracting as many listeners as there were performers in the orchestra. . . . I could multiply similar instances.[39]

Given this analysis, there were a number of calls for some kind of spiritual regeneration.[40]

However, an unease with the situation was also evident in the local labour movement. One problem had to do with participation. People would shop at the Co-op, activists lamented, but they would not help run its affairs.[41] At the same time, the ease with which it was possible to switch jobs and the unofficial system of using contacts to gain preference in career moves to a certain extent undermined the potential for collective organisation at work. Certainly, though the unions were registering considerable success with recruitment, few attended meetings, and it was doubted by officials whether the membership would stand much strain.[42] But there was also a deeper frustration at the whole direction that events were taking. Hodgkinson made this point clearly in a debate over the 'austerity budget' of 1947:

> I cannot be a moralist . . . but I am bound to say that there is ability to pay in this city if people have the conscience to direct their money in the direction in which it can best be spent. It seems a scandalous thing that [£2,489,000] should be frittered away on the dogs when we are trying to build up brighter prospects for our children and that we have to stand here and do this cheese-paring.[43]

To cope with these problems, the Corporation began a number of initiatives designed to promote a more collective consciousness. Some of these were quite successful. Thus, two-hour 'Know Your City' bus rides, operated over the summer of 1948, proved popular.[44] *Civic Affairs*, the Council's newspaper, was also applauded, so that a circulation of 20,000 per month had been generated by 1952.[45]

But against these, there were several examples of failure or difficulty, which emphasised the gulf that had arisen between popular attitudes and Labour aspirations. An early indication of this problem occurred in 1947, when a proposal that volunteer labour be recruited for work on the city centre aroused little enthusiasm. As the *Standard* commented:

> There was a time – say at the moment when the scheme began and public imagination was kindled – when such an idea might have achieved some success, but since then interest . . . has flagged and many difficulties have arisen.[46]

The provision of new, local authority housing could also unlock, rather than ameliorate, tensions of this kind. Not all owner-occupiers, firstly, were pleased by the prospect of being near to the developing Council estates.[47] But nor, on the other hand, was the relationship between the authority and its tenants always free from conflict. Families moving into the new homes seem initially to have been very pleased with them, if a little critical of the lack of shopping and social facilities around them.[48] Yet problems soon began to emerge. For example, many tenants were not happy with the common open spaces surrounding their houses which the Council had provided instead of private gardens, in an effort to encourage community.[49] Against this, Council members were clearly disappointed in the behaviour of some of their tenants, and a network of 'Lady Housing Visitors' was set up to promote the required attitudes. However, the problem did not end here, since householders were often resentful of what they saw as 'snooping'.

This led *Civic Affairs* to a vigorous defence of the Corporation line:

> Houses now being provided by the Municipality are of the most excellent design and construction. . . . The Housing Committee do not desire that Corporation Housing Estates shall be 'different' in other respects from private estates, but in carrying out their duties . . . they provide accommodation for a section of the community for which the private profit-seeking builder does not cater, and this sometimes creates problems of re-orientation . . . The new conditions call for new habits and it is not easy for older people to make the change. It would be unfair to quote too many examples lest we be suspected of copying the comedians we have derided, but coals *have* been found in the bath, the washbasin *has* been used as a meat-safe and, recently, a Visitor *did* discover that the cupboard to the kitchen dresser had been transformed into a chicken-coop by the removal of the doors and the substitution of wire-netting.[50]

One outcome of this sort of tension was the Corporation-sponsored investigation by Birmingham University sociologists into tenants' views on the recently constructed Canley estate. But this, in turn, can only have generated further anxiety for officials, since it revealed the widespread continuing existence of those very individualistic attitudes that the Council had hoped would be fast disappearing.[51]

The evidence gathered in the preceding paragraphs, then, seems to suggest that working-class Coventry was considerably more conservative than might at first sight be supposed. Labour, no doubt, drew upon support from convinced socialists and particular client groups. But its wider popularity was squarely based upon a particular conjuncture – the 'moment' of 1940–1 – and a particular promise – to provide a range of civic improvements to which Coventrians felt they were entitled. Given this situation, the party could well be anxious about its longer term prospects. Sentiment generated by the experiences of war could not last forever. On the other hand, the continuing ability of the party to assuage popular enthusiasms for housing and amenities was being undermined by a whole range of physical and financial factors. Lastly, certain social developments appeared less than comforting. Above all, there was little sign of that transformation in popular attitudes which Labour activists had assumed, more or less explicitly, would accompany (and thus prolong) their period in office. A sympathetic journalist's characterisation of the city, as an 'ugly and half-painted backcloth to huge and clamorous factories, and, for the moment little more', underlined the scale of the problems that remained to be solved in this respect.[52]

6 Planning the 1950s: the construction of the 1951 Development Plan

One important stipulation of the 1947 Town and Country Planning Act was that each local planning authority should by mid-1951 have prepared and submitted to the Minister their first Development Plan – 'a fairly broad but definite statement of policy' showing how land was to be used and how development was to be programmed.[1] This chapter looks at the way in which Coventry formulated its main proposals to satisfy this stipulation, and in particular at how the Council proposed to continue its pursuit of the 'welfare city' objective in the light of the kind of difficulties (of population influx, industrial concentration and resource scarcity) which had impeded progress so much in the immediate post-war years.

The first stages of the re-evaluation process were largely concentrated on questions of population size and composition, especially after the contents of the advisory West Midlands Plan became known in mid-1948. For this document, drawn up at the Minister's request by Sir Patrick Abercrombie and Herbert Jackson,[2] suggested that, in the light of the considerable problems of congestion in the Black Country, movement of population into Coventry could not be curtailed,[3] so that the city's population would be likely to have risen to 306,000 in 1962 (from around 250,000 in 1948). Furthermore, it appeared from this plan that an extra 34,000 people living in neighbouring areas (Rugby and Warwick Rural Districts) would at that date be dependent largely on Council services.[4] In real terms, the city might have to cope with a 36 per cent increase in population over, perhaps, the next 15 year period.

Reaction to these projections was mixed. Gibson felt that the city was already too big, but his pessimism was not shared by other Council officials.[5] Doubts were also raised in the Ministry of Town and Country Planning, because of the fear that Coventry and its neighbours would in the end grow together, squeezing out what little Green Belt still divided them.[6] Nevertheless, there was increasing official agreement that

Coventry would have to be a 'reception area' if the West Midlands' problems were ever to be sorted out, and so the Council was in the end advised that it ought indeed to plan for 306,000 by 1962.[7]

This recommendation caused considerable consternation in the Coventry planning department, because it was by no means clear how or where the extra population would find work. One set of anxieties centred on the narrow range of local industries, and the possibility that the kind of seasonal fluctuations experienced in the 1930s might return, once the initial pent-up demand created by the war was assuaged. More specifically, the problem of firms that needed to be moved from the centre had still not been solved: would new industrial estates on the city's periphery be acceptable both to the entrepreneurs concerned and to the national planning authorities? Given this context, there was a strong emphasis, once again, on the need for 'diversification' – the existing balance should be maintained and augmented by the introduction of new concerns – and an insistence that this could only be achieved if the local planning authority was allowed more of a say in decision-making about industrial location.[8]

Civil servants agreed 'in principle' that the development of further industry in Coventry was necessary 'over and above existing industry'.[9] But immediate exigencies meant that this would be unlikely in the short term. Production ministries, for example, emphasised that the requirements of current export and armament firms must come first: in fact 'the industrial building programme . . . for at least the next five years' would most likely be taken up 'almost exclusively with provision for Coventry's existing industries and other needs'.[10] The Board of Trade at the same time underlined its policy of helping depressed areas, and let it be understood that it might well seek to persuade firms thinking of relocating to or from Coventry that their futures lay, for example, in South Wales, at least as long as there was no serious unemployment in the city.[11] Finally, all were agreed that, given the existence of significant returns to scale, further concentration of the car industry in Coventry would be 'not . . . avoidable'.[12]

How, then, was the possible future imbalance between population size and employment opportunity to be bridged? Here departments offered a number of different solutions. Firstly, there was some emphasis on the potential offered by what was alleged to be the current state of undermanning in local industry.[13] Secondly, departmental attention continued to focus on the low proportion of the city's female population who were in employment, which implied a hidden reservoir of labour, and thus the means of attracting some light industry.[14] At the same time, it was alleged that 12,000–14,000 people were coming into the city every day to work, a situation that might allow a growth of population not needing new jobs if more houses were built in Coventry, or a growing number of local employment vacancies if further homes were built elsewhere.[15]

Corporation officials did not accept much of this reasoning (they pointed out, for instance, that some women would continue to choose not to work as long as their husbands could earn high wages in the engineering sector)[16] but they received little support from others in Coventry. The Chamber of Commerce saw diversification as a real need, it is true, yet it also argued that the city could not afford to turn away firms in the motor vehicle industry, and insisted that a priority must be the retention of all existing local concerns.[17] Trade unions and employers in the engineering industry apparently believed that the first essential was 'a balanced labour force' – 'an adequate labour force to meet current demands'. There could be little justification for building, say, offices, since this would only lead to further competition for already scarce kinds of labour.[18] The real need, on the contrary, was for more housing, a development which would benefit both sides of industry.[19]

In the light of such argument, it was of little surprise when the Board of Trade's official advice to Coventry on what assumptions it should use in the Development Plan proved to be extremely cautious. The case for diversification was recognised, but the overwhelming concern remained throughout on shorter term requirements:

> It is essential that emphasis should be placed for some time on devoting resources to catering for the needs of existing industry and the provision of more non-industrial building rather than the development of sites or buildings for new industries.[20]

As a rider to this, the city was also informed that it would not be granted its wish to be consulted in the detailed process of decision-making over industrial location.[21]

Alongside these various questions about population and industry, Coventry's planners had also begun to examine a wide range of issues concerning the provision of housing and amenities. The starting point here was an accurate and detailed series of investigations into the whole problem of building labour in the city. These noted that the work-force available for construction of all kinds in Coventry had fallen from 5,788 in August 1946 to 4,249 in May 1949. Put another way, only 1.67 per cent of the local population were now engaged in this sector, when the national average was 2.0 per cent. But against this, the scale of demand had continued to increase, so that there was a considerable backlog of projects. Gibson calculated that, with the current amount of labour available, even after 20 years, only half of the required building (homes, facilities and amenities) would have been completed.[22]

The Council's reaction to these points was once again to argue that the problem could only be solved by Government intervention. Specifically, it wanted the Ministry of Health to allow the importation of building labour for municipal housing in Coventry, and the Ministry of Works to allow the Corporation much more say in the allocation of building licences.[23] But these appeals were received with little sympathy in official circles, particularly because, as one civil servant noted, Ministry of Supply and Board of Trade sponsored building programmes were 'already overloaded'.[24] In this situation, the Council was forced to conclude that future development would have to proceed in order of strict priority. Thus, it was decided that the civic centre could not be tackled as one project, but should gradually be pieced together, with the college of art being completed first, followed by some police buildings, a city hall, a swimming baths, a new central library, courts and a health and community centre.[25] Furthermore, development would not always be possible on the scale once envisaged: e.g. it was agreed that blocks in the precinct would have to be built with fewer storeys than originally intended.[26]

In addition to examining the overall scale of provision, the Council also gave some considerable thought to various more qualitative aspects of future urban development. One problem that seemed pertinent in Coventry was the question of social balance. Some Labour Ministers had begun suggesting in the post-war years that mixing between classes was an important element of healthy social development.[27] Yet Coventry was, as one planner put it, 'a workers' town', almost entirely lacking an indigenous middle class.[28] How could this pattern be righted?

The answer here seemed to be the provision of more salubrious housing areas. Consequently, though it seemed likely that overall densities would have to rise as the population increased, it was agreed to keep certain areas more sparsely developed with detached and semi-detached houses.[29] Nevertheless, not everyone was agreed that even this kind of measure would work. According to the Chamber of Commerce, for example, the 'executive class' lived outside the city 'because Coventry was too large and they did not feel themselves to be part of the community'. No amount of planning, it was stated, could alter this fact.[30]

But if the consequences of this kind of discussion were largely for the future, the Council was also obviously interested in the social effects of its already existing policies. Had the, albeit limited, housing development fostered 'community consciousness', for example? To this end, it was decided to commission some research into local attitudes, and a project was set up, using Birmingham University sociologists, in November 1948. At first, the idea was to use a random sample in gauging popular reactions to a wide range of questions (from details of house design to cremation), but the researchers were quickly forced to recognise that a more limited focus on one specific locality would probably be of more use in the construction of the Development Plan, and so they opted instead to concentrate on one of the new housing developments, a group of B.I.S.F. units in Canley.[31]

The results obtained were salutary, in that they questioned some of the more simplistic assumptions that had been prevalent in Council and local planning department circles. The key finding was that neighbourhood identity or community consciousness did not just emerge, given the construction of a particular arrangement of buildings and amenities, because residents would already have a range of attitudes to social contact, based on factors like status and imputed 'respectability'. The Council could not therefore simply rely on building one, universal type of neighbourhood unit, but would have to experiment with several, based on detailed knowledge of the preferences of different types of potential tenant. The need, in other words, was 'to shift the emphasis from the physical determinism of the expert bureaucratic plan to the activities of the residents themselves'.[32] Moreover, the researchers also warned that the desire for privacy was more cherished and widespread than had previously been imagined:

> The requirement of high standards of privacy is not confined to the upper income groups. Residents in the lower income groups may be willing to forgo some of the amenities of the house in order to secure these higher standards of privacy.[33]

Again, the implication was that the Council's pursuit of any group identity (civic consciousness, for example) would have to be directed through channels other than the built-environment.

How, then, did the Development Plan look when it was finally approved by the Council for submission to the Minister in late 1951?[34] The first section dealt, as might be expected, with the city's recent history and outlined its main problems – the shortages of housing, schools and other amenities and facilities; the over-specialised nature of the local economy; the tangled and inefficient urban road system; and the unsatisfactory nature of some older, central slums.[35] Subsequent chapters then outlined, subject by subject, how the city might be expected to develop over the following years. It was suggested that the populace would indeed number about 340,000 by 1971, including 40,000 incomers from Birmingham's overspill.[36] Housing development was to be such that the bulk of people would not live at densities of more than 60 rooms per acre (roughly the standard recommended in the 1944 *Housing Manual*) though there would be areas of greater concentration in the inner city, and some 190 acres of low density units elsewhere.[37] Amenity provision was to be considerably augmented, through, amongst other things, the completion of the original central area scheme, and the provision of 44 new schools, 13 new libraries and 14 health centres.[38] In addition, the document promised that open space in the city would be doubled to 3,060 acres.[39] The neighbourhood unit idea was not completely rejected, but now presented in modified form. The city would be broken up into constituent units of 5,000–20,000 persons, but these were to be defined simply in terms of the siting of facilities and the means of welfare provision. If this grouping produced an increase in neighbourhood spirit, the document concluded, it would be 'an additional advantage'.[40]

The section on trade and employment accepted that over the following five years the amount of new industrial development in the city would be 'almost negligible'.[41] This was, at least in part, because the Council had been forced to accept that diversification and increased amenity and welfare provision were largely mutually exclusive possibilities:

> it is strongly felt . . . that the social disadvantages of new industrial development – even when this is by way of extensions to existing factories – now far outweigh all other factors. Coventry is seriously short of all social and cultural amenities, and has an enormous housing list to clear, and these jobs must take priority over industrial development where there is no conflict with overriding national considerations.

Nevertheless, it seemed unlikely that there would be any serious unemployment problem in spite of the population increase, since existing industry was certainly short of labour, while the number of people working in the city but living elsewhere would most likely decline. Furthermore, in the long term, diversification might occur, as a consequence of the Birmingham overspill.

The Plan ended by specifying some elements of an immediate five-year programme. Special emphasis, it was suggested, would be placed on concentrating resources in two inner-city neighbourhoods – Spon End (39 acres) and Hillfields (163 acres) – which it was proposed might be designated as Comprehensive Development Areas by the Minister (thus allowing the Council augmented rights of compulsory purchase).[42] More generally, a committee by committee breakdown of projected building expenditure to 1956 revealed, once again, the prioritisation of housing (49 per cent of the total), central redevelopment (21 per cent) and education (20 per cent).[43]

The publication of Coventry's Development Plan met with generally favourable reviews in the local and specialist press,[44] though the enthusiasm generated was in no way comparable with that which had surrounded the war-time plans. More interest greeted the release of findings from the sociological survey, not only because (as has been suggested) these posed questions about a pervasive interpretation of neighbourhood unit planning,[45] but also because they seemed to point to the need for a closer relationship between planner and public.[46]

In a real sense, then, the Development Plan represented both continuity and change from previous attempts at shaping Coventry's future. In constructing the final document, the Council had become perhaps less sanguine about planning in general, both in terms of its impact on people and in terms of the overall degree of autonomy which might be available to any one local authority. But it had certainly not just jettisoned ideas from previous plans, and indeed Gibson's original scheme for the city centre was retained almost unchanged in the new proposal. Above all, the Council had kept faith with the vision of what Dennis Chapman called a '"suet pudding" kind of city' – a city where, amongst other things, there would be 'relations of friendship and social contact . . . and not withdrawal or conflict'.[47]

7 Sustainable growth? Coventry's local economy in the 1950s

In the post-war years, it has been suggested, Coventry's economy was largely shaped by proscriptions and stimuli originating from Whitehall. Growth was strong, but the symbiotic relationship between the Government and local entrepreneurs that gradually emerged brought its own problems, both in terms of structural character and in terms of actual performance. The tendency to 'overheat', especially, was a constant difficulty which became serious enough during the early phase of the Korean war rearmament programme for the Government to impose a ban on further military spending in the city.

This chapter looks at how the local economy developed in the 1950s, and in particular at the characteristics of the growth that occurred over that decade. Were the problems experienced after the war still manifest, or had Coventry been able to move towards a more secure and sustainable pattern of expansion?

The Government's ban on further armaments spending in Coventry took effect from December 1951, but, by early the following year, it was already the subject of some controversy. For as the policy had become operative, there had been a simultaneous but coincidental deterioration in the commercial situation of the motor vehicle trade. Firms continued to experience difficulties over steel, of course, but there was now also a growing list of other shortages involving 'hundreds of components and accessories'.[1] From early 1952 a deterioration in export markets added to the bleak picture,[2] and several companies were left with embarrassing stocks, which had to be sold at a loss.[3] In response to these problems, there was some redundancy (with 800 being discharged from Rootes)[4] and considerable short-time working.[5]

In this climate, unease about the Government's intentions could only grow. Was it true, for example, that steel allocations were being deliberately manipulated to damp down civilian production, and ease the predicament of armaments manufacturers?[6] Departments recognised the potentially damaging features of this situation very quickly, but there was some disagreement about exactly what should be done about them. The Treasury apparently opted for a hard line, and advised against any easing of the ban.[7] At the other extreme, the Ministry of Labour was quick to emphasise the political repercussions that might accompany any further redundancy.[8] More pragmatic reasoning also favoured a change of tack. The Ministry of Supply, for example, was concerned that labour 'should not be dispersed unprofitably' during the 'temporary dislocation'.[9] The Services pointed out that the re-location of contracts simply meant increased costs to the Government.[10] Mounting evidence seemed to show, anyway, that much arms work continued to go to Coventry, for the simple reason that it could not be undertaken anywhere else.[11]

Matters finally came to a head at the end of 1952. The ban had been relaxed somewhat during the summer,[12] but its continued imposition in any form now came to be strongly questioned by the Admiralty, which wished to place a number of contracts in Coventry as a matter of urgency. In the end this pressure, the prospect of further short-time working as the car industry entered its traditionally slack winter period, and the wider reassessment of the whole armaments programme that was going on, together proved irresistible and the ban was finally lifted altogether in early 1953.[13]

Over the following three years, Coventry enjoyed almost unprecedented boom conditions. Growth, once again, was based not on the arrival of fresh industries (Industrial Development Certificates issued for new factory building related to an area about one-fifth that granted for extensions and repairs, 1953–5)[14] but rather on existing sectors. Armaments work continued to be of importance, firstly, even if the overall national programme had been curtailed. In fact 'defence' orders were sufficient to provide continuous employment for 20,000–30,000 throughout this period,[15] and embraced, amongst other things, Armstrong Whitworth's sub-contract work on Meteors, Sea Hawks and Hunters,[16] G.E.C.'s provision of communications equipment to N.A.T.O.,[17] and Standard's supply of Avon jet engines to the Ministry of Defence.[18]

But the most dynamic sector was undoubtedly motor vehicles. The stimuli here were home demand, which was increasing at unprecedented rates,[19] and very healthy interest in specialist markets abroad (particularly the U.S.A.).[20] The consequences were impressive. Thus, between 1951 and 1955, the work-force grew in size by one-fifth to around 50,000,[21] while the annual output of cars from Coventry rose from 125,000 to 203,000.[22] This expansion in turn allowed increased wages[23] and record rates of return for the companies concerned, with, for example, Standard's net profit figure rising from £853,069 in 1950–1 to £1,934,044 in 1954–5.[24] Given such statistics, it was of little surprise to find that Coventry's reputation as the 'Klondike City of the Midlands' had once again become firmly established in popular mythology.[25]

Nevertheless, despite all of this, the expansion in the motor vehicle industry was perhaps less securely based than it at first sight appeared. For the two firms at the heart of the trade – the volume producers Rootes and Standard[26] – though ostensibly healthy, continued to be plagued by a variety of production and financial difficulties, such that their future viability was periodically in question.

The basic fact about both firms was that they were not really generating sufficient unit returns. In part, this reflected longer-running factors – Standard's high-wage strategy,[27] Rootes's scattered factory locations.[28] But it was also a consequence of the particular pattern of growth experienced in the early 1950s. For the expansion of demand and output that occurred during these years did not follow a linear trend, but was (as in the late 1940s) frequently interrupted, due amongst other things to changes in consumer taste,[29] variations in government tax policy[30] or foreign tariffs and quotas,[31] and shortages of raw materials.[32]

This meant, in turn, as Table 7:1 indicates, that production was often at levels well below capacity, a situation that could only result in inflated unit costs and deflated unit returns.[33]

What made this lack of profitability particularly threatening, of course, was that it compromised the possibility of future expansion. For, in the absence of sufficient internally generated funds, the firms had to

Table 7:1 The Standard Motor Co.: daily output of cars and tractors, various dates, 1951–4[34]

Date	*Output of cars*	*Output of tractors*	*Output of all units*
April 1951	259	300	559
Nov. 1951	236	304	540
April 1952	176	ncf	ncf
July 1952	ncf	320	ncf
[Target set December 1952	320	400	720]
April 1953	ncf	265	ncf
June 1953	222	265	487
March 1954	300	245	545
June 1954	ncf	ncf	632

Note: ncf = no comparative figure available

consider raising money on the open market, always a relatively expensive option.[35] The possibility of self-perpetuating decline – with low profitability and low investment levels reinforcing each other – therefore began to appear ever more likely.

What, then, were the companies doing to protect themselves from this threat? One strategy, pursued particularly by Standard, was to bank on the inelasticity of demand and charge relatively high prices to the consumer.[36] Both firms, secondly, were keen to expand their product ranges, with Standard concentrating on its existing tractor capability[37] and Rootes developing its position in the commercial vehicle market.[38] The hunt was on, too, for further capacity through take-overs or mergers, so that the early 1950s saw Standard involved in talks with, in turn, Ferguson, Rover, Dennis and (inevitably) Rootes.[39]

But none of these initiatives proved very successful. The scope for price variation was obviously limited by competition. Moreover, alternative products were not necessarily any more profitable than cars: *The Economist* noted that tractors provided Standard with 'a satisfactory bread and butter business', but it added that the butter always appeared to have been 'spread thin'.[40] Finally, though merger talks were easy to initiate, they were more difficult to satisfactorily conclude, and neither firm was in the end able to find a suitable partner.

In the face of these constraints, and given the projected ambitious expansion plans of the other members of the 'Big Five',[41] the Coventry firms were persuaded more and more that they would have to make fairly fundamental modifications in their basic cost structures. Rootes began to explore whether it would be possible to move more of their operation out of Coventry, in order to bypass the high labour costs they incurred in the city.[42] But their more central strategy, which was shared by Standard, involved a large investment programme, financed from the market[43] and aimed at transforming the production process by introducing new machinery, so as to cut the size of the work-force[44] and thus move a stage nearer 'automation'.[45]

This was a high-risk option for several reasons. As has been suggested, going to the market was, in any case, an expensive way of raising capital. Furthermore, it was recognised that the new machinery would only be economic if volume production could be maintained.[46] But the greatest problem for the companies stemmed from the fact that automation seemed likely to lead to some kind of confrontation with organised labour.

Trade union strength was increasing in Coventry throughout the early 1950s, so that by 1955 there were about 75,000 members with high concentrations in the engineering industry.[47] The membership in general was not very militant,[48] as the data on strikes in Table 7:2 confirm, but it had won considerable concessions in day-to-day decision-making at the different factories. Thus, the unions were generally successful in their attempts to persuade companies to ride down-turns, not by redundancy, but by introducing short-time working.[49] Furthermore, there was considerable informal control of hiring and firing. The position at Standard, as outlined by the District Secretary of the T. and G., was certainly extreme, though by no means untypical of the general trend elsewhere:

> We have no agreement with the Standard Motor Co. which says that they must obtain labour from the Trade Unions, but it has been the practice for some time for the Company to recruit . . . from Trade Union sources, and arrangements are made by the Shop Stewards within the establishment to see that vacancies are allocated to the Unions, roughly pro rata to the membership within the establishment.[50]

Table 7:2 Number of strikes and aggregate days lost, the Coventry motor industry, 1945–55.[51]

Year	*No. of strikes*	*No. of days lost (agg.)*	
1945	3	37,850	
1946	13	146,985	(includes 80,000 at Humber, 58,000 at Daimler)
1947	5	14,726	
1948	4	5,118	
1949	6	2,952	
1950	6	2,746	
1951	5	32,959	(includes 20,500 at Jaguar)
1952	3	2,939	
1953	2	4,612	
1954	2	34,580	(all at Standard)
1955	4	7,500	

Given such 'unfortunate deficiencies in [the] management of labour',[52] as William Rootes saw it, few could be confident that automation would be introduced peacefully.

For some firms, the early 1950s boom continued well into the second half of the decade. Jaguar's production increased from 10,000 units in 1954 to 19,450 four years later, based on the seemingly inexhaustible appetites of U.S. consumers. Alvis, producing Leonides aero-engines and Saladin armoured cars alongside a dwindling number of expensive cars, were very successful, too, so that gross trading profits increased from £374,000 to £562,000 between 1954 and 1958.[53] But, elsewhere, the situation was very much less favourable, as some of the problems that had been latent in the late 1940s and early 1950s began to assume a more overtly threatening demeanour. In fact, between 1956 and 1958 Coventry was rocked by a series of down-turns – first in motor vehicles, then in aircraft and finally in machine tools – the scale of which had not been seen before in the post-war years.

Problems began in the motor industry during the early months of 1956. The initial difficulty was a government credit squeeze, which cut demand sharply, and thereby caused widespread short-time working at Rootes, Standard and a number of other companies.[54] In this climate, popular anxieties were further heightened when Standard announced that they intended to lay off 2,500 employees (over one-fifth of the total work-force) during the summer, in order to reorganise its tractor line and thereby facilitate the introduction of various new machine tools.[55] The union response here was to argue that the 2,500 should not be discharged but rather placed in the company's car plants, with every worker employed then being allotted a reduced number of shifts. However, management rejected this solution as administratively impossible and reiterated its original plans. The end product was a company-wide strike by all 11,000 employees, beginning in late April.

Over the following few weeks, media interest in this dispute ensured that it became an issue of national, not just local, concern. In part, this was because of the alleged role of Communist party members in fomenting discontent and dominating the Standard shop stewards' organisation.[56] But the strike also attracted attention because it seemed so clearly to be about automation, this becoming the *angst* word of 1956. According to the *Financial Times*, it was no less than 'a test case for the reaction of British industry and British workers to the stimulus of economic change'.[57]

This kind of coverage no doubt suited the company, but it did less than justice to some of the issues involved. Standard had certainly been moving towards a harder line position on labour relations for some time,[58] and there is some suggestion that their stance was part of a wider initiative by local employers to redraw the boundary between management and union functions.[59] At the same time, amidst all the talk of automation, there was very little detail about what might actually be at stake in terms of long-term job losses. Yet Dick, the Managing Director, was very clear about the labour-saving potential of the new machinery he had ordered:

> We are not installing £4 million worth of equipment to employ the same number of men. We cannot carry people for fun. The number of men taken back will depend on car production at the time.[60]

Nevertheless, if the media played down this issue, its immediacy was not lost on the work-force, so that the unions had no trouble in sustaining the strike well into May. In fact, a return to work only took place after the company had gone some way to meeting the union case, by agreeing that, though redundancy could not be avoided altogether, at least some transfer from the tractor plant to the car lines would also be possible. Yet, by early June, it was clear that the scope for this kind of compromise had significantly diminished. Hawks within the Standard management were no doubt encouraged by veiled declarations of support from the Government. At the same time, the local union leadership was to a certain extent undermined by the actions of national officers, who saw the dispute as an opportunity to forge a path-breaking redundancy agreement which could be copied elsewhere. Finally, there was a definite crumbling of solidarity between the different company plants, and a growing hostility amongst the car workers (encouraged by management) towards the principle of work-sharing. The episode ended with the company reverting to its original plans and declaring 2,000 redundancies. Considerable publicity accompanied Standard's payment of £15 to each man discharged, since this was allegedly the first time that a firm had granted such compensation. But it was not until some years afterwards that the company admitted that it had also used this opportunity to sack some known militants.[61]

However, if managements in the motor trade hoped that this victory would pave the way for a return to prosperity, they were soon disappointed. For the industry was next shaken by a major drop in demand for its products, caused first by variations in overseas nations' trading arrangements, and then by the ramifications of the Suez crisis (which included petrol rationing).[62] The consequence, inevitably, was further short-time working – Standard and Rootes's plants were kept on four- (and sometimes three-) day rotas over the autumn and winter of 1956–7[63] – and considerable redundancy.[64] At a peak, more than 10 per cent of the city's insured population (of about 172,000) were affected by these measures.[65] Most attention focused on the fully unemployed, who increased in number from 720 in March 1956 to a peak of 5,781 (3.3 per cent of the insured population) in March 1957.[66]

Recovery from this down-turn, when it eventually came, was fairly slow, and it was not until late 1957 that plants were producing at anything like full capacity, largely on the basis of a fortuitous upsurge in American demand for small cars.[67] In effect, then, production had been badly down for a period of more than a year (Standard's output of cars fell from 85,000 in 1955 to 57,000 in 1956 and 54,000 in 1957)[68] with inevitable consequences in terms of revenues. Rootes was particularly badly hit – it was in the middle of re-tooling when the down-turn began, and had no small car to offer as petrol rationing bit[69] – though as the data in Table 7:3 demonstrate, Standard did not do much better. A

Table 7:3 Rootes and Standard net profits (£s), 1955–7 (Rootes year to 31/7, Standard to 31/8)[70]

	1955	1956	1957
Rootes	1,503,367	687,736	(268,948)
Standard	1,934,044	573,004	330,104

Note: figure in parentheses = loss

number of small car producers suffered considerably too, and edged nearer leaving the trade altogether.[71]

But if Coventry had been badly hit by the motor industry recession, it was next faced with a variety of problems in two of its other main industries. One set of difficulties stemmed from the overall reassessment of military expenditure that had peaked with the Macmillan Cabinet's proposals of early 1957.[72] For it now appeared likely that contracts in a number of areas, especially aircraft, would be curtailed, with drastic consequences for several local firms.[73] One early casualty was a project that had been placed with Armstrong Siddeley to produce an engine for the P.176 supersonic bomber, a cancellation that led directly and indirectly to over 1,000 redundancies. Elsewhere, the position was hardly more encouraging. Armstrong Whitworth was told that it could continue to rely on the production of the Sea Slug guided missile for the Navy, but in the light of projected output levels of armaments in general, its future seemed to hinge on the self-financed AW 650 civilian transport plane, the success of which could only be rated as 'doubtful'. What made all this particularly worrying was that there appeared to be no real hope of any future return to prosperity; indeed, informed official projections suggested that the total work-force employed by the two Armstrong firms would drop from around 15,000 in 1957 to the 7,000 mark by 1960.

Meanwhile, there were also growing signs of a recession in the local machine tool industry.[74] Orders from abroad had been falling since 1956, but this trend was especially noticeable at the beginning of 1958. The problem, it seemed, was that British companies had simply fallen behind in terms of innovation, so that they had little to offer in the way of new electronically controlled systems.[75] Again, the immediate consequences were falling returns and redundancy: Alfred Herbert, for example, suffered a 22 per cent drop in profits between 1956–7 and 1957–8, and as a result opted to prune over 1,000 workers (or one-quarter of the total) from its pay-roll.[76]

As a consequence of these various difficulties, there was considerable discussion in Coventry as to where the city's industrial future might lie. The ruling Labour party was particularly concerned by the course of events, and in February 1957 went so far as to set up a working party to investigate the causes of local unemployment.[77] This body met 24 times over the ensuing months – interviewing many trade unionists, including Roy Reuther of the American auto-workers, and visiting the Volkswagen works in Germany – and eventually produced a 38 page report towards the end of the year.[78]

The working party's central recommendation, perhaps unsurprisingly, once again highlighted the need for diversification. There was a great need, it was argued, to reduce the city's dependence on motor vehicles and aircraft, and this might possibly be done by encouraging the development of other kinds of engineering, 'such as participation in the railway modernisation programme, and . . . the atomic energy industry'. The Council certainly had a role to play here, and it was suggested that positive initiatives might include the appointment of a full-time Industrial and Commercial Development Officer and the provision of a new trading estate. Furthermore, pressure should be put on the Board of Trade for 'a measured relaxation of the present ban on factory building in Coventry'.

But the working party was also keen to emphasise that future prosperity would only be possible if all the interested parties in Coventry co-operated in its pursuit. Management, it was suggested, could no longer afford to treat labour as subservient; while the unions should develop a 'responsible' and 'modern' stance on questions such as automation. To foster such attitudes, there was a need for 'some kind of civic act', which would celebrate industry's wealth-creating role, and emphasise 'the value of united action by all those who . . . [had] a common interest in the maintenance of full employment'. To this end, it was suggested that the Lord Mayor should convene a special conference of employers and unionists, which might then develop into a permanent forum, able to examine such issues as 'the Common Market and its problems in Coventry' and 'the social responsibilities of industry'.[79]

In early discussions as to how this latter idea could be put into practice, it soon became clear that some care would be needed in selecting what subjects should or should not be included in a projected agenda.[80] A few issues were clearly too controversial (this applied to 'the social responsibilities of industry'), while others would be regarded by the two sides of industry as matters for direct negotiation. In the end, it was decided that 'planning for industry' might be a suitable topic, especially since it seemed to open the way for extensive local authority participation.

But even here, it was acknowledged, the need for tact would be at a premium. For example, as one prominent member of the Council's planning department reflected, the subject of diversification was not without its own pitfalls:

> Experience in the past with both sides of industry has been that this tends to be a loaded question in view of the fact that Trade Unions do not want particularly to have competition, nor do employers of labour want to have firms brought in. . . . I personally think it is still a highly important and controversial matter but I am now very sceptical as to whether either side of industry will look at the problem dispassionately.[81]

Of course, it was also recognised that unilateral declarations from Coventry would in any case be irrelevant unless Government departments showed some signs of moving from their present restrictionist position. But the likelihood of this was slim, as a Board of Trade officer informed the Council:

> [he] was firmly of the opinion that the recession in the motor car industry of 1956 was a very temporary feature and saw no reason to modify the original attitude of the Board . . . namely, that no substantial new industry was necessary in Coventry. On the other hand if a major enterprise . . . were to undertake expansion or new construction in the city, no obstacle would be put in the way.[82]

Given these circumstances it came as little surprise, when the Lord Mayor's Conference did finally occur in December 1958 and January 1959, that incisive debate between the various parties was hardly much in evidence.[83] Discussion ranged over topics such as the city's communications and sewerage systems, and was only really remarkable for a strong attack by the employers (supported by some trade unionists) on the whole basis of previous local authority planning. Coventry would have to decide, it was suggested, whether it wished to remain a leading industrial city or become 'a spa or garden city'. Certainly the present policy, which allegedly 'sought merely to eliminate an unpopular industrial process by "zoning out" over a period of 10 to 20 years', when coupled with the practice of issuing short-term planning permissions, could only have 'disastrous effects in terms of local employment'. Industry, the employers argued, had frequently come off second best in the present Development Plan, and this would have to be rectified in the quinquennial review that was about to be begun.[84] Accordingly, the only real innovation that came out of the whole initiative was a permanent committee of representatives from the Council, the employers and the unions to 'enable informal consultation to take place on town planning matters affecting the City's industries'.

Part of the explanation for the complacency which marked these discussions stemmed from the fact that, while they were proceeding, the economy had once again begun to boom. A sharp upsurge in demand for motor vehicles was experienced at the end of 1957,[85] and there then followed three years of more or less sustained growth, with Rootes's output of cars and commercial vehicles, for example, increasing from 97,000 units in 1957 to 175,000 units in 1959.[86] This in turn meant enhanced profits – Standard's net returns more than doubled between 1957 and 1958 alone[87] – and higher wage levels.[88] By 1959 memories of the events of 1956–7 had dimmed.

However, as more critical observers of the local economy recognised, the sudden upsurge did not mean that all was well or that Coventry's underlying problems had been cured. Coventry's volume car producers were still distinctly lightweight in terms of their capital resources. Moreover, some of the commercial strategies being followed were clearly risky – with Standard's decision to sell their tractor interest, and use the money gained to launch the Herald, attracting particular comment.[89] Finally, it was also apparent that various problems in relation to the work-force still remained debilitating. Coventry firms had generally moved to harder positions on industrial relations after Standard's 1956 victory, but this management offensive had produced its own problems in terms of a growing number of unofficial strikes.[90] At the same time, smaller companies continued to find themselves unable to compete against their bigger competitors when it came to attracting labour.[91]

The pattern of development which characterised Coventry's local economy in the 1950s was, therefore, broadly similar to the one which had been experienced in the immediate post-war years. Growth was, once again, very considerable – employment in the city grew at about 2.4 per cent per annum over the decade, compared to a national rate of 0.8 per cent per annum[92] – and there was the same narrow range of really dynamic sectors (principally aircraft and motor vehicles). In addition, the Government's influence continued to be pervasive, with the Board of Trade in particular maintaining a pivotal role – exercising 'the power of life and death in this City', as the Secretary of the Chamber of Commerce put it.[93]

Extending this comparison, it may be suggested, too, that the balance of advantages and disadvantages which flowed from this particular trajectory also remained very mixed. Coventry's affluence could be exaggerated in popular accounts,[94] but the great majority of its workers did certainly go on earning relatively high wages throughout the 1950s, and unemployment stayed well below the national average for all but a few months.[95] However, the economy was no more securely based in 1960 than it had been in 1950, both because of the flawed nature of much of the existing enterprise, and because of the continuing lack of diversification. Fifteen years of growth had therefore provided considerable well-being, but no very safe platform for the future.

8 City reconstruction: building a new Coventry, 1952–60

In the first six years after the ending of the war, as Chapter 4 has shown, little progress was made with the construction of a 'new Coventry'. The Council had planned the precinct, for example, around five large blocks, each costing around half a million pounds, but by 1951 building work had really only started on one. A similar lack of achievement was evident in the provision of the planned welfare and recreational amenities. Most seriously, the Council remained saddled with a major housing problem. The waiting list for municipal property was still over 9,000 applications long at the end of 1951, with the difficulties over accommodation being complicated still further by the high rents it was necessary to charge on post-war dwellings.

The following paragraphs focus on attempts to resolve these various problems, and fulfil the kind of promises that had been made in the 1951 Development Plan, during the period 1952–60. These were years, of course, in which Coventry's local economy was often buoyant, which meant that the Corporation continued to have to deal with substantial migration into the city – as many as 20,000 people (equivalent to one-thirteenth of the 1951 population) arrived over the 10 years.[1] But, if this was a familiar problem, the Council also had to cope with new factors, the most important of which was a changed legislative and financial framework, consequent upon successive Conservative victories at Westminster. The first question to explore, therefore, must obviously be concerned with the initial thrust of Conservative policy: how did the new Government of late 1951 propose to deal with the whole reconstruction problem?

The Conservative approach was based on a number of different premises. One kind of reasoning was purely pragmatic, so that Macmillan, for example, could argue that while a larger programme of blitzed city reconstruction was not defensible in economic terms, it might be justified on grounds that were 'political and perhaps moral'.

The aim, above all, was to avoid 'agitation' – 'deputations, adjournment debates and so forth' – which would be especially likely, given any Conservative failing, in those cities where local power was held by Labour.[2]

But there was also a more ideological strand to the new Government's thinking, which was most evident in discussions over the key question of housing.[3] Conservatives recognised (however reluctantly) that the central role allotted to local authorities in the post-war housing drive would have to be maintained for some years to come, though they added that in future the emphasis in the public sector would have to be more on output pure and simple and less on maintenance of 'extravagant' standards of provision. But it was also felt that activity should, from the outset, reflect a new strategic goal – the creation of a widely-based property-owning democracy. In practical terms, of course, this meant freeing private enterprise builders from the controls that had been exercised under Labour.

How then were these various requirements translated into actual policy? An early indication of the new thinking came in December 1951 when Macmillan dropped the compulsory one to five ratio that had lately been introduced to allocate building licences between private and public housing schemes. Within a little over a year, the licensing system itself had been abolished for some kinds of private sector building.[4] Meanwhile, local authorities had come under increasing pressure to adopt new designs for houses, featuring smaller superficial areas and lower room heights, with the additional carrot before them that, if they did so, they would be allowed larger overall allocations. The controlling Ministry also made it very clear that it was in favour of extending the use of non-traditional types.[5] Coventry, to be more specific, therefore found that Macmillan had re-negotiated the standard prices of 'no fines' units above the level that had previously been agreed between the local authority and Wimpey, in order to give that firm an extra incentive to expand its operations.[6]

Coventry Council's response to these various initiatives was varied. There was unanimous agreement that the process of reconstruction should be speeded up. However, Councillors also continued to reaffirm their belief that there should be no deviation from the paths mapped out in the various local plans. In particular, it was felt necessary to underline the need for those developments that had already been characterised in some quarters as marginal components of the new city, e.g. the civic centre.[7]

On housing there was also some equivocation. The Corporation certainly disagreed about the need for an enhanced private sector, and continued to use the five to one principle in dividing up allocations as long as it was legally able to do so.[8] On the other hand, it was recognised that some economies might be possible, given a re-examination of housing and estate design. Some dimensions, such as room height, were regarded as sacrosanct.[9] But in the circumstances, a range of other measures – smaller floor areas, tighter overall densities, eleven storey blocks of flats – seemed inevitable.[10] Finally, it was clear that the Corporation's reliance on Wimpey's 'no fines' system would now have to be increased. The arrangement was already producing very quick results – over 1,000 units were completed on the initial contract at Tile Hill in just over two years.[11] But as the restrictions were lifted from private enterprise builders, and the scramble for local labour and raw materials increased, the advantages of dealing with a large national firm, controlling its own workforce and capable of delivering significant economies of scale on sizeable orders, were becoming ever more important.[12]

But whatever the merits or otherwise of these various positions, all the parties interested in Coventry were hamstrung during the early phases of the new Government by a very familiar problem – the inadequate size of the local construction sector. Again, the essence of the problem was unplanned and chaotic stimulation from London. Housing was the agreed priority, at least ostensibly, of the whole Government, but this did not stop the Home Office from lobbying hard for a new £400,000 police headquarters.[13] Nor did it deter the Ministry of Supply, co-ordinating the rearmament programme, from trying to build, as one observer put it, 'more factories in Coventry than . . . [could] be manned with industrial labour'.[14] In this situation, it was inevitable that completion rates on the city's civil programmes would once again begin to deteriorate.

The Corporation's response to this problem was to repeat the argument that since Coventry had special difficulties it should also be awarded special assistance. This point was made very forcefully by a deputation that saw several Ministers in June 1952:

> They said that even in 1939 the population was already far short of the normal amenities of urban life and that the blitz and subsequent increases in population and industrial development had made life in the City now intolerable. There was a desperate need for more shops, hotels, public houses, health centres, swimming baths, libraries etc. . . . Coventry must be given the labour and investment needed to provide the amenities and should be treated as though it were a new town . . . if the [building] labour force could be increased to the national average of 2% of the population, this would enable the maximum building requirements to be met in the next five years.[15]

Departments responded to this kind of plea in rather different ways. All were agreed that there was a problem of 'overloading', but the difficulty was to see in which direction a solution might be sought. The Treasury argued for a total ban on all new building contracts for a fixed period, in order to clear the backlog, but the Ministries of Supply and Housing insisted that their programmes should remain untouched.[16] Another solution, the importation of building labour, was opposed by the Ministry of Works, on the grounds that it would only mean debilitating other projects.[17] Underlying all of this, perhaps, was a degree of scepticism about Coventry's predicament. As one senior civil servant remarked: 'I don't myself think that there is anything to be done for Coventry, where life no doubt is very uncomfortable – but there are worse things than a boom.'[18] In the end very little action was taken, with the Government limiting itself to reserving some places in its own local hostels for builders, should they wish to come to Coventry.[19]

Yet despite these problems, 1952 ended and 1953 began with a resurgence of optimism on all sides. Housing completions were much better than had once been feared, and at 1,382 units for 1952 easily outshone the performance in the next best post-war year.[20] Coventry had certainly benefited from the Government's eventual cuts in the rearmament programme, but the key to its success here was the growing proportional importance of the 'no fines' system, with Wimpey being responsible for one-quarter of the units under construction in early 1950 but about 42 per cent three and a half years later.[21]

Furthermore, the Government, at least, seemed to be signalling that it expected progress to continue. Thus the capital allocation for central area reconstruction during 1953 was up on the 1952 figure.[22] More significantly, the targets announced for the next two annual house building programmes – 1,650 units for 1953 and 1,900 for 1954 – were considerably larger than anything that had been accomplished so far.[23]

Two further events also boosted hopes. Firstly, the Corporation was at last able to find a developer who was willing to take on the hotel block at the top of the precinct in a way that would not jeopardise the integrity of the whole Gibson scheme.[24] At the same time, local morale received a considerable fillip in February 1953 with the public inquiry into the Development Plan. For although over 540 statements of criticism or disapproval had to be dealt with during the hearing, the Corporation could draw considerable satisfaction from the Inspector's overall conclusion that 'considering the positive nature of the Plan the objections of weight were not many'.[25]

Over the following three years, the promise evident in 1952–3 was more than fulfilled. Progress was marked in most of the main spheres of reconstruction. In the city centre, to begin with, the precinct now began to take on a more definite shape, following the opening of the main blocks – Broadgate House (May 1953) and then Woolworth's (August 1953), Marks and Spencer (April 1954), Owen and Owen (October 1954) and British Home Stores (May 1955).[26] Meanwhile, there was also some advance in the Council's plans for civic amenity provision. The partial opening of the College of Art in March 1955 was clearly an important marker, particularly since the project was the first of its type to be attempted in post-war Britain.[27] Definite progress seemed to have been made, too, with the Council's attempt to provide Coventry with a municipal theatre. Negotiations over an existing building had to be abandoned because the price of purchase was simply too high, but subsequent plans for a custom-built auditorium were proceeding well, and a loan application had been lodged with the appropriate Ministry. Further optimism was generated on this front when, at the public enquiry of December 1954, only two objections were raised against the project.[28]

At the same time, the school building programme planned during and just after the war at last began to be realised. One or more parts of five new secondary schools were completed, allowing an extra 4,500 places. Progress in the primary sector was also considerable, and in fact 21 infant, junior or junior mixed schools were opened over this three-year period.[29]

But the biggest leap forward came in the sphere of housing provision. Large contracts for 'no fines' units – at, amongst other places, Tile Hill, Willenhall and Bell Green[30] – ensured a steady stream of Corporation completions, numbering altogether 4,806 in the years 1953–5.[31] The months of 1955 were particularly successful ones, so that the total for the whole of that year, which included units in Coventry's first 11-storey flats at Tile Hill,[32] broke all previous post-war records. Inevitably, this meant a decline in the Council's waiting list, despite the fact that over 9,000 new applications were made over this period.[33] However, the most spectacular changes were registered in the private sphere. Annual completions here had rarely reached above the 300 per annum mark to 1953, but as the restrictions and controls on builders were lifted, there was an upsurge in activity, so that the combined total for 1954 and 1955 – 3,915 units finished – was more than the entire output of the eight previous post-war years.[34]

But if Coventry Council could be gratified at the extent of this progress, it had also cause to be concerned at certain other developments that were occurring during this period. One worrying trend was a string of decisions by various Ministries which seemed designed to limit or re-shape crucial elements of the Council's plans. Furthermore, there were also adverse movements in the Corporation's financial position, resulting both from the statutory mechanism which had to be used for the acquisition of land, and from the Conservatives' wider move away from the 'cheap money' policy of the post-war years.

Evidence that the Government's wish for expansion did not extend to all aspects of the Council's plans first surfaced in 1952, when the controlling Minister made it clear that he would not be willing to sanction the proposed health centre at Tile Hill, which was to be the first of 14 that the Council had originally intended.[35] A further blow came one year later, with the Minister of Housing's decision not to enforce the removal of the Singer factory from Hillfields as the Council wanted. The point here was that the position of the plant effectively limited the kind of development, featuring blocks of flats and open spaces, that the authority had planned, so that its retention meant a considerable delay in beginning the reconstruction of this 'blitz and blight' area.[36]

The third incident of this kind came at the beginning of 1954. For some months the Council had been looking at how to build the link blocks (the two-tiered rows between the main buildings) at the eastern end of the precinct. Ravenseft, the developers of the hotel site opposite Broadgate House at the top of the pedestrian way, were very keen on the contract, and emphasised that their connections with the builders McAlpine would allow fast completion. But though this offer appeared attractive to some Labour Councillors, a majority in the end decided that, because of 'the potential asset to the City of this property', they should rather seek to repeat the procedure used with Broadgate House, and develop the project themselves. However, when this proposition was put to the Minister, he turned it down, arguing that 'the wiser course' would be to accept the offer made by Ravenseft, since that company was better equipped to deal with the risks inherent in the situation. In the end, the Council had no alternative but to accept this decision.[37]

The final incident (which was also perhaps the most damaging politically) occurred a few weeks later, when the Cathedral Reconstruction Committee, which had been planning a new cathedral for some years previously, finally decided that the time was now opportune to begin actual building. Its request for a licence was received enthusiastically in parts of Whitehall, with Eccles, the controlling Minister, especially 'anxious to make an early start'. But the Council was far less impressed, since it was feared that this kind of initiative might well deprive higher priority projects (specifically housing and schools) of building labour and resources. Again, however, events unfolded very much as the

Government wanted, and the Council was simply told that its objections were invalid and that the licence would be granted.[38]

Meanwhile, alongside these specific reversals, the Council also found itself troubled by the more general problem of a deteriorating financial situation. The administration recognised, as before, that the possibilities for increasing rate income were fairly limited, because of the political backlash that might be thus engendered.[39] But they could also not ignore the fact that costs were rising steadily, for a number of different reasons.

One set of problems stemmed from the Conservatives' general policy of raising interest rates on local authority borrowing. The expansion of the early to mid-1950s had of course meant increased expenditure, with the rate-borne part of the education account alone being 86 per cent up in 1954–5 on the figure for 1949–50.[40] Increased spending was partly covered by grants from the centre, but it also meant a heavy extension of borrowing, so that the Council's net loan debt rose from 13,331,098 in 1951 to 26,116,235 in 1955, a jump of 96 per cent.[41] The problem with this was that the cost of borrowing was increasing too – new loans could be had at around 3 per cent in 1951, but at over 4 per cent three years later[42] – which added an extra burden onto the Council's annual budget. In fact by 1953–4, interest payments on all the various loan accounts amounted to over one million pounds, or about 18 per cent of that year's gross expenditure.[43]

As if this was not enough, the Council now also began to experience some of the financial difficulties that had long been forecast by critics of the 1944 and 1947 Town and Country Planning legislation. The Corporation's general policy was to acquire land in the 270 acre Declaratory Order area as and when it could be specifically used in the reconstruction programme. But the existence of a clause in the statutes which compelled purchase from owners who were prevented by planning decisions from economic use, meant that there had been considerable over-buying – amounting to 9.5 acres or one-fifth of the total area amassed by 1955.[44] Furthermore, the prediction that betterment would be bound to accompany piecemeal acquisition now proved correct, so that the Council found itself paying more and more for each unit purchased.[45] On the other side of the account, receipts from leases were often disappointing, since clauses guaranteeing periods of peppercorn rent had had to be inserted in many of the contracts to compensate the signatories for the unfinished state of their particular building or the precinct in general.[46]

The position over Broadgate House seemed to symbolise all the Council's wider problems over finance. This building had originally been started, with the Corporation as developer, in January 1949, but shortages delayed completion until mid-1953. By opening day the authority had already had to service the original loan of £400,000 obtained to finance the project over a period of nearly four years without any balancing rent income. But even with lessees in place, and rents set very much at market levels, the budget on this account was completely out of balance. Indeed in March 1954 it was calculated that, for the previous 12 month period, loan charges were two and a half times the size of received rents. Given this situation, it was of little surprise when the Council eventually decided to use monies from its Capital Fund to pay back some of the original loan.[47]

The period from the end of 1954 to the end of 1956 was one of reassessment in Coventry. The trends described in the preceding paragraphs would, no doubt, on their own have given rise to some questioning about the future of reconstruction. But Donald Gibson's resignation as Chief Architect[48] and his replacement by Arthur Ling, together with an increasing amount of outside critical interest in what had already been achieved magnified the mood of introspection. Furthermore, the Council now found itself suddenly with very much less room for manoeuvre over all its building programmes, as a consequence not only of the Conservative Government's growing recourse to deflationary controls, but also of a decisive swing in the city's electoral balance.

Ling's appointment was the first of these various catalysts. A one-time assistant to Walter Gropius and Maxwell Fry, Ling had risen to become Senior Planning Officer of the L.C.C., on the way gaining an enormous amount of experience about reconstruction problems, particularly in relation to the East End of London.[49] He clearly was well suited to follow Gibson, not least because he had come to believe, like his predecessor, that the technical skills inherent in good architecture and planning were not enough on their own, but had to be meshed with a close appreciation of the user's attitudes and needs:

> To put several thousand people in one block of flats on stilts just because the designer thinks it is a good idea and gives scope for his designing ability is not a sure way of achieving successful results. On the other hand, I think it is essential that the technician should not compromise his integrity to the extent that he gives people what they want without bringing his specialised knowledge and designing ability to bear on the problem of their demands. The result must satisfy both the architect or town planner and the people for whom he designs and builds. This requires effort on both sides, and a first essential is that people should be in a position to feel that they are the initiators as well as the recipients.[50]

What questions were being asked, then, about the kind of reconstruction that had already taken place? There seemed little need, firstly, to challenge the general trend that had been established. Indeed, Coventry could rightly take pride in the considerable official praise that continued to be heaped on its efforts.[51] Equally, the favourable view that seemed to be emerging in Whitehall about the city's Development Plan – with detail only, and not substance, the subject of criticism – could be taken as further comfort.[52] Moreover, press coverage was, with few exceptions, at least favourable. *The Economist*, for example, comparing reconstruction in Coventry, Plymouth and London, had concluded that the Midlands city's efforts were by far the most successful. R.Gardener-Medwin, in a survey for the *Listener*, extended the comparison to Rotterdam and some German cities, but still found Coventry worthy of considerable commendation.[53] Nor was the specialist architectural press very much less positive. Writers disagreed about specific details (with only Broadgate and Tile Hill receiving wide acclaim) but there was universal praise for the attempt at overall co-ordination and strong positive reaction to the feel of the new developments.[54]

But, if the general trend established appeared about right, this did not mean that more specific criticisms were inappropriate. Ling, seeing the city with new eyes, was especially struck by two kinds of failing.[55] Firstly, he noted that, inspite of the various planned intentions, little had been done to solve Coventry's traffic problems. The centre of the city was still congested, while parking on outlying estates, which were largely without garages, continued to cause widespread damage to forecourts and grass verges.[56] Street accidents had regained their pre-war level by 1948, and then continued to grow, so that the total for 1955 was some 59 per cent greater than that for 1938.[57] But despite these trends, ameliorative measures were few and far between, and even so central a feature of the overall plan as the inner ring road had been caught up in a bureaucratic tangle of muddle and delay, and thereby not even begun.[58]

At the same time, Ling was also critical of what he described as the over-rigid segregation of the zoning used in the planning approach. This was a particular problem in the central areas, where the exclusion of residential developments meant that a feature like the precinct was almost unused both at night and at the weekends.

What could be done about all of this? Clearly there was a need to lobby further for some already planned features, like the ring road. But Ling was also keen to make the segregation of traffic a more prominent principle in all planning questions. Would it be possible, for example, to return to the original conception of the precinct, and pedestrianise the north-south, as well as the east-west, axis? Furthermore, could the

Radburn system of design for residential developments – 'whereby the approach to the houses and garages was from the rear, and the front was free from traffic'[59] – be incorporated into the future planning of the new estates?

The problems with the centre might also require some departure from existing principles. One obvious need was for some further positive features, to make the precinct generally more attractive. But Ling also felt that the time had come to move away from extensive suburban development and concentrate instead on intensive inner-city growth, using tower blocks set in open space to bring people back into living near the centre.

Ling's ideas clearly impressed the Council, so that there were some fairly immediate modifications of policy. It was agreed, for example, to plan a new estate at Willenhall specifically on the Radburn system.[60] Decisions over aspects of the precinct's design also reflected some fresh thinking. One of the second group of major blocks, the Corporation proposed, should be built so as to include a substantial dance hall.[61] In the same spirit, the western link rows would be built by the Council so as to encourage the widest possible range of retailers, and thereby avoid the situation that was held to mar Ravenseft's existing eastern development, where some shops had been allowed to occupy both upper and lower tiers of the twin decks.[62] Most significantly, the Council also agreed to accept Ling's advice on the north–south axis and revert to Gibson's original intention that it should be fully traffic free – a decision that was praised in the *Guardian* as a 'Triumph for Radical Replanning'.[63]

Yet, before very much else could be achieved, the Council once again found itself entangled in a multi-faceted political and financial crisis. One aspect of this was a growing anti-Labour mood amongst the local electorate, confirmed by the Conservative gains in the 1955 local elections, and the near loss of Coventry South in the subsequent national contest.[64] At the same time, the Corporation also found itself having to face major restrictions on its capacity to initiate investment, imposed by the Conservative administration as a reaction to balance of payments problems.[65]

The beginning of the deflationary spiral had been signalled by the Chancellor in a speech of October 1955, which called for restraint on investment expenditure, and announced the virtual termination of the system whereby local authorities had previously been able to obtain at least some specially priced funds. A few months later 'restraint' was replaced by 'standstill', to cover all new building, except where it concerned housing, schools or some main roads. In October 1956, this ban was made indefinite.[66] Meanwhile interest rates had been gradually moving upwards, so that housing loans which had cost 4 per cent on the open market at the start of 1955 were being priced at 5.75 per cent 20 months later.[67] Finally, and most seriously perhaps, major changes were instituted in the whole basis of local authority housing finance, with the withdrawal of the 'general needs' subsidy – which had previously supported most provision – and the substitution in its place of a system aimed largely only at slum clearance.[68]

The Council's initial reaction to all this was narrowly political, in that it was decided to shore up support in Coventry by using the opportunity offered by a national re-valuation of property to cut the annual rate from 23s. 6d. to 16s. 4d.[69] Subsequently, local officials began an extensive process, once again, of consultations and re-evaluation, so as to shape the various municipal programmes into forms that would be both permissible and possible in the future.

It was obviously necessary to establish, for example, how government departments now intended to vet investment projects submitted to them. Recent decisions suggested no fixed pattern. Permission to proceed with the theatre project had been granted in early 1956. But an application at about the same time to build community meeting places on municipal estates, by contrast, met only with refusal.[70] Again, what credence would be given in future to the Corporation's increasingly strongly held conviction that the precinct would only make sense commercially – in terms of both rentals and rateable values – if it were allowed to go forward as a continuous and ever increasing programme of works, rather than as a series of isolated projects in a miasma of incompleteness?[71]

Some guidance on these kinds of problems was provided at a meeting with Ministry of Housing and Local Government officials in November 1956. A measure of restriction on future building, the civil servants reported, could not be avoided. But in general the position was not as bleak as it might appear. In fact, the city could expect more lenient handling than most other places: 'Coventry . . . would be treated as the Government's new town ie. . . . there has to be some slowing down, but . . . the work must be kept going, and . . . there must be continuous development.' In detail, this meant that work already started (the theatre and the police headquarters) or in the pipeline (a new retail market, the south link block, and some new Council offices) would be allowed to proceed, while other projects were not necessarily to be discouraged.[72]

The situation over housing was rather different, in that the new measures introduced by the Government clearly offered hardly any room for manoeuvre. In strict terms, Coventry faced less of a slum problem than many of its neighbours, since much dilapidated property had been destroyed in the raids of 1940–1.[73] But there remained substantial areas of 'blitz and blight' near the core which the Council had long wished to redevelop. Given the new housing subsidy structure, and in the light of Ling's arguments about the need to bring people back into the inner city, it seemed logical to conclude that such areas should in future be at the centre of the authority's strategy.[74] Accordingly, a considerable amount of time was spent looking at how best to initiate such development, and in particular at whether it would be feasible to follow the example which seemed to have proved successful at Tile Hill – and was being pursued in various parts of London – and plan for high densities through the use of tower blocks.[75]

Yet in the end all this re-planning counted for very much less than might have been expected. For in the final three years of the decade, it became clear that, whatever had or had not been promised in late 1956, Coventry was certainly not going to be given any special status in its dealings with the Government. Consequently, the authority found itself, like many of its counterparts elsewhere, continually buffeted by deflationary pressures designed to limit its overall spending. In this situation and given the delicate electoral balance in the city, even the new, reduced objectives that had been adopted in the mid-decade reassessment became quite problematic.

Of course, the picture was not all bleak. On the positive side, a number of projects that were either at an advanced design stage or actually building in early 1957 now reached completion – notably the Belgrade theatre (March 1958) and the dance hall (August 1960).[76] School building continued too, while years of Corporation negotiations over health centres eventually produced some result with the opening of the Tile Hill facility.[77] In addition, a significant advance seemed to have been made with the ring road scheme, when the Ministry of Transport finally granted permission for the first phase of construction to begin during 1958.[78]

However, if the Council was thus able to oversee some limited degree of progress, it was also aware that many of its other ambitions were effectively undermined by aspects of government policy. A certain amount of control from the centre was exerted directly. Thus, some schemes put up to departments by the Council were simply judged superfluous – a fate that befell a projected municipal swimming pool, for example.[79] On other occasions, pressure was exerted in a more subtle way. Ministerial approval was granted when the Corporation applied to build a café in the western part of the precinct, but a rider was added that the authority should not operate the enterprise itself. As it happened, this did not finally deter the Council, though it did, of course, remove another good, potential source of income from the municipal budget.[80] Finally, the official insistence that, wherever possible, returns from completed units in finished parts of the precinct should reflect market rates was also damaging, since it prevented the Corporation from obtaining the wide range of shops it planned,[81] and led to numerous complaints about extortionate rents and narrowness of choice.[82]

But the Government's most potent weapon in controlling all local authority spending was the *de facto* power it had in keeping the price of borrowing relatively high.[83] Coventry's net loan debt, as has been suggested, was considerable in this period, so that inflated interest rates in the end meant that servicing payments were accounting for a higher and higher proportion of gross annual expenditure, perhaps one-fifth of the total by 1960.[84] One way out of this predicament, obviously, would have been to raise local rates. But here, once again, the Council faced considerable difficulties. The cut allowed by the re-valuation in 1956–7 had had to be reversed the following year, due to rising costs and a Government concession – worth 25 per cent of their rateable value – to shops, businesses and commercial premises.[85] Subsequently, political considerations remained strong enough to make a rate-stabilisation policy unavoidable and any advantages that came to the Council (such as a change in the industrial de-rating regulations)[86] were in fact used to this end. But this of course inevitably meant question marks over the reconstruction process: how could the present pace of building possibly be kept up? Labour activists were obviously unhappy at any suggestion of cut-backs in the various programmes, but they also had to recognise, with Hodgkinson, that there was 'a limit to the burdens one generation . . . [could] carry in furtherance of the enjoyment of another'.[87] After some debate, therefore, it was finally agreed that a diminution of investment budgets was inevitable, and a new set of greatly reduced targets was announced for the years around the turn of the decade.[88]

The position over housing presented a particularly clear microcosm of the Council's wider predicament during this period. Private building tended to remain largely impervious to government restrictions, so that houses in this sector continued to be finished in quite considerable numbers to 1960.[89] But the situation with municipal provision was very different. The number of units completed here had reached a record level (1,998) in 1956, as the big 'no fines' contracts of the early 1950s came to fruition.[90] However, over the following years, this sphere of the Council's activity (like every other) was subject to growing financial strain, the result of declining subsidies and increasing interest rates. Again, it was felt that no further burden should be imposed on the rate fund,[91] and so the Council had only the choice of raising rents or curtailing spending on the account. The former option was implemented in early 1958,[92] but as the overall financial position still continued to deteriorate, the Council could also not avoid programme-cutting.[93] The end products were a dwindling number of completions (1,082 in 1957, 905 in 1958, 689 in 1959 and 293 in 1960);[94] very little progress with the kind of inner-city redevelopment that had been so carefully planned as the new focus of Corporation strategy;[95] and a waiting list that continued to hover above the 4,000 applications mark (despite several revisions).[96] The decline in the Council's capital expenditure on housing – from £2,898,296 in 1956 to £1,044,109 in 1960 – summed up the whole sorry story.[97]

How much, then, had the Corporation been able to achieve between 1952 and 1960? Hannen Swaffer,writing for the *Daily Herald* at the turn of the decade, suggested that there was quite a lot to celebrate. Coventry, he argued, was 'England's finest example of proletarian tenacity and courage', since the Labour Corporation had not only seen the 'Vision Splendid' – 'the dreams of William Morris and the early pioneers' – but had also gone out and 'realised it'.[98] To what extent was this latter judgement justified?

No one could deny that the Council had done a lot. The new shopping precinct, to start with, which had gradually taken on a definite shape in the 1950s, was a great success, both with customers and traders, so that the previous trend whereby Coventrians went to other cities for their major purchases was more than reversed.[99] Furthermore, some municipal developments in the precinct were beginning to look like quite good business propositions, in yielding a degree of profit for the Corporation coffers.[100]

Progress with rectifying Coventry's long-standing deficiencies in housing, schools and recreational facilities had also been impressive. Over the period, for example, 10 new secondary schools and more than 11,000 extra dwellings were added to the Corporation stocks.[101] Moreover, the decision to build a municipal theatre (which Ken Tynan called 'one of the greatest . . . in the history of local government')[102] did much to reduce Coventry's previous reputation as a cultural desert.

Finally, the Corporation had also good reason to be pleased with the *way* in which reconstruction had evolved, in two different senses. On the one hand, Councillors were able to point out that, in spite of all the building, rates in the city had never been particularly high.[103] At the same time, on a rather different tack, they could also draw pride from the fact that, though architectural standards and fashions had changed sharply over the 1950s, reviews of Coventry by specialists in the early 1960s remained positive.[104]

Nevertheless, the dimensions of this impressive record should not be exaggerated. In a relative perspective, for example, Coventry's achievements in the fields of, say, housing and recreational provision[105] were by no means exceptional. Furthermore, even taken on their own, some of the Corporation's initiatives were, perhaps, not quite so successful as they might at first sight have appeared. There was certainly a problem with damp in 'no fines' dwellings, for example, though its extent remained a subject of dispute.[106] The precinct, too, was not without its problems. Visitors from outside Coventry were struck by the sameness of the shops, and the lack of life there in mid-week ('Like Aberdeen on a flag day') and at night.[107] It was also clear that the Council's architects had not solved the problem of what to do with the areas behind the shops fronting the pedestrianised ways, so that they had become, as one observer put it, 'in effect inferior and slightly dangerous parts' of the whole.[108]

But perhaps the Corporation's greatest failing had been its inability to deal more fully with the needs of those it had originally set out to help the most, the less well-off. Rents in the municipal sector, for example, were not particularly low,[109] since the Council had always opted to keep the rate-funded element in the total housing budget at relatively modest levels.[110] Nor were the new municipal estates very well served with amenities. The contrast between planned and actual provision at Tile Hill in 1959, shown in Table 8:1 was typical.[111]

Table 8:1 Planned and actual amenities at Tile Hill, 1959

Neighbourhood buildings planned	*Neighbourhood buildings in existence*
Community centre 1	Churches 3
Church 1	Pubs 3
Youth centre 1	Health clinic 1
Branch library 1	
Pub 1	
Day nursery 1	
Swimming bath 1	
Cinema 1	

Most seriously, significant sections of the poor had remained quite untouched by the ameliorating initiatives emanating from the authority. In 1961, for example, 23 per cent of households in the city still did not have regular access to piped hot water.[112] Given such statistics, it is unsurprising to find, as well, that infantile death rates for inner-city areas were very much higher than those found in more salubrious neighbouring suburbs.[113]

In the end, therefore, the 1950s turned out very much like the years 1945–51, with actual achievements, substantial though they sometimes were, falling a long way short of planned targets. How should this 'gap' be explained?

Conservative administrations after 1951, of course, were keen to present themselves as practitioners of a very much less directive style of government than that which had allegedly been employed by their Labour predecessors, but as this chapter has made clear, whatever these claims, the reality of the situation was that, at least when it came to centre–periphery relations, Whitehall continued to dominate. Indeed, in relation to the provision of local authority services, central government policies were often decisive, shaping not only levels of supply (through variations in the cost and availability of resources) but also levels of demand (since decisions over industrial location tended to determine the scale of labour inflows).

Yet, having accepted all of this, it would be wrong to conclude that developments in Coventry were totally determined from outside the city. For the Council could, and did, exercise a certain degree of choice, as when it made decisions, for example, over rate levels. It remains, therefore, to elaborate on the logic and circumstances that informed such judgements – a task that will be attempted in the following chapter's analysis of the local political balance.

9 An 'affluent society'? Politics and culture in Coventry, 1952–60

In Chapter 5 it was suggested that Labour's 'hold' on the Coventry electorate in the immediate post-war years remained considerably more precarious than some contemporary and later accounts would suggest. The party's ascendancy was certainly not the final flowering of a deep-rooted radical tradition in the city, but rather the product of a particular kind of appeal – reform which would make Coventry both more equitable and more efficient – and a particular set of historical circumstances – above all the Blitz of 1940–1. This situation, in itself, was bound to cause problems with the coming of peace. But in the years after 1945, the local Labour party was also dogged by other difficulties. Government policy meant that the actual pace of reconstruction in the city continued to be significantly retarded. At the same time, Labour's hope that a new, more 'progressive' local society would emerge alongside – even because of – the new buildings seemed less and less realistic. By 1951, it had become abundantly plain that the party's ability to dominate local politics was hardly secure.

This chapter looks at how Labour attempted to resolve its difficulties against a range of developments that were occurring in the 1950s. How did the real progress that was made with physical reconstruction during these years affect the local political equation? And did the boom conditions of 1953–5 and 1958–60 drive another nail into Labour's coffin, by popularising the 'you've never had it so good' philosophy of the Conservatives? To answer these kinds of questions, it will be necessary to divide the whole period into two, and concentrate first on the years leading up to the 1955 General Election.

One certain fact about the early 1950s in Coventry was that the local political environment appeared to be becoming considerably more complex. Some developments, such as the increased tempo of municipal building, were potential vote winners for Labour. But against this, the party was forced to recognise that sections of the electorate who previously had been assumed to be very loyal to Labour were now increasingly becoming apathetic or even antipathetic.

On the plus side, Labour could no doubt draw considerable comfort from the popular approval which accompanied the upsurge in building completions. Tenants moving onto the new housing estates were usually generally very pleased with their recently completed dwellings.[1] Moreover, public reaction to developments in the precinct remained positive.[2] This favourable atmosphere was underpinned, finally, by the attitude of the press. For although both the *Standard* and the *Evening Telegraph* were not slow in criticising aspects of the Council's activities, and frequently argued that private enterprise should be given a greater role in the civic reconstruction process,[3] they also continued to broadly uphold the consensual position on reconstruction that had been generated in the early 1940s. A *Standard* editorial of late 1953, entitled 'The Post-war Renaissance of Coventry', was typical of its general line:

> There is no denying that all of us feel a pride in the great work now being done to construct . . . a new heart to the living organism. . . . The ideas we are now expressing . . . are the best that this generation can devise and we hope that posterity will say that we have builded well. . . . These are wonderful times for the citizens, and especially for the younger generation.[4]

But despite this kind of praise, the Labour party was also aware that it faced a number of actual and potential difficulties. The 'responsible society', so desired at the end of the war, seemed to be as far away as ever. A flourishing local economy focused attention still further on money wages and consumption, and provoked more disparaging comment about Coventry's materialism and lack of soul.[5] Moreover, there was growing concern about the scale of the city's social problems (drunkenness, marital breakdown, hooliganism)[6] and an often repeated worry that Coventry was becoming almost lawless – 'dangerous . . . after dark, and even sometimes before it is dark'.[7]

Furthermore, Labour activists could not help recognising that relationships between the party and key groups in the population who had previously been assumed to be very loyal were becoming strained. As has been suggested, tenants moving onto the new estates were generally very pleased with what they found, but this did not prevent specific complaints about mud or the lack of facilities.[8] Equally, the local authority had to face the fact that its policy of keeping forecourts open and common was very unpopular in many areas. Tension here stemmed not only from the questions of upkeep and maintenance, but also from the widespread popular desire for privacy.[9]

Alongside these difficulties, there were also problems in the factories and with the unions. Workers, it seemed, were becoming more apathetic and less inclined to become involved in collective organisation or action.[10] One worrying symptom of this was the criticism which greeted the local launch of *Labour Voice*, a paper specifically designed for the shop-floor, especially because many of the adverse comments focused on the overly-political character of the publication.[11] Meanwhile, strain was also evident in relationships with some of the local unions. The Corporation's attempt to deal with its transport undertaking's long-running deficit by altering manning levels led to industrial action, and considerable disruption, during 1953–4, on the bus network.[12] The Council had also cause to be concerned when various revelations about the extent of local racial discrimination were published in the Coventry press.[13] The problem, here, was that some union branches seemed to be at least implicated, a fact that was deeply embarrassing not only because it affronted Labour's cherished internationalism, but also because the party had traditionally drawn strong support from the city's Indian community.[14]

But what made these various developments particularly threatening to Labour was the fact that they coincided with a resurgence of activity from a range of its political opponents. In fact, the party was now not only subject to closer criticism than ever before in the post-war years, but it was also confronted by competitors who seemed very much more in tune with at least some of the social developments that were occurring in the city.

One focus of opposition was a network of ratepayers' organisations, co-ordinated into a Coventry-wide Federation, which vigorously campaigned each year for objectives like 'more economic' Council rents.[15] Yet the Conservative party itself had also gone through something of a rebirth at the beginning of the decade, so that by 1953 it could boast 8,000 members and a good range of contacts, not just in the business community, but also on the shop-floor.[16] What made the Conservative electoral challenge particularly potent was the fact that the party had, at least temporarily, been able to conclude a pact with Coventry's Liberals so that its candidates were guaranteed a straight fight against Labour for Council seats.[17]

One end product of this renewed activity was that illiberal views were much more openly expressed in election manifestos and the local press than they had been even five years before. A letter from 'F.H.' to the *Standard* was symptomatic of the right's new found confidence:

> 'The barrier of class distinction is gradually being broken down by the new housing estates', said the Lord Mayor of Coventry . . . at the

> Licensed Victuallers annual dinner.... Does it ever occur to him that bankers and bricklayers might not unreasonably find little in common in their respective vocations to justify this absurd Socialist dream of dukes and dustbinmen sitting in a utility self-service pub, with a nursery upstairs, drinking beer together and talking with sweet equality about housing development in Tibet? Equality is bunk.[18]

However, Conservative propaganda was not just concerned with Labour's supposed fallacies, and considerable effort was made to provide a series of more positive images, in order to illustrate how much better life would be under a changed local administration. An old argument was turned on its head, with the Labour Council now being characterised as an obstructionist vested interest, which, for the sake of 'socialist dogma', was perpetuating austerity, and denying people access to a whole number of freshly available possibilities.[19] On one level, this meant championing Council tenants in their agitation against common open spaces on the estates.[20] On another, it meant emphasising the Government's role in promoting the private house building boom and, indeed, affluence in general. A *Standard* editorial, discussing the city's shortages of skilled labour, made this latter point clearly:

> The dismal Johnnies who prophesied that under a Tory Government the standard of life would fall to zero have been confounded, and even if the cost of living rises a point or two we have very little real complaint in the midst of so much plenty.... Coventry today is suffering one of the penalties of prosperity.[21]

Labour's response to the changing political environment of the early 1950s was pitched at a number of different levels. Considerable emphasis continued to be placed on the party's long-term commitments to fairness and efficiency, commitments which were, it was claimed, helping to shape a new city which would be envied the world over.[22] At the same time, the party was also prepared to go at least some way to meeting the points raised by its critics. Thus, the Housing Committee agreed formally to adopt the recommendations that had emerged from the Birmingham University study of tenants' attitudes, which meant that estates were henceforth to be built with a greater emphasis on privacy.[23] Similarly, attempts were made to neutralise the ratepayers' organisations' lament about high levels of Council spending, by measures which ranged from the provision of a 'Civic Chest' booklet (explaining the working of the various accounts)[24] to an initiative which involved a Treasury Organisation and Methods team making a full assessment of all the Council's operations.[25] Finally, and most controversially, there was also some consideration (at the very least) of administrative methods which might be used to alter the composition of the city's political geography – principally by building new municipal estates in marginal wards.[26]

Yet, for all this, it was clear that the party was in fact finding it very difficult to fashion the kind of new strategy which was demanded by the changes that were going on around it. Rather, there was a growing emphasis on internal argument, as the membership became engrossed in the wider left–right battle which had been triggered by Labour's governmental eclipse.[27]

The key fact was that a majority of the local party were now well to the left of the national leadership – 'Bevanite with a capital "B"' one Coventry activist put it.[28] This inevitably meant that a substantial amount of time was spent in disputes – either with the National Executive Committee or with the city's M.P.s, or with the local rump of right-wingers.[29] But it also meant that when substantive issues were discussed, they most often concerned abstract principles or foreign affairs, since these were the policy areas in which the left's offensive was being most vigorously pursued. Thus, it could be reported in 1954, for example, that 'No single political event in the last few years . . . [had] stirred the members of the Coventry Labour Party so much as the decision to re-arm Germany'.[30] By contrast, debate about local affairs was usually stunted, and marked most, as one observer put it, by sloganising:

> What was certain was that the word 'socialism' had a magical effect. It was bandied about the Group a great deal, seemingly without there being the need to settle down to ideological discussion on the nature of the particular socialism which the Group was seeking in municipal affairs.[31]

The consequences which stemmed from this situation were somewhat debilitating. The acrimonious atmosphere may have suited some activists, but it was clearly unattractive to many others, so that party membership in Coventry fell from a peak of 5,670 in 1952 to 3,540 in 1955 – a rate of decline very much more serious than the national trend.[32] At the same time, activity levels in the wards remained very low, with enthusiasm often only being generated by social events.[33] Most seriously, the public presentation of policy was also marked by the prevailing internal currents, so that, particularly in the years 1953-5, the local party leadership found itself staggering from one political crisis to the next – the dispute with the local transport unions of 1953–4, mentioned above; the altercations over the construction of the eastern link blocks and the Cathedral in 1954;[34] and the Civil Defence[35] and Stalingrad delegation controversies of 1954–5.[36] In each case, what was damaging to Labour was not so much its final position on the issue itself, but rather the argument and the dogmatic assertion which inevitably seemed to be a feature of the decision-making process.[37]

How did all of this shape the course of electoral politics in Coventry during the early 1950s? Some relevant data are presented in Table 9:1. Labour had gained an exceptional result in 1952, very much in line with the national trend,[38] because of a backlash against the Conservatives' 1951 General Election victory. However, over the next two years, results were very much less satisfactory, and though the Labour vote held up in numerical terms, it was clear that the party was failing to interest a large slice of the electorate, many of whom, as evidenced by the declining overall poll, were apparently opting out of voting altogether.

Table 9:1. Voting in Coventry municipal elections, 1951–5[39]

Year	*Size of electorate*	*% voting*	*Labour votes: No.*	*% of total*
1951	178,440	50.2	43,605	49
1952		52.9	56,448	60
1953		44.7	41,712	52
1954		44.6	43,324	54
1955	182,379	51.0	41,712	45

At first, the Conservatives found it difficult to do much about this situation, because of problems with their own organisation and leadership.[40] But by early 1955, with the economy booming and a General Election likely, it seemed clear that a big enough push might bring results. Accordingly, the Conservatives decided to capitalise on Cold War paranoia, and focus on Labour's growing reputation for 'leftism', and in particular on its supposedly over-friendly links with the civil authorities of various war-damaged East European and Soviet cities. As a Tory representative told the *Standard*: 'We intend to fight as we have never fought before. The issue is simple. It is the Kremlin versus Coventry. It is Conservatism versus Communism.'[41] In the end, this kind of appeal, and the fact the Liberals declined to stand any candidates and instead encouraged their supporters to vote Tory,[42] proved too strong for Labour, and although the party's vote was little changed in numerical terms, its share of the poll declined considerably, which meant two fewer seats on the Council.[43] 'The results', as one of Labour's local agents put it, were 'disappointing all round'.[44]

But Labour's problems in 1955 did not stop there, since in the General Election a few weeks later there was ample confirmation of its latent vulnerability. The Liberals, once again, declined to stand candidates, even though they had polled around 12,000 votes in 1950.[45] The end product was that, while Labour still won all of the three city seats, it did so in the face of an abnormally high swing to the Conservatives (5.3 per cent), and in the knowledge that Coventry South (where Labour candidate Burton's majority came out at less than 2,000) now seemed to have become a marginal.[46] These results, in particular, were seen as deeply shocking in the local party.[47]

In the aftermath of the 1955 elections, there was considerable debate in Coventry about where exactly Labour had gone wrong. Burton and Crossman (M.P. in the East constituency) were very struck by the fact that the party had been deserted by young people.[48] Others blamed the 'office' – the local full-timers, and the organisation that was supposed to turn out the vote.[49] Against this, there was a widespread feeling that much responsibility for what had happened rested with the local authority, which had pursued a number of irresponsible policies. Hodgkinson was convinced of this argument:'The behaviour of the Council Group . . . has done more to undermine confidence in the Labour Party here, and that unfortunately includes our Parliamentary Candidates, than anything else.'[50]

However, as the months of 1955 passed, it became ever more apparent that, whatever the rights and wrongs of the past, the central fact about the party's current predicament was that it now seemed becalmed in a sea of indifference and mistrust. Internally, many activists had been extremely badly hit by the poor performances of 1955, so that membership roles were once again falling.[51] More unnervingly, some evidence now began to surface which suggested that the anti-Labour mood might well be snowballing. Party workers were clearly worried when a fund-raising initiative at Humber had to be abandoned because of lack of interest.[52] But, even more ominously, they now found themselves 'constantly under attack' in wards where there were large municipal housing estates – considered previously as Labour heartlands.[53]

Given these developments, the party eventually decided on a mixed bag of palliative measures. It was agreed, firstly, to set up a sub-committee charged with investigating internal organisation.[54] But the biggest changes were in spheres of public policy. For example, the Housing Committee now announced that it would drop its previous policy of keeping open spaces unfenced on municipal estates, and henceforth in most cases provide individual, demarcated front gardens.[55] More significant still was the Council's decision, in early 1956, to use the opportunity provided by the re-valuation of the city's rateable property for a decisive cut in the annual levy, so that a rate of 23s. 6d. in 1955–6 was followed by one of 16s. 4d. in 1956–7.[56] This was to be the start of a long process whereby the party sought to recapture what it saw as the middle-ground of Coventry politics.

The political landscape through which Labour needed to negotiate a path during the second half of the 1950s was in many respects similar to the one existing between 1951 and 1955, except that now the trends towards apathy, or disenchantment with the party, were very much more marked.

One positive fact which still worked in Labour's favour was public pride in the new central area. Of course, not everybody agreed on details, and some of the new developments attracted a fair amount of negative criticism, with the *Standard*, for example, calling the theatre 'the whitest elephant in the Socialists' menagerie'.[57] But a writer for *Architectural Design* probably gave an accurate summation of local opinion when he concluded that: 'most Coventry people take pride in their new city, even if they do not altogether approve of it.'[58] Nor was this merely a passive kind of response, in that exhibitions and displays on what was being built still drew healthy audiences – 13,000 to an event in 1958, for example.[59]

Yet, as in earlier periods, the situation was very much less satisfactory when it came to the new municipal estates. As has been suggested in an earlier chapter, the Council was largely unable, throughout the 1950s, to provide the kind of facilities that it had originally planned for the expanding neighbourhoods. Consequently, many municipal tenants felt themselves in some ways deprived, condemned to a world of inadequate amenities (especially shops and pubs) and infrequent bus services. Observers noted an abnormal number of T.V. aerials on the new estates, but careful enquiry established that this had more to do with a keenly felt sense of social isolation than with a burgeoning imitation of middle-class home-centreness.[60]

Two groups particularly suffered from this situation. Women resented the time and distances involved in shopping, and the almost total lack of local play-spaces for children.[61] Teenagers constantly complained of the boredom of life in Coventry, and the lack of even the most primitive kind of meeting-places.[62] The consequence of this was a sense of frustration, which could easily lead to other problems, as the *Standard* reported:

> A serious shortage of recreational facilities for the young people of Bell Green Neighbourhood Unit . . . is resulting in crowds of teen-agers roaming the streets aimlessly and causing damage to property, say local residents. They complain of broken windows and street lamps, stripped apple trees, broken down fences, and gangs of young people who gather in the . . . shopping centre and make themselves a nuisance.[63]

Meanwhile certain other kinds of social development seemed likely to pose problems for Labour. Private house building continued at a fast pace between 1956 and 1960, with 7,000 units completed, so that by the later date a narrow majority of dwellings in the city were in fact owner-occupied.[64] What made these trends all the more ominous was information from specific Labour canvasses which showed that Conservative and ratepayers' association agitation had managed to create a complete rift between many private owners and any conception of left politics.[65]

Finally, there was also a growing concern with what was happening to young people. Teenagers had often formed their own special interest groups in the years since the war,[66] but they were now increasingly becoming involved in what, to adult eyes, seemed bizarre and alienating fashion crazes.[67] The most notorious one of these was the Teddy Boy/Girl culture, which had come to Coventry in 1954, and caught on so widely that by 1957 the promoters responsible for bringing Bill Hayley to Britain felt it appropriate to open the star's tour at the city's 2,000-seat Gaumont theatre.[68] The result of all of this was an increase in tension on both sides of the age-divide. Some venues catered for a youthful audience – the Milano Club at Radford and the Yardbird Club in Hillfields,[69] for example – but teenagers and young adults who wanted to hear music or dance felt that their needs were being ignored.[70] At the same time, many adults clearly felt threatened by the new forms of dress and behaviour, particularly since the press frequently made a link between youth cultures and various forms of petty crime ('Estate Dwellers Tell A Tale Of "Teddy Terror"').[71] Both kinds of reaction hardly augured well for the Council.

How, then, did Labour attempt to deal with these various developments? Its central retort to the débâcle of 1955 involved, as has been described earlier, a renewed emphasis on the annual rate figure, and subsequent policy reviews did very little to diminish the importance which was ascribed to this particular indicator. Indeed, it was now broadly recognised that, in the interests of keeping the rate stable, even so important a part of the Council's activity as the reconstruction programme itself would have to suffer. In an interview with the *Standard* during August 1958, Hodgkinson was quite open about the political judgements that were involved here. Labour had had to decide 'how far the citizens of Coventry . . . [were] prepared to go', whether the current generation could be expected 'to shoulder a burden' for new development 'quite out of proportion to the enjoyment they . . . [were] going to get out of it'. In the end, it had been agreed that retrenchment was unavoidable since 'it was becoming difficult to receive public support "for schemes which seem remote from their point of view"'.[72] In line with this kind of thinking, therefore, the late 1950s saw a number of cut-backs in Council investment programmes (as Chapter 8 has indicated) and generally stable annual rate figures.[73]

Yet, if all of this suggested a rather traditional approach, there were also pressures for innovation. The catalyst here was a resurgence in internal political education and discussion,[74] while the outcome was an approach which began to centre less on Labour's traditional blanket appeal (with its underlying assumption that all citizens shared certain key interests) and more on some kind of recognition of differential needs. Nevertheless, this process of change was hardly an even one, because inertia and prejudice were as common in the party as in the city at large.

An early example of the new thinking came during the slump of 1956–7, when Labour responded to the growth of local unemployment by launching an enquiry into the whole question of Coventry's industrial future.[75] Some months later, it was decided to begin a review of housing policy, and an internal working party was set up to present recommendations. The individuals involved were clearly determined not to be intimidated by previous practice and they went out of their way, in particular, to stress how unsatisfactory relationships between the Council and its tenants had become: 'The tenant feels that the centre of authority is too remote from him. It is too centralised; too big and impersonal, despite the best efforts of the elected representatives and officers concerned.' Given this conclusion, it was agreed to begin a process of devolution, by the establishment, for example, of a network of district offices.[76] At the same time, the Council also decided that, given the virtual moratorium on municipal house building and the obvious popularity of home-ownership amongst the local population, there was a strong case to be made for the authority to begin erecting its own dwellings for sale.[77]

In addition to these initiatives, there was some movement on two other major issues. Labour activists had been aware for some time of the growth of racism in Coventry,[78] but riots against blacks in various British cities during the summer of 1958 at last prompted a degree of definite action, aimed at using the Lord Mayor's office as a focus for promoting better integration.[79] Meanwhile, various attempts were also being made to alleviate the frustrations and alienation of the city's teenagers. Considerable effort was expended, for example, in opening up the Belgrade theatre to young people, using ideas like a half-price Young Stagers' Club.[80] On the same theme, a 'Welcome to Citizenship' ceremony, aimed at each year's crop of new voters, was designed to popularise ideas about civic responsibility.[81]

To what extent were these various strategies effective in allowing Labour to recover from the reversals of 1955? In the years 1956–8, firstly, it seemed possible that the tide might have turned back in the party's favour, since, as the data in Table 9:2 show, Labour's vote held up quite well, while the seats lost in 1955 were first won back, and then successfully defended. Yet, as local strategists recognised, not everything was as rosy as it perhaps at first sight seemed. Part of Labour's achievement, for example, had to be discounted against the collapse of the Conservative–Liberal electoral pact, a development which saw the smaller party standing 16 candidates and gaining over 9,000 votes in

Table 9:2. Voting in Coventry municipal elections, 1956–60.[82]

Year	*Size of electorate*	*% voting*	*Labour vote no.*	*%*	*Conservative vote no.*	*%*	*Liberal vote no.*	*%*	*No. of seats won by Labour*
1956	185,130	49.0	42,515	47	30,204	33	13,804	15	10/16
1957		45.7	43,732	51	31,338	37	9,684	11	10/16
1958		43.9	40,746	50	38,299	47	2,698	3	10/16
1959		47.4	48,216	50	45,320	47	1,909	2	10/16
1960	193,497	44.1	39,287	46	43,702	51	527	1	9/16

both 1956 and 1957.[83] Moreover, the situation was further complicated by the declining overall size of the polls, which seemed to suggest both a general diminution of interest in politics and the potential for a more volatile pattern of future voting behaviour.

Alongside these quite general anxieties, there was growing awareness of a very specific problem which appeared to be developing in the Coventry South constituency. Labour had held this seat in 1955 with a greatly reduced majority, it will be remembered, but various developments over the following years now suggested that the party's ability to repeat even this result was substantially diminished. The key dimension, as activists saw it, was the changing complexion of the local housing stock. For while the electorates of the northern, inner-city wards in this constituency were declining, as the local authority moved tenants from its older property to the newly created outlying estates in Coventry North and East, the position further south was very different, because of extensive private building. Furthermore, the Conservatives had recognised the chance that this gave them, and were concentrating resources on winning over the new owner-occupiers.[84]

In the event, some of Labour's forebodings about the local political balance were proved quite correct during the elections of 1959 and 1960.

Both left and right could draw some encouragement from the municipal contest in May 1959, but the balance tilted firmly to the Conservatives a few months later in the national poll. For, although the general swing against Labour in Coventry at this election was by no means disastrous, in the South constituency it became magnified very much as predicted, so that the party lost the seat, and thereby suffered its first parliamentary reverse of the post-war years.[85] In May 1960, the Conservatives further underlined their growing potential when they took one seat off Labour at the municipal elections and for the first time polled more votes than all the other parties put together. A *Standard* editorial, celebrating this event and headed 'Road to Victory is Open', rammed home the message that the Conservatives' prestige had never been higher.[86]

Labour's electoral set-backs in Coventry at the end of the 1950s produced a considerable amount of comment. The local party explained its poor showing in terms of the hostility of new home-owners and the indifference of the 21 to 35 age group.[87] Butt, in a detailed review of the Midlands' car industry and its work-force for *New Left Review*,[88] argued that the problem was Labour revisionism. The workers were as militant as ever, he argued, citing the upsurge in shop steward organisation and the incidence of unofficial strikes to back up his point. But, what had changed was Labour's ability to communicate with this struggle, since the party had jettisoned socialist solutions, and opted, instead, for the crudities of auction room politics. Appealed to on this level, it was not surprising that many in the electorate rejected Labour – they preferred the real thing (the Conservatives' open celebration of self-advancement) to its shallow and unconvincing new competitor.

In contrast to these narrowly political explanations, several commentators saw Labour's failing as a consequence of deeper, social changes, and particularly the coming of popular affluence. A link between political apathy and economic stability had first been made in the early 1950s, and, for some, could be used to explain Labour's 1955 reversal.[89] However, in the second half of the decade, a new variation on this theme became popular. For it was now suggested that affluence was not just giving workers a sense of well-being, but also actively converting them to middle-class values, notably a propensity to vote Conservative. Surveying Coventry society, the *Standard* could, therefore, propose that class differences, at least in so far as they had traditionally been defined, were now disappearing:

> The factory technician – hand as they were once called – earns nowadays far more than the professional classes. The tradesmen have their Jaguar and Daimler cars. University life is open to all who have brains. The managing director usually consults his employees and the

> shop stewards about any schemes he has in mind. There is a general acceptance of the fact that the bricklayer and plasterer are quite as important as the accountant and bank clerk. . . . Most people have cars.

In this kind of society, division had come to be registered in terms of one-upmanship about names of houses and foreign holidays.[90]

The proposition that Coventry was a new kind of urban society reached its most exaggerated form in John Wiles's play *Never Had It So Good* which opened at the Belgrade during February 1960.[91] Wiles had spent some time in Coventry, apparently recording everyday conversations,[92] and was deeply shocked by what he found. In what the *Daily Mail*'s drama critic described as 'a slap in the contemporary eye of Coventry's proud new face', he confirmed the *Standard*'s diagnosis of what was happening, though disputing that paper's rather complacent overall conclusions:

> It is a verbal blitz which destroys the new city as violently as the blitz which destroyed the old. . . . One long litany of protest sounds throughout the play – at false values bred by bursting wage packets, the creed of greed and 'I'm all right, Jack', the scramble for bigger T.V. screens and glossier veneers, trade unions ('they are there to protect the worker from his own inefficiency'), failing churches, Coventry corporation, and 'the technicolour plastic boxes' of contemporary architecture with the emphasis on 'temporary'.[93]

How should these different propositions be evaluated? Obviously, Labour's own explanation of its decline begs more questions than it answers. After all, *why* was it that 21–35 year-olds were tending to desert it? Butt's thesis also appears unsatisfactory. Is it really correct to assume that all Coventrians made up their minds about voting solely in relation to experiences gained at, or because of, work? And what of the local political input: did a Bevanite party's agitation count for nothing in the face of national revisionism?

Given these points, it is little wonder that, for some, the third type of explanation – where Coventry is seen as a new type of affluent society – has continued to appear the most satisfying.[94] Whether or not this is justified will be explored in the next chapter.

10 Some conclusions

This chapter begins with a brief summary of the main points that have been made about Coventry in the preceding pages, and then moves to a consideration of what these conclusions mean for the two broader controversies that were introduced at the beginning of the book. Does the Coventry case support or refute any of the existing models of reconstruction? Secondly, can growing popular affluence really be made the key to explaining political changes in the city during the 1950s?

The starting point for a clear interpretation of developments in Coventry, it has been argued, must be an accurate understanding of what the local Labour party was trying to do there after the war. The party's commitment was not to some amorphous municipal socialism, but rather to a fairly precise programme which aimed to right long-standing defects in local welfare provision and urban form. The aim was to use the opportunity provided by the German bombing (and the subsequent election of a sympathetic government at Westminster) to produce a fairer and more efficient city, and thus – partly because of the assumed efficacy of environmental factors in shaping human behaviour – a more democratic and collectivist local society.

Yet if this programme was comparatively modest in its ambitions, it quickly proved far less easy to implement than had at first been envisaged. One problem for Labour was the fact that post-war Coventry remained very much more conservative – indeed, Conservative – than had seemed likely in 1945. Thus, though some of the party's objectives remained very popular, the scope for change, even in the late 1940s, was limited by factors like the keen rates consciousness of significant parts of the electorate.

But a bigger problem for the Council stemmed from the overall stance of the Government. Local planners had hoped, obviously, for adequate resource provision from Westminster, but they had also argued that key variables – like population size and industrial structure – should be closely controlled, so as to secure a sound basis for the desired urban reconstruction. But here, on both counts, the post-war years were to hold only disappointment. For it soon became apparent that what the Government wanted from Coventry was industrial production (of export goods and armaments) on as cheap a set of terms, measured by welfare provision, as was possible. The Council, therefore, found itself in the awkward position of constantly having to try and satisfy an increasing if unpredictable demand for its services (as immigrants were drawn in by the booming local economy) with a wholly inadequate set of resource flows.

Developments in the 1950s only reinforced the essential elements of this pattern. Labour's electoral support did not collapse, but the party's traditional appeal was tending to appear increasingly unsatisfactory, a phenomenon which several commentators linked to growing popular affluence. Meanwhile, the terms of the centre–periphery relationship tilted further towards Westminster, as Conservative administrations pursued a new, ideologically inspired campaign aimed at restricting all local authority spending.

Given these pressures, it was inevitable that the actual pattern of development that occurred in Coventry would be rather different from that envisaged in the early plans. In the period to 1960, Labour was able to achieve some real gains in its campaign to build a better city, but it was evident that many local initiatives had been undermined from outside, either because of inadequate funding, or because they conflicted with other, more pressing government priorities. The *quid pro quo* for ordinary Coventrians was 15 years of almost unbroken economic growth, with high wages and low rates of unemployment.

How, then, does this particular history fit in with the broader descriptions of reconstruction that were outlined in Chapter 1? Does the evidence produced support Barnett's contention that 'New Jerusalemism' was all-triumphant? Or does it reinforce the views of writers like Blackwell and Seabrook, who argue that the radical upsurge of the war years was in fact effectively emasculated, so that reconstruction became essentially a process of capitalist restoration? Here the answer must surely be that the Coventry case really supports neither set of contentions. It suggests, firstly, that Barnett may have greatly exaggerated the extent of 'New Jerusalemist' influence and achievement. Important parts of Whitehall and significant sections of the electorate were against visionary re-planning, both in the war years and after. Moreover, the progress of welfare reform during the late 1940s and throughout the 1950s was hardly the dramatic story which the reader of *The Audit of War* might expect. Indeed, as far as Coventry is concerned, it may well be that Barnett's argument should be stood on its head, since here it was the growing official concern with exports and rearmament that damaged the achievement of welfare goals and not vice versa.

At first sight, this conclusion seems to be congruent with the capitalist restoration thesis. But, again, the detailed evidence suggests that the situation was considerably more complicated than the abstract model would allow. Labour's aims in Coventry were, no doubt, quite modest when measured against its latter-day critics' ideas on socialism, but the party's achievements cannot simply be seen as functional to the continuation of capitalism. Secondly, though conservatism in reconstruction matters was no doubt encouraged by local industrial and commercial employers, it is also clear that many in the electorate wanted a quick return to the *status quo ante* after the war, since they valued the provision of homes and jobs before abstract questions about social justice. The pattern of reconstruction which occurred, therefore, was hardly just imposed by vested interests, as Blackwell and Seabrook et al. imply. Finally, the restoration thesis is also weak in relation to the Government's role during the 1940s and 1950s. Official interventions were often of paramount importance, but, again, they were rarely (if ever) just about preserving capitalism. Different Ministries had different policies for Coventry, and sometimes these conflicted quite drastically. Moreover, if any pattern can be detected from the various administrations' overall stances on reconstruction, the suggestion is that short-term, political considerations were usually most important in influencing policy determination at government level.

Of course, it might be argued in reply to these points that Coventry was exceptional, and that elsewhere the situation was very much more as might be expected from the existing literature. To evaluate this kind of claim, it will be necessary to turn away from Coventry for a moment, and focus instead on the reconstruction experiences of some other blitzed cities, particularly those of an approximately similar size like Hull, Plymouth, Portsmouth and Southampton.[1] Does what happened in these places over the key first post-war decade – when the die of future development was effectively cast – confirm Coventry's atypicality?

The period 1940–2, it has been suggested, was one of great hope in many British cities.[2] The Blitz had produced considerable suffering, yet it had opened up tremendous possibilities, too. Max Lock, a planning consultant working on Kingston-upon-Hull's future, summed up the euphoric mood:

> Hitler has at last brought us to our senses. We, the British public, have suddenly seen our cities as they are! After experiencing the shock of familiar buildings disembowelled before our eyes . . . we find the

> cleared and cleaned-up spaces a relief. In them we have hope for the future, opportunities to be taken or lost. These open spaces begin to ventilate the congestion of our cities and maybe also of our imaginations.[3]

In this climate of opinion, Lord Reith's instruction to 'plan boldly' was taken very seriously, and even Conservative authorities that had never intervened to control the built-environment before were now to be found commissioning and even, on occasion, endorsing, imaginative schemes for future reconstruction – as at Southampton in 1942, Portsmouth in 1943, and Plymouth and Hull (where Abercrombie was the main consultant) in 1944.[4] Most of the new plans adopted the 'clean sweep' approach and were designed to improve conditions for the user; many incorporated a common repertoire of features, and involved re-styled city centres (to provide centralised civic, educational, recreational and shopping facilities), ring road systems, and a multiplicity of completely new neighbourhood units.[5]

The move to visionary planning generally received strong public support, but even as the new schemes were being finalised, it was becoming obvious that their implementation would not be easy. Local authorities found civil servants often less than enthusiastic about aspects of the proposals (with the Ministry of War Transport blocking Southampton's ring road scheme altogether, for example).[6] They had to recognise as well that most traders wanted shopping centres rebuilt on pre-war lines (which had particularly severe implications for the Southampton and Hull plans).[7] Finance, too, was a major worry. The extent of war damage in the blitzed cities was daunting, and meant, for example, that just to deal with urgent or serious cases, Southampton, Hull and Plymouth would need 5,000, 13,000 and 19,000 new housing units, respectively.[8] But where was the required funding to come from? Many of the cities had experienced declining populations during the war,[9] and all had greatly reduced total rateable values.[10] Moreover, in most cases, the local economic outlook appeared bleak, with each of the cities dependent on only two or three sectors, and many of the existing trades badly disrupted.[11] Matters were hardly improved, either, when the terms of the 1944 Act became known, since the statute implied, as has been suggested above, less than generous financial assistance from the centre and the consequent spectre of very high rate levels.

Given these problems, the mood by the end of the war was more inclined to caution than experiment. In Portsmouth, the coalition of 'private builders and owners of commercial undertakings' which dominated local politics decided on a wait-and-see policy.[12] Along the coast, the incoming Labour administration at Southampton was only a little more adventurous, settling on a plan emasculated of all novel features and mainly designed to restore rateable value as quickly as possible.[13] In Plymouth and Hull, where Labour was also newly in power, there was no such blatant retreat and the war-time plans remained largely intact as the guide to reconstruction. But even in these cities optimism was at a premium, and it was agreed that housing and the restoration of economic prosperity would have to be the leading priorities, in line with the wishes of the local electorates.[14]

Over the next few years, the blitzed cities found themselves subject to a number of different influences in relation to reconstruction. Initially, the major government priority was housing, and local authorities were urged to complete as many new units as possible. At the same time, Board of Trade involvement, stimulated both by the need to promote exports and by the need to prevent local pockets of unemployment, meant that industrial regeneration continued to be a major focus of concern.[15] Silkin, the Minister of Town and Country Planning, was keen to encourage progress with city centre reconstruction, as well, and spent much time chivvying local authorities (like Portsmouth's) which had slipped behind.[16] But, against this, there was also a growing emphasis on 'realism' in all reconstruction matters, promoted directly by the Treasury,[17] and indirectly by the general conditions of austerity and economic crisis. A regional official's reassessment of the Abercrombie plan for Hull (which *The Times* called 'perhaps the most comprehensive scheme ever devised for a city of this size') illustrated the changing priorities:

> There is much in the . . . Plan . . . of great value. . . . But in many important respects the Plan seems remote from reality, and inappropriate to the true and inescapable character of Hull. Indeed it savours of a plain middle aged woman who might quietly dressed be beautiful taking refuge in powder and paint. . . . Generally it seems to me a tragedy both for Hull, Sir Patrick Abercrombie and planning generally that he ever went near the place, and the sooner Hull get away from his wilder ideas and face up to the practical job of replanning . . . in a sound, decent, ordinary way the better.[18]

Given such attitudes, the blitzed cities began to find it more and more difficult to gain a sympathetic hearing in Whitehall, and thereby obtain the level of resource support to which they felt they were entitled.[19] Their predicament was symbolised by a very conservative series of ministerial decisions over Declaratory Order Area applications, with Southampton, for example, getting 270 acres instead of the 514 it had proposed.[20]

What made these problems with officialdom all the more difficult for the local authorities was the fact that they coincided with a growing mood of disquiet about the reconstruction process amongst the public. In part, this was fuelled by impatience over the provision of new housing – 'Houses anywhere, at once, were preferred to houses in the right place five years ahead'.[21] But there was also a general feeling of irritation with controls of every kind, which appeared to be particularly threatening to any form of radical city planning:

> Economic planners were out of reach and were in any case incomprehensible to the ordinary citizen. . . . Town planners were much nearer, multiplied quickly in numbers and appeared both incapable of doing anything big, and tardy and niggling over trifles. The guidance of land use thus soon became unpopular.[22]

The implications of this change in the public's mood were made clear at the municipal elections in Southampton during 1950. Labour, as had been usual, campaigned on its record – a modest and realistic approach to reconstruction. But the Tory agitation against compulsory purchase – 'Southampton . . . was becoming a very controlled town, and it was up to the townspeople to see that it was de-controlled' – proved a bigger vote-catcher, and Labour was swept from office.[23]

The outcome of these different policies and pressures was that all local authorities were persuaded to become even more conscious of the need to do everything possible to secure jobs and homes, than they had been before, which in practice meant building housing estates wherever land was available, and allowing companies to rebuild on, or occupy, sites regardless of the overall planning implications. Conversely the visionary plan, and the interventionist stance its implementation required, appeared more and more inappropriate. Portsmouth's Conservative administration, to repeat, had never been very enthusiastic about radical re-planning anyway, but all pretence of comprehensive redevelopment was now dropped, in favour of limited schemes designed to ensure the speedy provision of homes and jobs, and the full restoration of rateable value. As one commentator put it, the city had first been exhorted to plan 'boldly', then to plan 'modestly', but its final proposals amounted only to a 'plan for essentials'.[24] Hull Corporation, troubled equally by a resurgence of Conservative activity in the city,[25] a housing list well into five figures,[26] and sustained opposition to the Abercrombie proposals from various commercial interests,[27] retreated too, so that by 1951 the agreed proposals for future reconstruction contained just 'a few details of the 1944 plan but none of the main concepts'.[28] Only in Plymouth was the situation any different. Here, war-time enthusiasm for the local authority's plan, fanned both by official propaganda and world-wide publicity, had left enough of a legacy to make all political parties wary of introducing major modifications, so that even the Treasury was only able to secure limited concessions.[29]

The Conservative success at the 1951 General Election did little to change the overall governmental approach to reconstruction that had been established since the war. Macmillan, it is true, early on urged his colleagues to give rebuilding work in the city centres a higher profile, and referred to the aid recently provided for Lynmouth (a town devastated by floods) in support of his case. But Butler, the Chancellor, was emphatically against changing priorities:

> From the political angle there is . . . a distinction to be drawn between Lynmouth and the blitzed cities, since many people were rendered homeless in Lynmouth overnight. I believe the public would recognise a difference between providing homes and other forms of help for those people immediately and building shops and offices now in blitzed cities, where the more immediate needs have long since been met. Many would agree that there are still a great number of building jobs which, on economic or social grounds, ought to be done before the shops and offices are attended to.

In this situation, any further protest seemed futile, and so Macmillan retreated, telling some Labour M.P.s a few months later that there had been 'a good deal of exaggeration' in accounts of the blitzed cities' predicaments.[30] Reconstruction policies over the remaining years of the Churchill Government therefore essentially followed the long-standing pattern that had been established under Labour, albeit with an enlarged role for every kind of private enterprise.

How, then, did these various pressures and policies shape what was actually built in the blitzed cities over the 10 years after 1945? Put another way, to what extent was the new building different from that envisaged in the war-time plans?

It is, unfortunately, impossible to give systematic answers to these questions because the data are so thin.[31] Nevertheless, some tentative conclusions may be derived from the scattered information in Tables 10:1, 10:2, 10:3 and 10:4.[32] It seems apparent, for example, that rebuilding in general had taken place on a very much smaller scale than that originally either planned (compare the totals of the completed dwellings to the war-time projections of need) or thought desirable (compare the extent of factory rebuilding to the amount of plant still in ruins at the end of the war). Within this somewhat unimpressive overall context, looking at the various types of reconstruction in a relative light

Table 10:1 Progress with reconstruction in selected blitzed cities, (1) housing, 1945–53[33]

City	*No. of houses destroyed 1939–45*	*War-time assessment of no. of houses needed urgently in post-war period*	*No. of permanent houses built 1945–53*	*Size of Council waiting list 1953*
Coventry	4,185	12,000	8,863	11,811
Hull	4,354	13,000	4,650	15,927
Plymouth	3,754	19,000	8,802	9,500
Portsmouth	5,064	ncf	4,604	15,056
Southampton	4,167	5,000	6,538	9,435

Note: ncf = no comparative figure available

Table 10:2 Progress with reconstruction in selected blitzed cities, (2) factories, 1945–53.[34]

City	*Amount of industrial space destroyed by bombing in the war and not yet repaired by 1945 (million sq. ft.)*	*Industrial building 1945–53 (million sq. ft.)*
Coventry	3.4	2.0
Hull	2.7	3.8
Plymouth	2.3	0.7
Portsmouth	0.3	0.7
Southampton	1.9	0.3

Table 10:3 Progress with reconstruction in selected blitzed cities, (3) amounts spent on city centre reconstruction, 1949–50 to 1952.[35]

	Amount spent (£s)		
City	*1949–50*	*1951*	*1952*
Coventry	118,000	317,500	375,000
Hull	91,000	386,000	563,000
Plymouth	475,000	781,000	683,000
Portsmouth	362,000	379,000	188,000
Southampton	434,500	220,500	302,500

Table 10:4 Progress with reconstruction in selected blitzed cities, (4) estimates made in 1953 of years needed at current or speeded up rates of building before all war damage in city centres made good[36]

City	*No. of years before war damage made good*	*Pace to be accelerated?*
Coventry	20	yes
Hull	5–7	yes
Plymouth	20	no
Portsmouth	15	yes
Southampton	5	yes

suggests that progress was most marked in the housing and industry sectors. By contrast, city centre reconstruction, which so many in officialdom regarded as a luxury, had proceeded fairly slowly, being starved of funds completely until the late 1940s and subsequently given only very small capital allocations. Some idea of the relative priorities in operation here can be gained from a close look at the figures on the use of building steel in 1949. City centre schemes that year were given altogether a mere 5,540 tons (0.5 per cent of the total available). On the other hand, a survey of industrial projects for the same period revealed, amongst other things, 14 developments using 1,145 tons of steel in Plymouth, and 128 developments using 2,544 tons of steel in Hull.[37]

The impression, then, from the data that are available is of a fairly prosaic achievement, and this conclusion also seems to be suggested by more qualitative data. It is significant, for example, that despite wartime promises, few of the new estates in the blitzed cities were provided with any community facilities, and ended up, therefore, looking like their much criticised 1930s predecessors.[38] Moreover, it is also clear that there was widespread disappointment at the architectural standards which continued to inform much of the new building, with *The Economist*'s verdict, that 'if the worst errors have generally been avoided, the full opportunity has rarely been seized', the mildest of many rebukes on this subject.[39] Visiting Europe to look at progress in rebuilding, the American Leo Grebler felt of Britain that what had occurred owed rather too much to the City Engineer, and rather too little to 'the sensitive consultant-planner of high professional rank and reputation'.[40]

This brief sketch of what was happening in some other blitzed cities, therefore, tends to confirm and not refute several of the more general conclusions that have been derived from the Coventry study. Reconstruction in Britain after the war, in these locations at least, was not a

'New Jerusalemist' jamboree, which contradicts the kind of argument that has been put forward by Barnett. But nor can it be seen as a simple story of betrayal, in which the high ideals of 1940–4 are subsequently sold out by pseudo-radicals. The consensus for visionary planning in the war had never been total, and had always excluded powerful national and local interests. Moreover, local authorities who persevered in the post-war world with radical schemes were considerably more hemmed in by difficulty than is often realised, since they had to deal not only with a range of problems stemming from their economic positions, but also significant adverse changes in public opinion. In this sense, then, their actual achievements, limited though they were, may well be thought more remarkable than they at first sight appear.

Turning away from reconstruction, some attention will now be given to the second major issue raised by the Coventry study, the relationship between political loyalties and improving popular standards of living. Specifically, can Labour's decline in Coventry over the 1950s be seen as connected to the growing affluence of the city's population. And if it can, does embourgeoisification or the more subtle process of spreading instrumentalism (as proposed by Goldthorpe et al.) better describe what was happening?

At first sight, the affluence thesis, in one variant or another, does indeed appear persuasive in this case, not least because, as Chapter 9 has demonstrated, it held considerable sway in contemporary opinion. But a closer examination of what is being proposed raises problems. Affluence theories depend upon a simple 'before' and 'after' juxtaposition. 'Before', there was relative poverty, a cohesive, 'traditional' working-class culture, and mass loyalty to the Labour party. 'After', there is popular material wealth, a growing tendency to adopt middle-class standards (the embourgeoisification theorists) or instrumental attitudes (Goldthorpe et al.), and a declining commitment to Labour. Do either parts of this couplet fit the Coventry experience?

As far as the 'before' scene is concerned, it is immediately obvious that the answer must be a negative. Coventrians had long been relatively well-off. Moreover, instrumentalism, in particular, had often been commented upon in relation to the Coventry work-force, with the lure of cash being understood as explaining lack of loyalty to firm and union alike. Finally, mass support for Labour had never existed in the city, so that even at the supposed radical high-points of 1937 and 1945, the Conservative share of the local working-class vote was fairly substantial.

But there are also problems with the 'after' part of the picture. Thus, there is no real evidence to suggest *growing* instrumentalism in the 1950s. In addition, the idea of affluent workers being propelled into a world of middle-class, individualistic concerns seems unconvincing in the Coventry case. Some authorities, to repeat, thought that they detected this type of change, and cited the life-style of the new private estate dweller – based on the television set, the home and the family – in support of their argument. But there was a good deal of exaggeration in such claims. For example, in the rush to emphasise home-centred life-styles, it was often forgotten that Coventry also boasted a strong and varied network of collective institutions at this time – a whole range of organisations embracing interests like fishing and cycling, not to mention at least 36 working men's clubs, with 51,000 members.[41] In fact even the degree of social change that was observable in the 1950s often had most to do with evolving ways of being working class. This point, and the underlying continuity it implied, was perceptively remarked upon in an account of Coventry by William Millinship, published in 1965:

> there are no very rich or very poor, and few real slums. High wages, status and material comfort have produced a peculiar class structure, based on money far more than accent and background. Highly paid workmen have an aggressive 'I'm as good as the next man, Mac' attitude. There is something of the toughness of New York, but this is a worker's city. There are no exclusive hide-outs. . . . The Bridge Restaurant in the city centre has table lamps and looks intimate and expensive from the outside. But men in pullovers march in without being intimidated.[42]

It may be concluded, then, that neither version of the affluence thesis seems really applicable in the Coventry case. The best that might be said is that the city's workers had long displayed attitudes close to the Goldthorpe et al. instrumental stereotype. But this does not explain why more of them were opting to turn away from Labour in the 1950s than had done in the late 1940s. Clearly, other factors must have been at play.

To find out what these other factors were, it is obviously necessary to focus very specifically on the ways in which Labour interacted with the electorate. Why had Labour originally been able to build a majority on the Council, and why did its appeal become so relatively unsatisfactory in the 1950s?

Labour had established itself in Coventry, it will be remembered, not on the basis of some enormous socialist advance, but rather after a couple of fairly narrow election victories. Many people remained completely unsympathetic to the party's politics, but just enough were favourable to allow a continuing majority on the Council. Support was drawn essentially from three groups in the population – convinced socialists (relatively few in number), direct clients of the local authority (principally municipal tenants) and a much larger aggregation of less committed voters, who were attracted by different aspects of Labour's programme, but most usually by its stance on local reconstruction.

What happened to this block over the 1950s? Certainly, there is little evidence of disintegration, and indeed commentators were often drawn to remark on the considerable numerical stability of the Labour vote.[43] But nor is there any suggestion of growth, either in terms of quantity or in terms of cohesion and loyalty.[44] Given this, and in a context where the overall size of the electorate was continuing to increase at quite a fast rate (on average, at about 1 per cent per annum between 1950 and 1960),[45] it was inevitable that Labour would become more vulnerable should any kind of reasonable challenge from the Conservatives materialise. Why had the party got caught in this predicament?

One possible way of approaching an answer to this question entails looking at how far Labour was involving people in politics, and whether or not its own approach to socialism was inducing apathy. It has been argued on a wider canvas, from a number of different angles, that social democracy failed in post-war Britain precisely because it was over-reliant on bureaucratic and paternalist solutions and under-reliant on encouraging popular participation in decision-making.[46] Planning, in this perspective, was too often about imposing abstract principles of social engineering, and too rarely about involving the community in gauging its own needs, a situation that bred apathy and cynicism. Moreover, the welfare reforms enacted after the war, it is claimed, tended to produce the same kind of unsatisfactory end products, because they precluded any kind of reciprocity between giver and receiver. Could it not be argued that the Coventry Labour party suffered exactly from these defects, and might not the growing local disillusionment of the late 1950s be seen as very much their logical consequence?

To provide an answer to this question, it is necessary, first of all, to look at what the Labour party was doing to create involvement in decision-making about, for example, planning, and then assess whether people in Coventry were satisfied or dissatisfied with these initiatives. Evidence on both these points is not particularly full, but it is enough, at least, to suggest that the participation argument might not be as persuasive as it at first sight appears.

The Labour party believed that people's interest in politics ought to be expressed, first and foremost, through the ballot box.[47] In other words, voting was seen as the way in which the citizenry could deliver a judgement on what was or was not being done at Corporation level. To this end, a lot of effort was put into schemes aimed at raising public awareness about Council policy and encouraging good electoral turn-outs, using such media as *Civic Affairs*.

But the Labour party also always understood that the electoral system might not be enough, and that to create the kind of community-orientated city they desired, it would be necessary to erect other channels of communication with the Coventry public.[48] There was, then, a considerable amount of consultation involving representatives of civic or special interest groups. But Councillors were also always ready to meet the ordinary citizen, as Hodgkinson remembered of the immediate post-war period: 'we bent ourselves backwards to reach out to the community at large and we had literally . . . dozens of ward area meetings in order to . . . give the citizens a chance . . . to come and express an opinion'.[49] Finally, it should also be remembered that Coventry Council was a pioneer of the questionnaire survey into tenants' attitudes, with Kuper's work at the end of the 1940s (see page 57) being only one of a number of initiatives of this type.[50]

What all this added up to, it may be concluded, was a fairly determined attempt to keep abreast of public opinion and stimulate criticism of an informed kind. Certainly, outside observers were impressed with what was going on. The Americans Bart and Cummings noted in 1956 that citizens' bodies had played only a 'peripheral role' in Coventry's re-development. But they also reported that the Council had taken part in a good deal of consultation on this matter, involving 'the chamber of commerce, the Ratepayers Association, the Newspaper Retailers Association, church representatives and many others'. In addition, Councillors retained, as these writers put it, 'close contact with community groups'.[51] Eight years later, a correspondent of *Town and Country Planning*, attending public meetings organised by the Council as part of the Development Plan Quinquennial Review, was also impressed:

> One could imagine, in other places, that such meetings would attract few: what probably makes the thing go in Coventry is the feeling that it is worthwhile: that the consumer will be treated with courtesy, and that his views matter.[52]

The evidence on how local people reacted to all of this is fragmentary, but it does not suggest, anyway, some deep-seated dissatisfaction at not being listened to. The first point to make is that, while people did care about what was happening in Coventry after the war, and were prepared to use their votes in greater than normal numbers,[53] their interest was not necessarily always overwhelming, so that though most meetings and events organised on reconstruction produced good audiences, some failed entirely.[54] But what about the issue of participation itself? Here, what little evidence there is does not suggest any great dissatisfaction with the existing channels. The 1945 'Coventry of the Future' essay competition, organised by the local evening paper, produced about 150 different suggestions from adults. But topics dealing with 'civics' made up only 3 per cent of the total, and invariably were mentioned by only a few of the participants. In fact 'Public Discussion with Councillors' came further down a ranked list of suggestions by popularity than the desire for a municipal zoo.[55] Seventeen years later, the Quinquennial Review meetings threw up a similar picture. All told, they produced 838 ideas from the public, but only, at a maximum, 30 to 40 of these (i.e. around 4 per cent) had anything to do with consultation or participation in decision-making, and not all of these were necessarily of a critical nature.[56]

All this suggests, therefore, that the argument about participation may be something of a red herring. But what about the second theme mentioned by the critics of paternalism and bureaucracy, the alleged apathy-creating impact of welfare reforms? On this, the specific evidence for Coventry is non-existent. Nevertheless, some comment on what is being proposed may be made from a tangent, by referring to aspects, already described, of the Council's relationship with its tenants. It might be expected from the paternalist/bureaucracy argument that people on municipal estates would be most likely to be dissatisfied with Labour, because they were most on the receiving end of the cold giver–receiver relationship. Yet in Coventry over the 1950s, the situation seems to have been rather more complicated than this simple proposition suggests. Significant dissatisfaction did exist on the estates, as has been fully documented – about mud, lack of facilities, damp and various other issues. But not all tenants were critical, and some families, notably those who had moved from the old central slums, remained grateful for their new surroundings.[57] Moreover, political activists continued to consider the estates as Labour heartlands, a perception that was largely (though not absolutely) accurate.[58] Consequently, it may be concluded that, for this period at least, the argument linking welfare reforms and apathy does not really hold good in the Coventry case.

How, then, can Labour's decline over the 1950s be explained? Having rejected the affluent worker and the bureaucratic/paternalist theses, can anything be put in their place? One way out of this impasse is to take Labour's own explanations of its decline more seriously, and look again at the party's relationship with the electorate, but this time from a perspective that is much more sensitive to the dialectic between politics and social change. For one of the most striking things about Coventry politics in the 1950s was the way in which Labour lost contact with precisely those groups who were at the centre of change – young people and new home-owners. Was this situation inevitable, or did it reflect problems within Labour's own ideology and organisation?

In the 1940s, it will be remembered, Labour had addressed the electorate as if it was a homogeneous whole, with identical experiences and interests. All would benefit, it was argued, if certain sensible reforms were enacted. This appeal worked to a certain extent, and for a number of reasons. But one thing that gave it some credibility was the fact that the community which was described in rhetoric at least resembled the one that existed in reality. Coventry could not, of course, be considered a static society (because of immigration) and nor was the indigenous working class undifferentiated (with divisions between respectable and rough, and home-owners and Council tenants, amongst others). But against this, there were other factors which welded the population together. Work and leisure experiences across the city were very similar, so that the majority of the population had similar life-styles. Critics could, in fact, write of 'too much sameness of income and habits':

> The private lives of most people are blanketed by a sort of sameness. . . . If one is a 'bit different' there is always the feeling 'What will the neighbours say?' This sort of thing always occurs and stifles personality in large industrial cities, but it seems to be exaggerated in Coventry.[59]

On top of this, a majority of the population had lived through the bombing and the publicity about bold reconstruction, and so were eager to see their city's re-birth.

However, over the 1950s, it seems, this kind of common identity began to decline. Memories of the war faded, and reconstruction, once it got into gear, seemed to cast much less of a magic spell. On the other hand, there is no doubt that the old working-class 'sameness' was rapidly becoming a thing of the past. In part this was because increasing money wages, the spurt in private house building, and a widening availability of goods in the shops, meant a growing diversity in patterns of living. But, in part, it was also a more subjective phenomenon, since national political and social discourse – the Conservatives' celebration of the property-owning democracy and the consumer society, and the proliferation of American cultural influences, to give some examples – promoted ideas about new life-styles and identities. People were not becoming middle class, to repeat a point made earlier, but there were an increasing number of different ways of being working class.

These latter changes were particularly noticeable in relation to two groups in the population. Home-ownership had always been widespread in Coventry, but over the 1950s there were quantitative and qualitative changes in its dimensions. In other words, the decade saw both a large increase in the number of private houses locally, and a sharpening of ideas about what home-ownership meant, made manifest, for instance, in the high-profile agitational activities of the ratepayers' associations. There were changes, too, in perceptions among and about young people. Leisure-centred youth cultures had, no doubt, always existed in Coventry to some extent, but during the 1950s there was a definite sense of them becoming more coherent and socially visible. Being a Teddy Boy or Girl, after all, meant not only conformity to a fairly strict and all-embracing code dictating dress, attitude and behaviour, but also being visibly different from every other section of the population.

Now, what is especially interesting about these changes is the way Labour failed for so long to react to them. The local press began recognising a link between home-ownership and support for the Conservatives from the early 1950s,[60] but Labour seemed to have accepted this as an almost natural state of affairs, which it could do little to alter. Thus, while the party did, of course, continue to emphasise its commitment to low rates, there was a complete absence of any more aggressive policy to woo the private house-owners. Labour's reaction to the emergent youth cultures was also unimpressive. Some recognition of what was going on became evident at the end of the 1950s, with the Young Stagers' Club and the 'Welcome to Citizenship' initiative. Yet, for the most part, there was only complacency or even hostility, as when the Council refused to intervene over a management ban on Teddy Boys and Girls at the precinct café in 1959.[61]

In the end, therefore, for many, Labour came to be defined only in terms of negatives. It was not the party for the people who lived in private houses. Nor was it a party that was much interested in youth, unless of a very wholesome and sanitised variety. It is these facts, more than any others, which explain the psephology of Coventry in the late 1950s.

But, of course, this begs a question. For why should Labour have been so slow to respond to what was going on? The party was, after all, well aware of the trends described. Was its lack of reaction due to some external barrier, or was it more of an internal failure, to do with Labour's own ideology and organisation?

The answer to this question must be that both kinds of explanation have some merit. Labour's room for manoeuvre on all political questions was certainly very limited because of the financial strait-jacket which it found itself in. Thus, to put it crudely, the indifference of the young might have been less pronounced if the party had actually been able to build the community and leisure facilities that had once been planned. But, having said this, it also seems undeniable that Labour's wounds were to a certain extent self-inflicted, a point that can be justified by briefly reviewing some of the party's salient characteristics.

The first point to make is that, over the specific questions of home-ownership and youth, there were immediate practical reasons why Labour struggled. One problem for the party was the fact that it had always shunned being involved in ratepayers' associations (on the basis that they were usually Tory fronts), so that the upsurge of agitation from this quarter in the 1950s proved difficult to counter at source.[62] On the youth issue, the problem was of a rather different kind. Here, the party's commitment was not in doubt, and there was a formal youth section in existence at all times over the 1945–60 period. But, in practice, the impact of this group was undermined by a high rate of membership turnover, due to National Service and 'young men leaving . . . for technical study in connection with their apprenticeship'.[63] The consequence was that Labour's profile in this key area remained low.

At the same time, there were also more deep-seated reasons why Labour found it difficult to respond to change, and particularly the types of change that were occurring in the 1950s. Two comments can be made, about the party's ideological disposition, and about its organisational style and key personnel.

It should be noted, firstly, that Labour was to some extent wedded to an ideology which made the careful handling of sociological or cultural trends relatively difficult. The local party had never been influenced by Marxism. Rather, it continued to be informed by a kind of moralism, which had its roots in the Independent Labour Party and Nonconformity.[64] This kind of approach had several strengths – it encouraged great conviction and clarity of purpose – but it was sometimes less than useful when used to identify trends in the make-up of the electorate.

Labour's analysis of society was based upon a belief in the overwhelming importance of mutual co-operation between citizens, whatever their social position: 'We are all members of one community, interdependent and helpless the one without the other. "One citizen differs from another, but the Salvation of the Community is the common business of them all"'.[65] The task of politics was to find a way of promoting this cause.[66] More specifically, since it was felt that people would generally want to reject 'the lowest impulse of human nature' for 'the high ideal of fair sharing', the objective for Labour was to isolate any forces (like 'vested interests') that might mislead or corrupt.

In the years after 1945, with the General Election victory and the consolidation of power in Coventry, it appeared that progress was being made to this end, and the party could congratulate itself on being 'in step with democratic opinion'. But from the late 1940s, this optimism was far less easy to sustain, since it was abundantly apparent that, despite the curbs on 'vested interests' that had been instituted, opposition to Labour's vision was certainly not dwindling away. There was considerable consternation, then, at why some people still chose 'Bacon and basic' in preference to improved homes and services.

One kind of response to this situation was a re-emphasis on the need for tighter organisation, so as to get the message across better. But for many, the inevitable consequence was a sense of frustration, and increasing cynicism about the electorate.[67] After all, if people had been told what was good for them, and still chose selfishness or frivolity, what might this say about them? It was only a short hop from here to a more

Table 10:5 Hodgkinson's record of service on Council committees, 1937 to 1959[68]

Total no. of committees served		*Main committees served*	*Other positions on Council*
1937	7	F, H	
1938	10	F, H	
1939	13	F, H, PAC	
1940	(no information available)		
1941	(no information available)		
1942	14	CR, F, H, PAC(C)	
1943	16	CR, F, H, PAC	
1944	7	PAC	Dep. Mayor
1945	9	CR, PAC	Mayor
1946	11	CR, E, F(C), PAC	
1947	9	CR(C), F, PAC	
1948	9	CR(C), F, PAC	
1949	10	CR(C), F, PAC	
1950	10	CR, F(C), PAC	
1951	9	CR, F(C), PAC	
1952	11	CR, F(C), PAC	
1953	11	CR(C), F, PAC	
1954	11	CR(C), F, PAC	
1955	10	CR(C), F, PAC	
1956	8	CR, F, PAC	
1957	5	CR, F, PAC	
1958	7	CR, F(C), H, PAC	
1959	6	CR, F(C), H, PAC	

Abbreviations: (i) Committees: City Redevelopment/Planning and Redevelopment = CR; Education = E; Finance = F; H = Housing; PAC = Policy Advisory (ii) Chair = (C)

Table 10:6 Stringer's record of service on Council committees, 1937 to 1959[69]

Total no. of committees served		*Main committees served*	*Other positions on Council*
1937	3		Dep. Mayor
1938	26	E, F, H	Mayor
1939	10	E	
1940	(no information available)		
1941	(no information available)		
1942	13	CR, E, PAC	
1943	12	CR, E, PAC(C)	
1944	12	CR, E, PAC(C)	
1945	14	CR, E, PAC(C)	
1946	11	CR, E, PAC(C)	
1947	11	E, PAC(C)	
1948	9	E(C), PAC(C)	
1949	7	E(C), PAC(C)	
1950	7	E, PAC(C)	
1951	8	E, PAC(C)	
1952	9	E, PAC(C)	
1953	9	E, PAC(C)	
1954	9	E, PAC(C)	
1955	8	E(C), PAC(C)	
1956	8	E(C), PAC(C)	
1957	8	E(C), PAC(C)	
1958	9	E, PAC(C)	
1959	8	E, PAC(C)	

Note: Abbreviations as in Table 10:5

overt sectarianism, in which certain groups could be stigmatised as actively antisocial.

Given this structure of feeling, it is not difficult to see why some activists would feel lukewarm (at best) towards home-owners and groups like the Teddy Boys and Girls. Against the grand, and endlessly difficult, task of rebuilding a city, the aspiration to own a private house might appear blatantly disregarding of the community's needs. Similarly, a life-style devoted to dress and pleasure, in which work was an inconvenience to be endured and community merely a gang of peers, could appear to be somewhat irresponsible.

What, to a certain extent, reinforced these tendencies was the fact that Labour itself, as a party, continued to be rather narrowly socially based and inward looking. Labour had recruited few intellectuals, and even Crossman, the local M.P. who was perhaps most concerned with the kinds of social change that were appearing in the 1950s, retained little influence.[70] In fact, throughout this period, the party remained essentially dominated by trade unionists, often connected to the shop steward

Table 10:7 Trade union background of candidates on Labour municipal lists, 1949–1959 (T=61)[71]

		No. of candidates who were:	
Union	*Member of union*	*Official in union*	*Shop steward in union*
A.E.U.	27	7	14
T. and G.	12	3	7
Others	22	8	2

movement, with which there were especially close relations.[72] At the centre of affairs, for example, both in the party and on the Council, were Hodgkinson and Stringer, elected representatives first in 1928, and once shop stewards and members of the I.L.P.[73] (Tables 10:5 and 10:6). Further down the hierarchy, activists from similar backgrounds tended to dominate, as the data in Table 10:7 demonstrate. In this situation, it would have been surprising, at least, if there had not been a bias towards traditional labour movement concerns, and a feeling that, perhaps, some of the newer kinds of popular aspiration were hardly the stuff of politics.

In a sense, then, the Labour party was partly a victim of its own ideology and traditions over the 1950s. The problem was not mass desertion by newly affluent workers, or bureaucracy and paternalism, but the party's inability to communicate with those groups at the centre of social change. There was a gradual realisation of this after 1955, as Chapter 9 has shown, but the evolution of Labour's politics was too slow to stop the rot, and the loss of Coventry South was the inevitable consequence.

Statistical appendix

Table A The population of Coventry County Borough 1939–60, with an estimate of the net impact of migration into the city

Year	*Total population (mid-year)*	*Impact of migration (calendar year)*
1939	220,000	+ 6,714
1940	229,500	− 15,706
1941	192,470	− 12,066
1942	207,000	+ 10,433
1943	214,870	+ 5,691
1944	222,210	− 75
1945	221,970	+ 2,903
1946	232,850	+ 7,935
1947	242,860	+ 5,898
1948	250,400	+ 2,906
1949	254,400	+ 821
1950	256,800	+ 123
1951	259,200	+ 953
1952	261,900	+ 1,219
1953	265,200	+ 990
1954	267,900	+ 1,208
1955	271,600	+ 2,719
1956	277,700	+ 3,604
1957	283,900	+ 2,708
1958	288,500	+ 2,507
1959	294,500	+ 3,081
1960	300,900	+ 2,310

[*Source*: T. Gregory *People and Housing* (Report No. D.P.R.49, Coventry City Council First Review of the Development Plan (April 1966) p.85]

Table B The relative prosperity of Coventry in the 1930s: selected indicators

City	*% of 'all private families in 1937 with incomes of less than 2 10s. per week'*	*% insured population unemployed, June 1938*	*% of working class 'overcrowded', 1935–6*
Coventry	10	7.4	1.9
Hull	29	14.4	3.0
Leicester	15	10.9	1.6
Newcastle	25	12.5	10.7
Nottingham	25	10.8	1.5
Plymouth	17	7.9	6.0
Portsmouth	14	7.0	1.8
Wolverhampton	17	9.9	3.2

[*Sources*: C. Chisholm ed. *Marketing Survey of the U.K.* (3rd edn, London, 1938); Ministry of Health *Report on the Overcrowding Survey . . . 1936* (London, 1936)]

Table C War damage in Coventry and other blitzed cities: selected indicators

City	*% of 1938 housing destroyed*	*Units damaged or destroyed and not repaired by 1945:*					
		Shops		*Commercial buildings*		*Factories/ warehouses*	
		(i)	*(ii)*	*(i)*	*(ii)*	*(i)*	*(ii)*
Coventry	7	826	290,000	149	351,000	108	3,394,000
Hull	5	407	1,200,000	415	850,000	313	2,650,000
Plymouth	9	930	3,700,000	150	800,000	150	2,250,000
Portsmouth	6	337	1,625,000	159	77,000	115	262,000
Southampton	9	824	1,124,000	311	1,642,000	141	1,915,000

(i) no. (ii) sq.ft. of floor space involved
[*Sources*: HLG 71/915 W.(S.N.)(45)(Final) Report of the Inter-departmental Committee . . . 23/5/1945; and ibid. Letter H. Wells–M. P. Winnington-Ingram 19/3/1945, enclosing War Cabinet Reconstruction Committee Special Committee . . . An Estimate of War Damage [n.d.]]

Table D Rateable value: Coventry and other blitzed cities, 1939–1950

City	*Rateable value* *April 1939* £	*April 1945* £	*April 1950* £	*April 1950 as % of April 1939*
Coventry	1,555,805	1,570,075	1,800,326	+ 15.7
Hull	1,804,870	1,654,861	1,747,958	− 3.2
Plymouth	1,868,945	1,547,587	1,725,851	− 7.7
Portsmouth	1,930,227	1,677,285	1,836,247	− 4.9
Southampton	1,632,255	1,428,679	1,535,915	− 5.9

[*Source*: Ministry of Health *Rates and Rateable Values in England and Wales*, various editions]

Table E Analysis of rateable property in Coventry, 1940, 1946, 1952 and 1960

	At 31/3/1940		*At 31/3/1946*		*At 31/3/1952*		*At 31/3/1960*	
	(i)	*(ii)*	*(i)*	*(ii)*	*(i)*	*(ii)*	*(i)*	*(ii)*
Houses								
£20 or less	59,509	48	57,131	49	60,635	45	ncf	ncf
£21–5	3,911	5	3,866	6	6,205	7	(55,320	23)[a]
£26+	3,509	8	3,376	8	3,658	7	34,364	24
All	66,929	62	64,373	62	70,498	60	89,684	46
Shops	4,018	12	3,406	8	3,579	11	3,881	13
Offices	528	1	393	1	407	2	(669	2)[b]
Industrial	493	4	447	5	561	8	630	17
Banks	25	(0.3)	25	(0.3)	27	(0.4)	ncf	ncf

Notes: Column (i) = no. of assessments
Column (ii) = % of total rateable value
ncf = no comparable figure
[a] refers to all houses rated at less than 26 p.a.
[b] includes banks in office areas

[*Source*: Coventry City Council *Abstract of Accounts*, various years]

Table F Rates in Coventry and other blitzed cities 1939–40 to 1959–60

Year	*Coventry*	*Hull*	*Plymouth*	*Ports-mouth*	*South-ampton*	*All County Boroughs' average*
1939–40	13/6	21/6	10/–	11/6	11/9	ncf
1940–1	14/–	21/–	10/2	13/6	11/9	14/11
1941–2	14/–	20/6	10/4	13/6	12/–	15/2
1942–3	14/–	20/6	10/4	13/6	12/–	14/11
1943–4	14/–	20/6	10/4	13/6	12/–	14/9
1944–5	14/–	20/6	10/4	13/6	12/–	14/9
1945–6	15/–	20/6	10/4	13/6	12/–	15/5
1946–7	16/6	21/6	13/–	15/6	14/10	16/9
1947–8	18/6	23/10	14/6	17/6	18/3	18/6
1948–9	17/6	21/–	17/6	19/–	17/6	18/1
1949–50	17/6	19/–	18/–	19/–	18/4	18/4
1950–1	20/–	21/2	18/–	19/–	19/3	18/8
1951–2	22/–	23/–	18/6	19/–	19/9	20/–
1952–3	23/–	25/–	19/4	21/–	20/9	21/–
1953–4	23/6	27/–	20/4	21/–	20/11	22/9
1954–5	23/6	26/10	20/8	21/–	21/4	23/3
1955–6	23/6	26/10	21/–	22/–	21/4	23/6
1956–7	16/4	18/6	15/2	12/4	14/5	16/5
1957–8	19/6	21/4	16/8	14/10	16/6	19/–
1958–9	20/6	22/6	18/6	14/10	16/10	19/5
1959–60	20/6	22/6	17/4	14/10	16/10	20/–

Note: ncf = no comparable figure

[*Source: Ministry of Health Rates and Rateable Values in England and Wales*, various editions]

Table G Applications for Council houses and the waiting list, Coventry, 1944–60

Year	*No. of applications over year*	*Waiting list at 31/12 each year*		
		Total	*A cases*[a]	*B cases*[b]
1944	2,900	nfa	nfa	nfa
1945	5,307	7,141[c]	nfa	nfa
1946	6,238	11,674[c]	nfa	nfa
1947	3,272	10,776[c]	nfa	nfa
1948	2,844	14,212	392	2,545
1949	2,428	12,067	140	1,974
1950	nfa	13,368	116	1,969
1951	2,668	9,593	99	1,776
1952	2,807	10,863	6	1,407
1953	3,482	9,015	78	1,319
1954	3,012	10,370	9	1,122
1955	2,681	7,076	13	905
1956	3,072	6,116	1	555
1957	3,244	5,152	3	382
1958	2,984	4,178	–	181
1959	nfa	4,247	1	277
1960	nfa	5,148	1	425

Notes: nfa = no figure available
[a] A cases were 'Highest Priority' (including T.B. sufferers, etc.)
[b] B cases were applicants crowded beyond 1936 Housing Act standards
[c] figures for 1945–7 relate to April of the year in question

[*Sources*: Housing Committee minutes, various dates; *Coventry Standard* 8/1/1949; *Annual Reports of the Coventry Medical Officer of Health*, various dates]

Table H Houses built in Coventry, for the Corporation and for private sale, 1946–60[a]

Year	*No. of permanent houses completed:*	
	For Coventry Corporation	*For private sale*
1946	128	492
1947	213	390
1948	863	103
1949	550	181
1950	383	284
1951	849	79
1952	1,382	272
1953	1,715	381
1954	1,351	1,017
1955	1,740	2,898
1956	1,998	1,624
1957	1,082	1,119
1958	905	1,295
1959	689	1,580
1960	293	1,573

Note: [a] does not include temporary houses

[*Source*: Ministry of Health/Ministry of Housing and Local Government *Housing Returns*, various dates]

Table I Political Coventry: General Election results and percentage voting Labour 1945–59; and municipal electorates, turn-outs, results and percentage voting Labour, selected contests 1945–59

	Municipal electorate: Size	*Turn-out %*	*No. of seats won by Labour*	*% voting Labour*
G 1945			2/2	61
M 1945	168,859	44.4	17/25	55
M 1947		54.4	9/17	45
M 1949		57.3	10/16	49
G 1950			3/3	57
G 1951			3/3	59
M 1951	178,440	50.2	10/16	49
M 1953		44.7	10/16	52
G 1955			3/3	54
M 1955	182,379	51.0	8/16	45
M 1957		45.7	10/16	51
G 1959			2/3	52
M 1959	190,343	47.4	11/7	50

Note: G = General Election, M = Municipal Election

[*Sources*: various editions of the *Standard* and *Civic Affairs*; material in MRC MSS 11/3/54; F. W. S. Craig *British Parliamentary Election Results 1950–70* (Chichester, 1971); Registrar General's *Statistical Review of England and Wales*, various editions]

Table J Political Coventry: percentage voting Labour by ward, selected municipal elections, 1947–59

Ward	*% voting Labour in:* 1947	*1949*	*1951*	*1953*	*1955*	*1957*	*1959*
Bablake	44	47	42	41	38	40	36
Charterhouse and Binley	50	57	58	63	54	64	61
Cheylesmore	39	38	37	37	28	34	31
Earlsdon	21	24	23	26	23	23	22
Foleshill	53	51	51	63	50	59	58
Godiva	47	48	51	63	50	55	52
Holbrooks	59	62	63	66	55	60	55
Longford	51	52	55	67	60	70	64
Lower Stoke	42	39	40	44	35	42	45
Radford	55	56	54	60	54	61	61
Sherbourne	35	40	33	29	30	34	31
St Michaels	49	56	58	66	54	61	62
Upper Stoke	55	57	56	62	54	59	59
Walsgrave	53	57	57	55	46	51	48
Westwood	52	63	61	65	59	70	66
Whoberly	40	43	46	45	40	42	34

[*Sources*: various editions of *Civic Affairs* and material in MRC MSS 11/3/54]

Guide to sources and abbreviations used in notes

This study is based on the following main archive sources:

1 Material in the Local Studies Section of Coventry City Library, particularly the minutes of the Council (abbreviated CCC) and its various committees – the City Reconstruction Committee, subsequently the Planning and Reconstruction Committee (CRC), the Finance Committee (FC), the General Purposes Committee (GPC), the Housing Committee (HC), the Policy Advisory Committee (PAC) and the Public Health Committee (PHC); and the local newspapers – the *Midland Daily Telegraph* (*MDT*), the *Coventry Evening Telegraph* (*CET*) and the *Coventry Standard* (*Standard*).

2 Material in the Coventry Record Office (CRO), particularly the files in the series Sec/CF/1 (compiled by the Town Clerk) and AP/CF/1 (on planning issues).

3 Material in the Modern Records Centre, the University of Warwick (MRC), especially the records of Coventry Borough Labour Party (MRC MSS 11) and Standard Motors (MRC MSS 226).

4 Various files in the Public Record Office, London (mainly those in BT, CAB, HLG, HO, IR, LAB, SUPP, T and WO).

Notes

1 Introduction

1 R. J. Waller *The Dukeries Transformed* (Oxford, 1983); R. C. Whiting *The View from Cowley* (Oxford, 1983).
2 C. Barnett *The Audit of War* (London, 1986).
3 R. Miliband *Parliamentary Socialism* (London, 1961); T. Blackwell and J. Seabrook *The Politics of Hope* (London, 1988); and J. Saville *The Labour Movement in Britain* (London, 1988).
4 M. Abrams ' "The Future of the Left." New Roots of Working-class Conservatism' *Encounter* Vol. XIV No. 5 May 1960 57–9.
5 H. Hopkins *The New Look* (London, 1964) p. 372.
6 *The Economist* 16/5/1959.
7 See, for example, material in T. Harrisson *Britain Revisited* (London, 1961); and S. Hall 'A Sense of Classlessness' *Universities and Left Review* Autumn 1958 26–32, and 'The Supply of Demand' in E. P. Thompson ed. *Out of Apathy* (London, 1960) pp. 56–97.
8 For this slogan, and its genesis, see A. Sampson *Macmillan* (Pelican edn, Harmondsworth, 1968) pp. 159–65. The 1959 contest is fully surveyed in D. E. Butler and R. Rose *The British General Election of 1959* (London, 1960).
9 M. Abrams and R. Rose *Must Labour Lose?* (Harmondsworth, 1960).
10 J. H. Goldthorpe, D. Lockwood et al. *The Affluent Worker: Industrial Attitudes and Behaviour* (Cambridge, 1968); *The Affluent Worker: Political Attitudes and Behaviour* (Cambridge, 1968); and *The Affluent Worker in the Class Structure* (Cambridge, 1969).
11 T. Blackwell and J. Seabrook *A World Still to Win* (London, 1985) p. 82.
12 I. Crewe 'The Politics of "Affluent" and "Traditional" Workers in Britain: an Aggregate Data Analysis' *British Journal of Political Science* Vol. 3 Pt. 1 Jan. 1973 29–52.
13 Car workers made up an important part of the Luton sample; while they are often cited in pro-embourgeoisement literature, too (e.g. F. Zweig *The Worker in an Affluent Society* (London, 1961)).
14 Note especially K. Richardson *Twentieth-Century Coventry* (Coventry, 1972), though see also R. W. G. Bryant 'The Reconstruction of Coventry' in H. Wentworth Eldredge ed. *Taming Megalopolis* (New York, 1967) pp. 765–83 and T. Gregory 'Coventry' in J. Holliday ed. *City Centre Redevelopment: A Study of British City Centre Planning* (London, 1974) pp. 78–134.

15 J. Seabrook *What Went Wrong?* (London, 1978) pp. 167–201.
16 J. Benington *Local Government Becomes Big Business* (London, second edn. 1976).
17 Seabrook (1978) op. cit.
18 J. Hinton 'Coventry Communism: A Study of Factory Politics in the Second World War' *History Workshop* Issue 10 Autumn 1980 90–118.
19 B. Lancaster and T. Mason 'Society and Politics in 20th Century Coventry' in B. Lancaster and T. Mason eds. *Life and Labour in a Twentieth Century City: The Experience of Coventry* (Coventry, 1986) especially pp. 351 and 356.
20 P. Thompson 'Playing at Being Skilled Men: Factory Culture and Pride in Work Skills among Coventry Car Workers' *Social History* Vol. 13 No. 1 Jan. 1988 45–69.

2 The politics of reconstruction: war-time plans for a new Coventry

1 This estimate appears in HLG 79/132 Note [?Wright] – L. Neal 26/7/1943.
2 This tension has received relatively little attention in the literature, although see material in P. Addison *The Road to 1945* (London, 1980) and J. M. Lee *The Churchill Coalition, 1940–1945* (London, 1980). For a cogent critique of the Government's backtracking over town and country planning, see G. J. G. Bruce *The Planning Act, 1944, and National Policy* (London, 1945).
3 For other views of the inter-war history of the city see F. Carr 'Engineering Workers and the Rise of Labour in Coventry 1914–1939' (unpublished Ph.D. dissertation University of Warwick, 1979) and various contributions to B. Lancaster and T. Mason eds. *Life and Labour in a Twentieth Century City: The Experience of Coventry* (Coventry, 1986).
4 Contemporary sources upon which much of this paragraph is based are J. B. Priestley *English Journey* (London, 1934) pp. 68–76 and unattributed observations in the Nuffield Social Reconstruction Survey Box A.6. 'Report on Coventry and East Warwickshire' Sept. 1941. Interesting comments on the state of union organisation in Coventry at this time may be found in J. Jones *Union Man* (London, 1986) p. 87. Comparative information on the city's prosperity during the 1930s is presented in Statistical Appendix, Table B. For Coventry's relatively high rate of owner-occupation, see M. Swenarton and S. Taylor 'The Scale and Nature of the Growth of Owner Occupation in Britain between the Wars' *Economic History Review* 2nd Ser. Vol. XXXVIII No. 3 Aug. 1985 387.
5 Anon. 'Factory City Thinks Again' in *Future Books* Vol. 3 1946 14.
6 A useful account of Coventry's urban geography at this time may be found in ibid. 14–15 and 18.
7 The total number of street accidents in Coventry grew from 1,499 in 1935 to 2,059 in 1938 (i.e. by about 30 per cent) (*Report of the Chief Constable for the Year Ended 31/12/1938* (Coventry, 1939) p. 9). It is not possible to estimate how many of these were in the central area, but some idea of the concentration is provided by the following:

> A map has been prepared showing all accidents at the principle accident points in the central area . . . out of a total of 841 occurring per annum . . . during 1937, 1938 and 1939, 112 were on the principal east–

west route between Whitefriars Street and St. John's Church, and 94 were on the north–south route between the north end of Bishop Street and Greyfriars Green, two stretches each only half a mile in length.

(A. R. Pugh and A. L. Percy 'Planning and Reconstruction in Coventry' *Journal of the Institution of Municipal and County Engineers* 3/9/1946 85.)

8 See, for example, the portrait of Stoke Aldermoor in *MDT* 10/3/1936; and the more general conclusions on pre-war suburbs in the *Standard* 4/5/1946.

9 See West Midlands Group *Local Government and Central Control* (London, 1956), Chapter Five, for a comparative perspective on Coventry Council spending in the 1930s.

10 BT 64/3409 Ministry of Town and Country Planning Advisory Panel A.P.C.C. 11 'Notes on Employment and Labour Conditions at Coventry' 9/7/1943 pp. 1–2.

11 For debate about how Coventry's built-environment could be improved see *MDT* 26/1/1937 and 12/7/1938 and CRO Sec/CF/1/7662 Coventry City Guild 'Report of the Civic Centres Committee' Jan. 1939.

12 Planning initiatives in the 1930s are covered in HLG 79/130 Report by H. R. Wardill on 'Bombed Areas – Re-development of Coventry' 23/1/1941 pp. 3–4 and CRO Sec/CF/1/9501 Memo. by Town Clerk 'Control and Development of the Countryside' Nov. 1941.

13 G. Hodgkinson *Sent to Coventry* (London, 1970) pp. 128–9.

14 In the *MDT* 27/10/1937 Labour was characterised as 'obsessed by a degree of modesty that is startling if becoming'.

15 Holtby's exhortation can be found in her *South Riding* (London, 1936) p. 5. George Hodgkinson, Labour official and prominent Councillor, was certainly impressed by this formulation: see the transcribed interview with him in the CRO (OH 11/1) p. 13. The quotation is also repeated in Labour's *Coventry Tribune* 26/10/1946.

16 *Coventry Searchlight* 1/11/1937.

17 *MDT* 2/11/1937. Labour's programme for Coventry – with its strictures about the need for efficiency and its commitment to financial orthodoxy – was very typical of the party's wider thinking on local government problems at this time: see H. R. S. Phillpott *Where Labour Rules* (London, 1934) and R. B. Suthers *Mind Your Own Business: The Case for Municipal Housekeeping* (rev. edn, London, 1938). But the success in Coventry was rather unusual, in that most boroughs with a Labour majority in the 1930s had 'a serious unemployment problem, and a heavy relief burden': D. E. McHenry *The Labour Party in Transition 1931–1938* (London, 1938) pp. 210–11.

18 On the PAC see material in CRO Sec/CF/1/6637.

19 As an incoming Labour Mayor put it: 'we find notwithstanding the extraordinary addition to the rateable value the demands from the growing city swallows it up faster than it is created' (CRO Acc. 204 S. Stringer Address on becoming Mayor [n.d. but 1939] p. 2).

20 PAC 22/12/1938.

21 *MDT* 14/4/1938.

22 Biographical information on Gibson may be found in *Architects' Journal* 20/1/1955 and *CET* 13/1/1972.

23 There is, unfortunately, no one very good account of Liverpool in the 1930s. But see inter alia C. H. Reilly *Scaffolding in the Sky* (London, 1938)

(particularly Reilly's 1934 Roscoe Lecture, reprinted as Appendix A); W. G. Holford 'The Work of the Liverpool School' *Journal of the Town Planning Institute* Vol. XXV No. 1 Nov. 1938 15–18; G. Stephenson 'The Planning Schools. (7) The University of Liverpool' *Town Planning Review* Vol. 22 No. 1 April 1951 84–7; and G. Stamp '. . . an interview with John Brandon-Jones' *Architectural Design* Vol. 39 No. 10–11 1979 96–101.

24 Gibson's most sustained credo – entitled 'The Third Dimension in Town Planning' – may be found in *The Report of Proceedings at the Town and Country Planning Summer School, 1947* (London, 1947) pp. 99–108.

25 Gibson visualised the town planner as 'the chief authority in all matters relating to the design, structure and appearance of the city' and argued that as a consequence:

> This planning officer should have authority in all matters which concern him, over all the other officers in any local authority. He should be . . . unhampered by the thousand and one legal and technical restrictions which have caused town planning today to degenerate into negative and sordid observations of rule of thumb regulations.

(D. Gibson 'Post-War Civil Development' *Camera Principis* Vol. 9 No. 53 Aug. 1940 3.) The Labour party believed, too, in bringing 'an expert mind upon the problem on town planning' and warned that, without 'vision about planning', Coventry, 'a city of mushroom growth', might well be spoilt: *Coventry Searchlight* 1/11/1938. It is not clear how far Gibson and the politicians agreed on wider questions, but note the assurances about the architect's Labour loyalties in Edgar Snow's piece on Coventry in the *Saturday Evening Post* (Philadelphia, U.S.A.) 6/3/1948.

26 See R. D. Manning 'Coventry. A new Official Architectural Department' *Keystone* July 1939 23–4. The history of the A.A.S.T.A. has apparently yet to be written, but see A. Jackson *The Politics of Architecture* (London, 1970) p. 76, where it is referred to as a 'militant centre of activity'.

27 Nuffield Social Reconstruction Survey 'Report' op. cit. 4–5.

28 For a list of the 'shadow' factories, see HLG 79/132 Letter E. H. Doubleday–A. M. Jenkins 13/8/1943.

29 A. Shenfield and P. Sargant Florence 'Labour for the War Industries: The Experience of Coventry' *Review of Economic Studies* Vol. XII No. 1 1944–5 39.

30 Nuffield Social Reconstruction Survey 'Report' op. cit. 5–8.

31 P. Johnson-Marshall 'Coventry: The Test Case of Planning' *Official Architecture* Vol. 21 No. 5 May 1958 225.

32 *Keystone* Nov. 1940 11; P. Johnson-Marshall *Rebuilding Cities* (Edinburgh, 1966) p. 263. The MARS Group is discussed in Louise Campbell 'The MARS Group, 1933–1939', *RIBA Transactions*, Vol. 4 No. 2(8) 1985 68–79. Their contribution to the exhibition in Coventry is satirised in *Camera Principis* Vol. 9 No. 50 May 1940 2–3.

33 Contemporary accounts of the damage can be found in HLG 79/130 Report by Wardill op. cit. 4–8 and CRO Acc. 483 Reports of the Coventry Reconstruction Coordinating Committee 3/12/1940 and 1/5/1941. Later official figures putting Coventry's predicament in a comparative light are presented in Statistical Appendix, Table C. Much interesting material on the Coventry raids can also be found in T. Harrisson *Living Through the Blitz*

(Penguin edn, Harmondsworth, 1978) pp. 132–41 and passim.

34 HLG 71/915 W. (S.N.)(45) 'Report of the Inter-departmental Committee on Special Needs of Particular Areas' 23/5/1945 Appendix One.

35 G. C. Firth *75 Years of Service to Education* (Coventry, 1977) p. 81.

36 See, for example, T. Harrisson in the *Listener* 21/11/1940; and R. Calder in the *New Statesman* 7/12/1940.

37 Reported in the *Standard* 7/12/1940.

38 Material on the meeting between Reith and the representatives from Coventry appears in HLG 68/66. See also *The Times* 3/2/1941.

39 CCC 3/12/1940.

40 The motion supporting Gibson was carried 43–6: CCC 25/2/1941.

41 The plan is included in HLG 79/130 Report by Wardill op. cit. as App. 5, and described in the *Architect and Building News* 21/3/1941.

42 The more conservative scheme – by Ford, the City Engineer – is in CRO Sec/CF/1/9464. The differences between Gibson and Ford's proposals are listed in *MDT* 27/2/1941. The engineer's general orientation is perhaps best summed up by his remark that 'one could not lead up to an architectural climax as was exemplified in Coventry Cathedral with a modernistic building of dead straight lines designed with no imagination' (*MDT* 4/3/1939).

43 See particularly HLG 71/914 D. E. Gibson 'Report to Housing Committee of the City of Coventry' 22/3/1943; Firth op. cit. pp. 90–3 for F. H. Harrod's 'Report on Educational Reconstruction in Coventry' of Dec. 1943; and CRO Sec/CF/1/9697 D. E. Gibson 'Report on Post-War Housing to the Housing Committee' 21/1/1944.

44 E.g. D. E. Gibson 'Problems of Decentralisation . . . Statement III' in F. E. Towndrow ed. *Replanning Britain* (London, 1941) p. 105; IR 34/268 Transcript by the Pacific Service of the B.B.C., 31/10/1941 'Today and Tomorrow' by Mallory Browne and D. E. Gibson; W. L. Hulley 'Coventry Re-development' *Journal of the Institution of Municipal and County Engineers* 11/11/1941; D. E. Gibson 'The Reconstruction of Towns' in E. A. Gutkind ed. *Creative Mobilisation Vol. II* (London, 1943) pp. 208–11; and Anon. 'Factory City' *Future Books* op. cit. passim.

45 L. Mumford *The Culture of Cities* (London, 1940) passim.

46 Le Corbusier's book, published in French in 1924 and in English in 1929, is cited as particularly important in Johnson-Marshall 'Coventry: The Test Case' op. cit. 225.

47 Gibson had certainly been influenced by Abercrombie during his time at Liverpool (see the unpublished interview with Donald Gibson by B. Lancaster and T. Mason 3/4/1985).

48 Alker Tripp's *Road Traffic and Its Control* (London, 1938) included a diagram of a precinct scheme, for example.

49 Sharp's most influential work, *Town Planning*, had come out in Penguin in 1940. His general influence is discussed in K. Stansfield 'Thomas Sharp 1901–1978' in G. Cherry ed. *Pioneers in British Planning* (London, 1981) pp. 150–76.

50 D. E. Gibson 'Some Matters Concerning Post-War Reconstruction' *Architectural Association Journal* Vol. LVI No. 648 Feb. 1941 72; Johnson-Marshall 'Coventry: The Test Case' op. cit. 226.

51 Anon. 'Factory City' *Future Books* op. cit. 18; and the interview with

Coventry's Mayor in the *Standard* 31/8/1946.

52 For which see W. Russell Taylor 'The Neighbourhood Unit Principle in Town Planning' *Town Planning Review* Vol. 18 No. 3 July 1939 174–86; and J. Dahir *The Neighbourhood Unit Plan* (New York, 1947).

53 Nuffield Social Reconstruction Survey Box L.G. 152. Interview by J. H. Glaisyer with E. H. Ford and D. E. Gibson [n.d. but 1942] p. 14.

54 D. E. Gibson 'Coventry Housing' *Journal of the Town Planning Institute* Vol. XXVI No. 5 July–Aug. 1940 162–6.

55 CRO Sec/CF/1/9697 D. E. Gibson Report op. cit.

56 HC 27/1/1944, CCC 7/3/1944.

57 ibid.

58 See a speech by the Mayor, reported in the *Standard* 31/3/1945.

59 See, for example, HLG 79/130 Report by Wardill op. cit. Appendix 3(i)–(iv) and the editorial in the *Standard* 8/3/1941.

60 For local opinion pro and contra flats, see HLG 79/130 Report by Wardill op. cit. Appendices 2(ii) and 3(iv) and *MDT* 31/3/1941.

61 HLG 79/132 Coventry Chamber of Commerce. Coventry Retailers Advisory Committee on Town Planning. 'Report on Re-development of Coventry Shopping Facilities' 18/1/1944 p. 3.

62 HLG 79/130 Report by Wardill op. cit. 4 and HLG 88/9 Advisory Panel Minutes No. 3 7/7/1943 10(r).

63 *Truth* 7/3/1941.

64 E. g. *Daily Herald* 26/2/1941; *News Chronicle* 26/2/1941; *Reynold's News* 2/3/1941; *CET* 12/12/1942.

65 A typical pamphlet reference is [anon.] *Your Inheritance . . . an Uncomic Strip* [n.d. but 1942?]. For the genre see L. J. Wright 'British Town Planning Literature 1939–1945: A Survey of Planning Titles in General Pamphlet Series' (unpublished B. A. dissertation, Leeds Polytechnic, 1983).

66 See, for example, Alker Tripp *Town Planning and Road Traffic* (London, 1942); R. Tubbs *Living in Cities* (Harmondsworth, 1942); J. Forshaw and P. Abercrombie *County of London Plan* (London, 1943); F. Osborn ed. *Making Plans* (London, 1943); *Architectural Review* Vol. XCIII No. 556 April 1943 (a special edition on 'Rebuilding Britain'); José Luis Sert (for C.I.A.M.) *Can Our Cities Survive*? (Cambridge, 1944); R. L. Reiss *Municipal and Private Enterprise Housing* (London, 1945); and Association for Planning and Regional Reconstruction *Housing Digest* (London, 1946).

67 *MDT* 26/2/1942.

68 For which see material in HLG 52/1509 and HLG 101/516.

69 Rubble was cleared from the central area between March and August 1942: see HO 207/1169 Letter Group Surveyor, War Debris Survey–The Earl of Derby 16/9/1942 and enclosed report.

70 See, for example, HLG 71/914 Comments by Research Division on 'City Architect's Report . . .' 29/7/1943 and Memo. by E. H. Doubleday on 'City Architect's Housing Report' 8/9/1943.

71 The Advisory Panel's membership and terms of reference may be found in its final Report of 2/8/1944 (HLG 88/9). Some material on its formation and the circumstances of its visit to Coventry appears in HLG 79/132.

72 Gibson's report had in fact tended to dismiss the whole question:

> The cost of constructing the buildings will be similar whatever the plan may be, although if anything it will be more economical to build in more

continuous larger blocks, than in many individual small buildings. The cost of the buildings need not therefore be considered at the moment.
(HLG 79/130 Report by Wardill op. cit. App. 5 p. 6.)

73 *CET* 9/10/1943.
74 HLG 88/9 'Report of the Advisory Panel' 2/8/1944 App. 1B.
75 HLG 79/131 A.P.C.C. 32 Memo. by the City Treasurer 21/1/1944; and A.P.C.C. 38 Notes of a Meeting Held at Coventry 24/2/1944.
76 For the genesis and drafting of this Bill see J. B. Cullingworth *Environmental Planning 1939–1969 Vol. 1 Reconstruction and Land Use Planning 1939–1947* (London, 1975).
77 HLG 79/131 Letter E. H. Doubleday–B. Gillie 16/5/1944.
78 The development of Ministry thinking can be followed in the voluminous HLG 79/131; for a flavour, see Notes Gillie–G. L. Pepler 18/5/1944 and Doubleday–Gillie 22/8/1944.
79 See, for example, the interchange of mid-1944, when the Council, under pressure to specify progress to Whitehall, immediately raised questions relating to post-war factory policy and the proposed ring road – issues which had not been settled between relevant Ministries (HLG 79/131 misc. correspondence 19/5/1944–14/7/1944).
80 For the Chamber's plan, and Council discussion on it, see CRC 19/6/1944. A critical judgement of the scheme is recorded in HLG 79/131 Doubleday–Gillie 16/5/1944.
81 HLG 71/1020 Memo. for New Minister [n.d. but Aug. 1945] p. 2.
82 CRC 14/2/1944; HLG 79/131 Coventry Chamber of Commerce. 'Memo. on Shopping Facilities' [n.d. but Feb. 1945]; CRC 11/4/1945, 11/7/1945; *CET* 12/7/1945.
83 HLG 79/131 'Notes for Meeting with the Redevelopment Committee' 15/3/1945.
84 *Standard* 27/1/1945, 21/3/1945.
85 HLG 79/131 Note E. S. Hill–H. E. C. Gatliff 20/7/1945.
86 See, for example, Gibson 'Some Matters' *Architectural Association Journal* op. cit. 70.
87 HLG 88/9 Advisory Panel Minutes No. 4 13/7/1943 p. 2. The views of other Council officers can be found at ibid. and in HLG 79/132. See also Nuffield Social Reconstruction Survey Box L.G. 152. Interview op. cit., where it is claimed that Councillors wanted expansion so that their Mayor would gain the status of Lord Mayor.
88 HLG 79/131 'Note of Meeting at Coventry' 24/2/1944 and Letter Doubleday–Gillie 30/5/1944.
89 BT 106/17 Letter A. D. Carmichael–P. A. Warter 19/3/1943 enclosing A. D. Carmichael Report on 'Reconstruction – Midland Region No. 9' 20/3/1943; and WO 185/224 'Notes on Visits Paid to Car Manufacturers by Col. R. T. Grantham' 3/2/1945.
90 For attitudes to wages, see the weekly reports of the Regional Industrial Relations Officer in LAB 10/444 and LAB 10/554.
91 BT 177/1508 B.D.I. 4/44 (23/11/1944).
92 E.g. the work of Shenfield and Sargant Florence cited in notes 29 and 94 (below); and M. P. Fogarty *Prospects of the Industrial Areas of Great Britain* (London, 1945) pp. 352–3.
93 The proportion employed in engineering had in fact risen from 48 per cent

in 1938 to 67 per cent in 1943: see BT 177/1519 Memo. 'Coventry. Survey of Present Industrial and Employment Situation' 25/10/1946 p. 4.

94 A. Shenfield and P. Sargant Florence 'The Economics and Diseconomics of Industrial Concentration: The Wartime Experience of Coventry' *Review of Economic Studies* Vol. XII No. 2 1944–5 98.

95 HLG 79/131 Correspondence between Doubleday and Gillie 30/5/1944 and 1/6/1944.

96 HLG 79/131 Letter Town Clerk–Secretary, Ministry 22/5/1944.

97 HLG 79/131 Letter Town Clerk–Secretary, Ministry 7/2/1945.

98 HLG 79/131 Letter Gillie–D. Jay 1/6/1944.

99 For elements of the Board's thinking, see HLG 79/132 Note Gillie–Pepler 30/9/1943; BT 177/1508 B.D.I. 4/44 (23/11/1944) and 9/44B (11/12/1944); and WO 185/224 Interdepartmental Committee on the Post-War Resettlement of the Motor Industry . . . 1st Meeting (29/12/1944).

100 WO 185/224 Interdepartmental Committee passim.

101 BT 96/188 Location of Industry Committee I.L. (45) 12th meeting 7/2/1945.

102 The negotiations on 'shadow' factory allocation are far from easy to track down in official material, but note anyway the limited information in BT 106/49, BT 177/1369, BT 208/32, CAB 124/419 and CAB 185/224, together with the reference cited in note 96.

103 See material in BT 177/26.

104 Gibson 'Some Matters' *Architectural Association Journal* op. cit. 73.

3 Economic reconstruction: Coventry's local economy 1945–51

1 See, for example, for Armstrong Whitworth, BT 170/72 R.B.I. 6/45 (19/11/1945) and 13/46 (11/2/1946). Unemployment in Coventry during this period was as follows:

Year	Month	Total unemployed
1945	July	1,508
	October	3,808
	November	5,000
	December	5,135
1946	January	4,844
	March	4,582
	April	4,064
	June	2,514
	July	2,093
	September	1,787

(BT 177/1519 Memo. 'Coventry. Survey of Present Industrial and Employment Situation' 25/10/1946 p. 6.)

2 For a good example of a typical production difficulty see SUPP 14/395 Letter W. Lyons–W. Strath 9/3/1946. The problem of pricing new work is stressed in WO 185/224 Letter K. M. F. Hedges – Sir G. Turner etc. enclosing K. M. F. Hedges 'Memorandum on the Progress the Motor Industry has made in its Reconversion to Civil Work' 5/9/1945.

3 Information on the (variable) extent of damage to plant in Coventry can be found in T 229/346 I.P.C. (W.P.)(49) 14. Cabinet Investment Programmes Committee 'The Motor Industry. Note by the Ministry of Supply' 12/1/1949 pp. 4–5.

4 BT 177/1508 B.D.I. 4/44 (23/11/1944) and 9/44B (11/12/1944); and *CET* 27/4/1945. Rover moved (because of shortage of space) to a 'shadow' factory it had been operating in Birmingham.

5 BT 177/1508 B.D.I. 106/45 (19/10/1945) and BT 177/1519 Memo. 'Coventry' p. 5.

6 BT 170/72 R.B.I. 15/45 (10/12/1945) 1/46 (4/1/1946) and 5/46 (14/1/1946); WO 185/224 Letter H. A. R. Binney–Hedges 2/5/1945; and *CET* 5/4/1945 and 7/9/1945.

7 Daimler, for example, was certainly interested in leaving Coventry – it claimed it had lost 0.5 million sq. ft. in the bombing and wanted a 'shadow' factory near London. But its application ran into strong opposition from the Board of Trade on both 'distribution of industry' and 'strategic' grounds. See CAB 124/803 Letter Sir B. Docker–Lord Woolton 15/9/1944 and Minute [signed A.S.?] 19/9/1944; and BT 177/1470 Letter P. A. Warter–H. R. Camp 11/7/1945.

8 See, for example, for Standard's immediate post-war production policy, H. G. Castle *Britain's Motor Industry* (London, 1950) p. 219.

9 Rootes and Daimler certainly benefited from large government orders: see WO 185/224 'Notes on Visits Paid to Car Manufacturers by Col. R. T. Grantham' 19/1/1945 and *CET* 1/6/1945.

10 Precise figures on output company by company over this period are not available. For an estimate of the market shares held by Standard and Rootes see G. Maxcy and A. Silberston *The Motor Industry* (1959) p. 117.

11 *People* 10/9/1950. As a result of this article 2,000 enquiries were received at the local Labour Exchange while 'many hundreds more' got in touch directly with companies or the unions. Few of the applicants were placed in jobs though, and many found the lack of accommodation a particular deterrent (T 229/582 Note [unsigned] 'Boom Town' (n.d. but 1951) and *People* 17/9/1950).

12 D. Thoms and T. Donnelly *The Motor Car Industry in Coventry Since the 1890's* (London, 1985) p. 160.

13 Respectively by Standard Motors, Courtaulds and G.E.C.

14 Migration into Coventry was especially significant between 1946 and 1949, being responsible for about two-thirds of the city's overall 9 per cent population increase. See Coventry City Council *Coventry. The Development Plan* (Coventry, 1952) p. 64; and Statistical Appendix, Table A.

15 Chisholm's 'Income Level Index' for 1951, it is true, does not give Coventry a particularly high score, but the figure quoted is noted as a definite underestimation: C. Chisholm ed. *Marketing Survey of the United Kingdom* (London, 1951 edn) pp. 40–1.

16 Exact comparisons are difficult here because there are no completely consistent sets of official statistics. But it seems certain, anyway, that engineering industries retained their dominance, employing about 60 per cent of the insured population in 1946 and around 56 per cent in 1950 (BT 177/1519 Memo. 'Coventry' p. 4 and T 229/582 'Report of the Working Party on the Labour Position in the Coventry Area. August 1951'

Appendix III Table 1).

17 The broader picture is well represented in D. W. Parsons *The Political Economy of British Regional Policy* (London, 1986) pp. 96–134. Nevertheless Parson's perspective does not shed much light on the type of situation Coventry represented.

18 BT 177/1801 Official Committee on the Distribution of Industry. Panel A.B.D.I. (A) 78th Meeting (19/11/1946); BT 177/1800 Official Committee on the Distribution of Industry. Panel A.B.D.I. (A) 68 'Survey of the Present Industrial and Employment Situation in Coventry. Note by the Board of Trade, Nov. 1946' and B.D.I. (A) 82 'Survey. . . . A Note by the Secretary, Feb. 1947'.

19 This table has been compiled from information in BT 177/1802–1807.

20 The figures here are derived from Table 3:1 and the *Financial Times* 8/11/1950.

21 Nor was it common for new companies to get round the licensing system by occupying old premises: T 229/582 'Report' para. 23.

22 ibid. para. 24. It should be noted that the low incidence of unsuccessful applications for I.D.C.s reflects the fact that many firms knew of the strict Board policy on Coventry and therefore did not even bother contemplating a move to the city.

23 For favourable assessments of various markets supplied by Coventry firms see *Planning* Vol. XV No. 292 20/12/1948 (machine tools); T 229/346 Note by Statistical Division, Board of Trade 'Prospects of U.K. Exports of Wool and Rayon Piece Goods and Motor Vehicles' [n.d. but 1948]; and the *Financial Times* 29/11/1948 (which reports the Society of Motor Manufacturers and Traders as suggesting that the home market for cars and commercial vehicles was such that there were possibly one million orders on the books).

24 See, for example, CRO Acc. 926/1/1/1 Alfred Herbert Board Minutes 26/3/1946.

25 The Government's policy on the motor trade is summarised in W. Plowden *The Motor Car and Politics in Britain* (Pelican edn., Harmondsworth, 1973) especially pp. 309–34.

26 See, for example, *The Economist* 5/1/1952.

27 See, for example, *The Economist* 5/2/1949.

28 See, for example, SUPP 14/332 Memo. by W. M. Millar 'Steel Allocation – Period IV/1952' 28/7/1952.

29 SUPP 14/332 for National Advisory Council for the Motor Manufacturing Industry M.M.I. (50) 9 'The Market for British Cars in the U.S.A. Note by Ministry of Supply' (8/9/1950) enclosing 'Extracts from a Report Prepared by the Embassy, Washington, on the Market for British Cars in the U.S.A.' (July 1950); Note 'The Market for British Cars in the U.S.A. . . . passages which concern Jaguar Cars Ltd.' [n.d.]; and Letter W. Lyons–Sir A. Rowlands 20/9/1950.

30 See, for example, *The Economist* 20/3/1948.

31 *The Economist* (15/11/1952) dated the end of the post-war boom for British car manufacturers to 1952, but some Coventry firms had certainly experienced sharp competition abroad before this.

32 Note, for example, Jaguar's use of the capital market and the loan facilities of a local bank, cited in the 'Notes to Shareholders' filed with its Annual

Reports and Accounts for the Years Ended 31/7/1945 and 31/7/1946 (held in the Local Studies Section, Coventry City Library).

33 For which see inter alia T 229/582 'Report' para. 17.

34 Daimler was thus apparently prevented from rebuilding at Radford: BT 177/1470 Memo. A. A. Mansell–C. J. Schinas 25/11/1947.

35 The Working Party of 1951 calculated that, of 89 expansion schemes sanctioned between 1945 and 1950, only 38 had been fully completed by the time of its enquiries: T 229/582 'Report' Appendix IX.

36 See, for example, SUPP 14/332 for the Chairman of Singer Motor Ltd.'s Address to the A.G.M. 20/11/1950, and a Memo. by L. H. Robinson 19/3/1952 (on Daimler).

37 P.E.P. Motor Vehicles (London, 1950) pp. 23–4.

38 CRO Acc. 985/1/2. Alvis Board Minutes 3/9/1945 (65); and MRC Standard Motor Co. Minutes of Executive Directors' Meetings MSS 226/ST/1/5/1 24/7/1952 (163(2)).

39 *Financial Times* 29/11/1948 includes a comprehensive review of raw material costs.

40 Unfortunately, the detailed records of steel allocations to car manufacturers in the period 1945–50 appear not to be available (though see SUPP 14/331–2 on 1951–2). For a 'representative' steel problem, see SUPP 14/865 Min. by Second Secretary (Supply) 19/1/1948 enclosing 'Joint Statement by Sir John Black and Mr. Harry Ferguson to the Minister of Economic Affairs' (28/10/1947).

41 Machine tool companies' labour costs were proportionally the highest (see *The Economist* 5/6/1948 on Coventry Gauge and Tool Co.). Car manufacturers' requirements varied: some specialist firms used much skilled labour, though volume manufacturers depended on less (T 229/582 'Report' para. 16). Overall, probably 40 per cent of the engineering labour force was skilled: see the detailed breakdown provided by the Coventry District Engineering Employers' Federation, ibid.

42 In 1951, the *Standard* reported that local officials of the A.E.U. believed that membership in the Coventry area – then standing at 27,000 – 'could be doubled if all who were eligible joined the Union'. It went on to note that 'even today some Coventry engineering factories have a minority trade union representation among their workers' (10/8/1951).

43 Control over entry was to some extent exercised through the apprenticeship system, for example. Note that in 1951 there were 1,740 apprentices to 22,613 adult male skilled workers in engineering (T 229/582 'Report' para. 16).

44 Many firms seem to have normally promoted from within their own ranks (LAB 8/1740 Note W. E. Davis–Dame Mary Smieton 5/2/1952). But opportunities were certainly not open to all, with women, for example, being excluded from most well-paid positions (disputes about women's employment can be found in the Engineering Employers' Federation archive at the MRC, e.g. (1946) F(6)92 (MSS 237/3/1/90) and (1946) W(9)5 App. 83 (MSS 237/3/1/218)).

45 On Coventry wage rates see K. G. J. C. Knowles and D. Robinson 'Wage Movements in Coventry' *Bulletin of the Oxford University Institute of Economics and Statistics* Vol. 31 No. 1 Feb. 1969 1–21 and R. A. Hart and D. I. Mackay 'Engineering Earnings in Britain 1914–68' *Journal of the*

Royal Statistical Society Vol. 138 Pt. 1 (1975) 32–50.

46 On this point see T 229/582 'Report' para. 31; CAB 134/856 E.A. (E)(51)15 Cabinet Economic Policy Committee Sub-committee on the Economic Situation 'The Labour Situation in Coventry. Note by the Chancellor of the Exchequer' 11/12/1951 Annex p. 2; and *Financial Times* 8/11/1950.

47 See, for example, reports in the *Standard* 4/5/1946, 15/6/1946, 4/1/1947, 1/3/1947, 23/4/1948, etc.

48 Unfortunately there does not appear to be any way of providing quantitative data on the frequency of under-capacity working. For examples of, or comments on, aspects of this problem see the *Standard* 7/4/1948 (Rootes's Ryton plant working at 50 per cent of capacity due to steel shortages); SUPP 14/328 'Note of Meeting at the Daimler Company on 12/10/1949' [unsigned] (Daimler, beset with steel difficulties and facing reduced demand due to heavy purchase tax, was at this time operating at a rate 'close to the minimum economic production level of the factory'); and T 229/582 'Report' paras. 19–21.

49 P.E.P. *Motor Vehicles* op. cit. 129: 'Volume output is undoubtedly the most important factor in low costs'.

50 On retooling costs in general, see the *Financial Times* 29/11/1948. Model changes could certainly deflate profits quite substantially: e.g. Jaguar's results for 1949 – a profit of £63,469 but down 53 per cent on 1948 – were blamed on the introduction of the XK120 (Jaguar Annual Reports and Accounts etc., for Years Ended 31/7/1948 and 31/7/1949, Local Studies Section, Coventry City Library).

51 Note, for example, the successful lobbying on this point at a National Advisory Council Meeting, reported in CRO Acc. 985/1/4 24/2/1948 (680).

52 See, for example, the Alvis Board discussions on an export price for the T.A. 21: CRO Acc. 985/1/4 7/3/1950 (1084), 13/10/1950 (1174), etc.

53 Castle op. cit. 218. Alfred Herbert also enjoyed similar advantages: *Planning* Vol. XV No. 292 20/12/1948.

54 Lord Montagu *Jaguar. A Biography* (London, 1961) p. 64; A. Whyte *Jaguar: The History of a Great British Car* (Coventry, 1981) pp. 128–37.

55 G. Robson and R. Langworth *Triumph Cars. The Complete 75-Year History* (London, 1979) pp. 146–7; *The Times* 2/3/1949.

56 SUPP 14/331–2 passim.

57 Standard, for example, built its own castings plant soon after the war: MRC MSS 226/ST/1/1/10 28/10/1946 (830).

58 MRC MSS 226/ST/1/5/1 29/3/1951 (77(a)).

59 Standard's approach is well covered in S. Melman *Decision-Making and Productivity* (Oxford, 1958) passim. It should be noted that no strikes are recorded at this company between 1945 and 1951 in the Ministry of Labour record books (LAB 34/60–67).

60 There were major strikes at Humber in 1945 and 1946, Daimler in 1946, and Jaguar in 1951 (LAB 34/60 D.E. 13/1; LAB 34/61 D.E. 54/1 and D.E. 27; and LAB 34/67 D/A 13). The most important of these was the 1946 dispute at Humber, which saw the employer prevent the adoption of a Standard-type agreement, thus, in the words of an Engineering Employers' Federation official, making 'a very considerable contribution towards cleaning up the Coventry situation' (MRC MSS 237/S/1/269 Letter A. Lowe–A. W. Weekes 5/4/1946).

61 The tool-room rate, for example, did not regain its 1945 high until 1950: see the *Standard* 30/4/1948 and the *Financial Times* 8/11/1950.

62 T 229/582 'Report' para. 51.

63 Standard and Alvis strategies here can be studied through their archives in the MRC and CRO respectively. Armstrong Siddeley also adopted this approach: CRO Acc. 1060/1/4 Armstrong Siddeley Minute Book No. 3 Board Meeting 15/9/1949.

64 The firm in question was Armstrong Whitworth: see AVIA 54/1207 D.G.T.D. (A) Working Party on Development of Seaslug. Notes of a Meeting 5/4/1950 p. 2.

65 Unfortunately very few of the primary sources examined contain much useful information on defence contracts. However, some idea of the norms involved can be obtained from the Alvis Board Minutes (in the CRO) and material in T 225/520 (especially 'Extract from the Comptroller and Auditor General's Report on the Civil Appropriation (Class X) Accounts for 1946–7' [n.d.]) and T 229/374 (especially 'Notes of Meeting Held at the Treasury' 8/11/1951). Secondary sources, too, are disappointing, though there seems to be general agreement that 'cost plus' contracts were still very common in this period. See inter alia R. Worcester *Roots of British Air Policy* (London, 1966) pp. 39 ff.; C. Turpin *Government Contracts* (Harmondsworth, 1972) pp. 166–99; and G. Kennedy *The Economics of Defence* (1975) pp. 126–33. Interesting evidence on methods of costing work also emerges from Cmnd. 2428 *First Report of the Enquiry into the Pricing of Ministry of Aviation Contracts, July 1964* (P.P. 1963–64 XVI) and Cmnd. 2581 *Second Report, Feb. 1965* (P.P. 1964–65 XIX).

66 Of the 117 firms employing more than 50 persons sponsored by the Ministry of Supply, Board of Trade or Ministry of Materials in 1951, at least 48 were on defence work. Firms employing more than 100 on defence included (with the per cent proportion of defence employees to total employees in parentheses): Alvis (85), Armstrong Siddeley (80), Armstrong Whitworth (100), Bluemel Bros. (20), Bretts Stampings (84), British Piston Ring Co. (10), Cornercroft Ltd. (72), Coventry Gauge and Tool (75), Coventry Precision Engineering (86), Coventry Rad. (25), Daimler (5), Dunlop Rim and Wheel (53), G.E.C. (7), Alfred Herbert (5), Humber (1), B. O. Morris (50), Peerless and Ericsson (35), and Unbrako Socket Screw Co. (25). See CAB 134/116 C.P.C. (51) 75 Cabinet Committee on Productive Capacity 'Note by Joint Secretaries on Labour Situation in the Coventry Area, Covering Supplementary Report by Working Party' 26/10/1951.

67 Information on this directive apparatus can be found in Parsons op. cit., P.E.P. *Government and Industry* (London, 1952) pp. 102–6 and A. A. Rogow *The Labour Government and British Industry 1945–1951* (Oxford, 1955) passim.

68 Amongst other things, the Government helped with steel, currency (for imported engines) and planning permission: E.P. Neufeld *Global Corporation* (Toronto, 1969) p. 112; MRC MSS 226/ST/3/F/1/28 Letter H. Ferguson–Sir John Black 2/10/1945; BT 177/1801 B.D.I. (A) 55th Meeting (18/6/1946).

69 SUPP 14/395 Letter H. Bailey–Sir J. Helmore 21/8/1952.

70 SUPP 14/331 Minute by W. M. Millar 8/2/1951 and Minute by H. Bailey 16/2/1951; and SUPP 14/332 Memo. by L. H. Robinson 19/3/1952; and

material in W.O. 185/324.

71 Case by case discussion of expansion proposals may be found in the Minutes of the Official Committee on the Distribution of Industry. Panel A. (BT 177/1801). A couple which emerged at a higher level (because of interdepartmental disagreement) involved G.E.C. and Courtaulds. Both companies put forward plans to expand their facilities in Coventry during early 1950. The Cabinet Distribution of Industry Committee immediately granted the former permission, since its work had considerable strategic significance. Courtaulds' case was seen as legitimate on production grounds by all departments, but it could be faulted in terms of the wider distribution of industry strategy. The company eventually achieved a compromise – a modified expansion scheme. See material in CAB 134/132 and BT 177/252.

72 HLG 71/736 Minute from Research Officer Region No. 9 (R. K. Kelsall) to Miss Green 12/12/1949.

73 On this point see particularly T 229/582 'Report' para. 22 and CAB 134/856 'Note by the Chancellor' Annex p. 4.

74 Notably, with the Armstrong Whitworth Apollo: see material in AVIA 54/180.

75 This seems to have been the case when Jaguar was asked to produce Meteor tank engines as a condition of being given a shadow factory: see the interview with Lyons in *Autocar* 15/5/1969.

76 Note, for example, this exchange at a Midlands Region Interdepartmental Committee on the Distribution of Industry discussion about Coventry:

> *Mr. Davis* (Min. of Supply) asked whether there was a comprehensive plan for relating war-damage replacements and re-developments to the necessary restrictions in capital investment; and to guard against the use of building resources on less vital projects. *Sir Walter Gurner* (Min. of Town and Country Planning) said that there was no comprehensive plan for rebuilding blitzed areas, and *Mr. Allen* (Min. of Works) said that fundamentally the matter was in the hands of the sponsoring departments which could exercise discretion in supporting or rejecting applications for building licences. (BT 177/1512 B.D.I. 177/49 (16/12/1949).)

77 On the rearmament programme, see P.E.P. *Growth in the British Economy* (London, 1960) pp. 138–51, R. Fletcher *£60 a Second on Defence* (London, 1963) pp. 31–8, and K. O. Morgan *Labour in Power 1945–1951* (Oxford, 1984) pp. 422–35.

78 CRO Acc. 985/1/4 20/6/1950 (1133) and 13/10/1950 (1178).

79 Sheet steel allocations to Standard and Rootes, for example, declined as follows (1950 III Index = 100):

	Period			
	1950 III	1950 IV	1951 I	1951 II
Standard	100	100	95	86
Rootes	100	100	94	85

(SUPP 14/331 Note by F. F. D. Ward 19/5/1951.)

80 LAB 8/1740 'Note of Meeting Held at Ministry of Supply' 11/6/1951.

81 CAB 134/231 Cabinet Economic Policy Committee Sub-committee EPC(DP)(51)(3) Memo. by Ministry of Labour 'Short Time Working in the Motor Industry in the Coventry Area' 16/7/1951; and T 229/582 'Report' Appendix VIII.

82 CRO Acc. 985/1/4 6/6/1951 (1278), and see for Armstrong Siddeley reactions Acc. 1060/1/4 3/5/1951.

83 T 229/582 Correspondence Weekes–Rowlands 25/6/1951, 26/6/1951, 6/7/1951 and 19/7/1951; *Daily Mail* 27/8/1951.

84 CAB 134/231 E.P.C. (D.P.)(51) 1st Meeting 10/7/1951 Min. 1, 2nd Meeting 25/7/1951 Min. 1.

85 See, for example, articles in the *Financial Times* 25/8/1951 and 17/11/1951.

86 T 229/582 'Report' paras. 53 and 56.

87 CAB 134/856 'Note by the Chancellor'.

88 CAB 134/856 E.A. (E.)(51) 6th Meeting Min. 3.

89 BT 171/180 Report on 'Vulnerability of the Sub-Regions of Great Britain to Localised Unemployment in the Event of a Substantial Recession' April 1951 passim.

90 An interesting breakdown – from which these figures are taken – appears in CAB 134/856 'Note by the Chancellor' Annex pp. 3–4.

91 Data in T 229/582 'Report' Appendix III Table 2 show that in June 1951 the 31 biggest firms in Coventry were together employing 82,505 persons. This figure represented about 84 per cent of the total number employed by all the firms with 10 or more persons.

92 See, for example, the following figures measuring Standard's position against two other volume producers (column A = trading profit per vehicle (£), column B = trading profit as a percentage of turnover):

Year	Standard		Ford		Vauxhall	
	A	B	A	B	A	B
1950	31	8.9	63	17.3	47	13.1
1951	27	7.8	66	16.1	59	12.9
1952	24	6.2	72	14.0	95	16.9

(Standard figures from MRC MSS 226/ST/2/1/34–42, Ford and Vauxhall from Maxcy and Silberston op. cit. 169).

93 See, respectively, SUPP 14/867 Memo. by Ward, ?/3/1954; and references cited in note 36 (above).

4 City reconstruction: building a new Coventry, 1945–51

1 From Hodgkinson's Foreword to Coventry City Council *The Future Coventry* (Coventry, 1945) p. 2.

2 HC 13/1/1944 and the *Standard* 20/1/1945.

3 See Statistical Appendix, Table G.

4 See, for example, the *Standard* 17/3/1945.

5 See, for example, Ministry of Health and Ministry of Works *Housing Manual 1944* (London, 1944) and Ministry of Health *Design of Dwellings (London, 1944)*. A useful summary of contemporary reports, etc., can be found in Association for Planning and Regional Reconstruction *Housing*

Digest (London, 1946).

6 HC 3/10/1944, 12/10/1944 and 16/11/1944.

7 FC 1/5/1945.

8 ibid. and the *Standard* 10/3/1945.

9 *Standard* 19/5/1945.

10 HC 14/6/1945; and PAC 18/7/1945 and 24/10/1945.

11 HC 21/8/1945 and the *Standard* 25/8/1945.

12 The main parties' positions on housing and town planning can be found, respectively, in *Housing Digest* op. cit. and the *Architects' Journal* 28/6/1945.

13 HLG 71/600 Meeting between Minister and Blitzed Towns Advisory Committee of M.P.s, 6–7/12/1945; J. Campbell *Nye Bevan* (London, 1987) p. 157.

14 *Camera Principis* Vol. 14 No. 114 Nov. 1945 3.

15 See Statistical Appendix, Table I.

16 On Labour's stance during the campaign see the *Coventry Town Crier* Jan. 1945, and the *Standard* 20 and 27/10/1945. Some ideas about popular priorities can be gauged from entries submitted to an *Evening Telegraph* 'Coventry of the Future' competition of late 1945. Here the 10 most popular suggestions for a better Coventry concerned, in order, 'Children's Playgrounds and Nurseries', 'Better Hotels and Restaurants', 'Housing Improvements', 'Revision of Transport Routes and Schedules', 'Community Centres', 'A New Civic Centre', 'Subway Pedestrian Crossings', 'Public Conveniences', 'Car Parks' and a 'Theatre and Concert Hall'. An 'Arcaded Shopping Centre' was the 20th most popular suggestion. See the tabulated listing at JN 711 in the Local Studies Section at Coventry City Library.

17 PAC 19/12/1946.

18 CRC 7/1/1946, 21/2/1946; CCC 5/2/1946, 5/3/1946.

19 See, for example, comments overheard at the 'Coventry of the Future' exhibition, reported in *Camera Principis* Vol. 14 No. 114 Nov. 1945 3. More general impressions of the Coventry electorate's interest in 'bread and water politics' were recorded by Crossman during the 1945 election campaign: see his piece in the *New Statesman* 30/6/1945.

20 CRO Sec/CF/1/9929 Letter Town Clerk–Regional Controller (Board of Trade) 19/9/1949.

21 Material in BT 177/26 relates to Board of Trade views on land purchase for industrial location. For the 'costs of works' controversy – the controversy about financing rebuilds – see HLG 79/131 'Discussion . . . on Coventry between the Minister and . . . the City Council . . . 30/1/1946' p. 2.

22 CRO Sec/CF/1/9937 Memo. by Estates Surveyors Section 20/2/1948.

23 Gibson's views can be found in D. Gibson 'Problems of Decentralisation' in F. E. Towndrow ed. *Replanning Britain* (London, 1941) pp. 100–5' and E. A. Gutkind ed. *Creative Demobilisation Vol. II* (London, 1943) pp. 208–11. The Council's attitude was summarised to the Advisory Panel as follows: 'The Council certainly intend to buy the land for the shopping arcade but have not considered whether they also wish to build it. If they don't build it themselves they will certainly wish to have some say in its architectural appearance' (HLG 88/9 Advisory Panel Minutes No. 4 13/7/1943. 16(d)).

24 Local authorities could build themselves where private enterprise was unable or unwilling to do so, and provided the Minister gave his express

sanction. On taking office, Silkin quickly recognised that this part of the Act was unsatisfactory: see HLG 79/131 'Discussion' 30/1/1946 p. 2.

25 Though in exceptional circumstances they might run for up to 15 years. See F. Osborn ed. *Planning and Reconstruction* (London, 1946 edn) p. 85.

26 CRC 7/1/1946; HLG 79/128 Letter Town Clerk–Secretary, Ministry of Town and Country Planning 3/4/1946.

27 PHC 7/6/1945, 7/3/1946.

28 *Report of the Medical Officer of Health for 1946* (Coventry, 1946) p. 6 and the same *for 1953* (Coventry, 1953) p. 16.

29 HC 13/7/1944; *Standard* 4/5/1946, 27/8/1949.

30 See material in CRO Sec/CF/1/8774.

31 *Standard* 2/3/1946.

32 *Standard* 11/5/1946 and 7/12/1946.

33 HC 21/3/1946.

34 For a description of these units see the *Standard* 10/8/1946 and R. B. White *Prefabrication* (London, 1965) pp. 161 and 178–9. Costings data, etc., are given in HC 21/3/1946.

35 *Standard* 25/8/1945.

36 This table is constructed from material in HC 21/8/1945 and various parts of the Ministry of Health *Housing Return for England and Wales, 1946* (London, 1946).

37 HLG 79/131 'Discussion' 30/1/1946 passim.

38 CRO Sec/CF/1/10625 C. Barratt 'Final Report of the Town Clerk on the Public Inquiry' 12/8/1945, and A. R. Pugh and A. L. Percy 'Planning and Reconstruction in Coventry' *Journal of the Institution of Municipal and County Engineers* 3/9/1946.

39 *CET* 28/6/1946.

40 *Standard* 20/7/1946.

41 *CET* 25/6/1946.

42 MRC MSS 11/3/2/52 Coventry Borough Labour Party Report for 1946 p. 4: 'In every ward except St. Mary's, Longford and Cheylesmore the vote was down by comparison with the figures in November 1945. The political pendulum has obviously swung a little to the Right.'

43 Joad felt that Coventry people had 'no civic spirit, no common consciousness . . . no cultural interest . . . no nothing but football and the dogs'. The *Telegraph* noted drily that Joad had recently addressed an audience in Coventry on 'The Future of Civilisation','and the theatre was full': *CET* 20/11/1946.

44 E.g. the *Coventry Tribune* 7/12/1946.

45 See material in CRO Sec/CF/1/8774.

46 *Standard* 2/3/1946, 25/1/1947.

47 See Statistical Appendix, Table G; and HC 11/4/1946.

48 *Standard* 20/4/1946.

49 *Standard* 12/10/1946.

50 HC 22/8/1946.

51 *Standard* 24/8/1946 and 4/1/1947, and material in CRO Sec/CF/1/9959.

52 See, for example, *Municipal Review* Vol. 18 No. 207 March 1947 85.

53 See data presented in A. Burton Stibbon 'Financial Aid to Housing', paper presented to the 19th International Congress for Housing and Town Planning, Zurich 20–6/6/1948.

54 For the Council's labour policy see MRC MSS 11/3/2/52 Report p. 4, and *Camera Principis* Vol. 15 No. 119 April 1946.
55 Coventry City Council *Abstract of Accounts for 1952–53* p. 4, *Abstract of Accounts for 1958–59* p. 5.
56 The 1946 Act is summarised in Ministry of Health 'Housing Policy', paper presented to the 18th International Congress for Housing and Town Planning, Hastings 7–12/10/1946.
57 Note, for example, the popular outcry when the Council proposed a general rent revision in 1946: HC 7/5/1946.
58 Burton Stibbon op. cit.; and H. W. Singer 'The Economics of Planning' in Association for Planning and Regional Reconstruction ed. *Town and Country Planning Textbook* (London, 1950) p. 486.
59 See Statistical Appendix, Table D. Reasons for Coventry's relatively advantaged position are examined in HLG 71/2222.
60 Coventry Chamber of Commerce 43rd Annual Report, presented to the A. G. M. 18/2/1947: 'This sterile interim period is having a deadening effect on the life of the city.'
61 *Standard* 4/1/1947.
62 See Statistical Appendix, Table E. Industry had of course been 'de-rated' – i.e. assessed at only 25 per cent – since 1929, at considerable cost to the city (Coventry City Council *Abstract of Accounts for 1952–53* pp. 4–5). Equally, Coventry did not gain much from government property within its boundary, unlike some south coast ports for example.
63 FC 29/1/1946 and 19/3/1946. Other towns did receive special help – e.g. the £605,000 paid to Hull, 577,500 paid to Plymouth, 546,000 paid to Portsmouth and 395,000 paid to Southampton, 1946–51 (HLG 101/516 Table 'Financial Assistance to Local Authorities' [n.d.] and Note by F. L. Edwards 6/2/1951). Coventry had previously received some help from the Exchequer, in that the £100,000 emergency loan granted in 1941 was not recalled at the end of the war; but it is likely that this facility was extended to all other blitzed towns, too (see ibid. and material in HLG 52/1509).
64 HC 3/10/1946.
65 HC 3/10/1946 and 13/2/1947.
66 HC 17/4/1947.
67 See Lanchester Collection of Audio Tapes on Local History of Coventry, Interview No. 50 with C. H. Dodson [Coventry Polytechnic Library]; and HLG 101/516 Minute by P. M. Johnson 6/12/1950.
68 There is unfortunately, so far as I am aware, no one good source on this machinery; but, for certain aspects of the system of control, see Burton Stibbon op. cit.,' E. Layton *Building by Local Authorities* (London, 1961) and D. W. Parsons *The Political Economy of British Regional Policy* (London, 1986).
69 For this episode, see material in CRO Sec/CF/1/9736 and HC 15/5/1947, 26/6/1947 and 2/9/1947.
70 HLG 79/127 Letter E. H. Doubleday–A. M. Jenkins 1/10/1945.
71 HLG 71/13 'Technical Dept. Reconstruction Areas Technical Examination Committee. City . . . of Coventry . . . Report' [n.d. but 1946] passim.
72 HLG 71/600 Letter L. Silkin–L. Middleton 18/4/1947, and material in HLG 71/601.
73 CRO Sec/CF/1/9464 Letter Ministry of Town and Country Planning–

Town Clerk 23/5/1947 (which notes that the Ministerial Order was 'designed to limit the land affected more closely to the area of extensive war damage') and the *Standard* 7/6/1947.

74 HC 13/2/1947.

75 *Standard* 8/3/1947 and 22/3/1947.

76 Quoted in the *Standard* 8/3/1947.

77 See, for example, the editorial in the *CET* 17/6/1947.

78 Monthly completions during 1947 (Corporation houses only) were: 8, 8, 16, 10, 8, 10, 21, 22, 21, 17, 30 and 52 (Ministry of Health *Housing Return for England and Wales, 1947* (London, 1947) all parts).

79 In fact, Coventry slipped from 13th position in the league table of county borough completions to 33rd over the year: ibid.

80 See Statistical Appendix, Table G.

81 The Standard 3/5/1947 noted, anyway, that the city was in the middle of a property boom at this time.

82 GPC 22/4/1947, 9/9/1947, 15/10/1947; and *Coventry Tribune* 5/7/1947.

83 See Statistical Appendix, Table I.

84 *Coventry Tribune* 29/11/1947.

85 For the debate over this proposal, and its eventual fate, see the voluminous reports in the *Standard* and *Evening Telegraph*, and material in HLG 79/125.

86 *Coventry Tribune* 6/3/1948 and MRC MSS 11/3/2/58 Minutes of the Fourth Annual Meeting of the C.B.L.P. 10/3/1948.

87 N. Lichfield *Economics of Planned Development* (London, 1956) pp. 203–7.

88 Singer op. cit. passim.; *Standard* 24/1/1948.

89 *Standard* 7/2/1948 and 5/2/1949.

90 Consequently, the city's Net Loan Debt rose from £7,287,885 in 1947 to £13,331,098 in 1951 (Coventry City Council *Abstract of Accounts for 1951–52* p. 7).

91 *Report of the Medical Officer of Health for 1949* (Coventry, 1949) p. 34.

92 See material in CRO Sec/CF/1/1161.

93 PAC 25/1/1949, 22/2/1949, 15/3/1949, 3/11/1949 and 29/11/1949.

94 HC 14/8/1947, 9/12/1948, 15/9/1949.

95 CRO Sec/CF/1/1178 Planning and Redevelopment (Industry) Sub-committee. Notes on Discussion with Regional Representatives of Government Departments 28/7/1948.

96 HLG 71/1265 West Midlands Plan Vol. 4 pp. 161–2 (for the suggestion that the target population for Coventry should be around 340,000).

97 HLG 79/126 contains material on this application.

98 Much of the most interesting discussion on this subject took place at the Sites (Allocation) Sub-committee, whose records can be found in CRO Sec/CF/1/9464 and 9937. The following paragraph is largely based on material in these files.

99 For the wider debate on leases, see inter alia a Report of the Central Advisory Committee on Estate Development and Management in War-damaged Areas (summarised in *Estates Gazette* 26/4/1947) and articles in *Estates Gazette* 11/10/1947 and 6/12/1947.

100 Betterment occurs where land gains in value from development around it.

101 CRC 26/4/1948; CRO Sec/CF/1/9464 First Report of the Sites (Allocation) Sub-committee [n.d.]; and CRO Sec/CF/1/9937 S(A)S-C Minutes 5/1/1949.

102 Statistical Appendix, Table H; and HC 16/2/1950.
103 CRC 16/6/1948.
104 *Standard* 13/12/1947.
105 O. Marriott *The Property Boom* (London, 1967) pp. 62–3.
106 CRC 15/9/1948, 28/9/1948, 17/11/1948 and 11/5/1949.
107 Note, for example, Silkin's statement at a Ministry Planning Conference with representatives from blitzed towns in October 1947:

> At the moment we are concentrating on such measures of reconstruction as will enable us to improve our economic position. Housing, the rebuilding of our blitzed towns, even the building of new towns, are for the moment regarded as luxuries, or rather as irrelevant in the rebuilding of our economic position.

(HLG 71/601 Conference on Reconstruction Problems 23/10/1947 Verbatim Report p. 5).
108 See Chapter 3, Table 3:1.
109 See HLG 79/133 Letters W. V. Wood–E. F. Muir 5/12/1949 (and enclosures), and D. P. Walsh–Wood 5/1/1950.
110 HLG 79/126 Letter Sir J. Maude–Dame E. Sharp 14/4/1949.
111 HLG 79/133 Letter Walsh–Wood 5/1/1950; HLG 71/610 Letter C. W. Gurner–W. B. Vince 19/11/1948 and Letter Regional Estate Officer–G. S. Wheelon 26/1/1949; and CRO Sec/CF/1/9464 Memo. by Town Clerk 'Central Redevelopment' 29/12/1948.
112 *Standard* 14/8/1948 and 15/1/1949, and HC 8/12/1949.
113 *Standard* 11/3/1950.
114 See material in CRO Sec/CF/1/1161 and note Stringer's statement (that other priorities came before the theatre) as reported in the *Standard* 26/11/1949.
115 This was the Woolworth's block in the precinct: see CRO Sec/CF/1/9870 Letter Gurner–Town Clerk 10/12/1948 and material in CRO AP/CF/1/6.
116 Allocations for 1950 and 1951 were in terms of a capital spending ceiling: for Coventry, see material in HLG 71/610.
117 Note, for example, the position in early 1950, as described by the Town Clerk:

> It will be appreciated that the first quarter of the year has already elapsed and the Council is not yet in a position of knowing which schemes are likely to go forward with a consequent inability satisfactorily to plan the redevelopment of the city, particularly the central area.

The reason for this delay was apparently a 'hopeless difference of view' between departments at Westminster as to what the programme should be (HLG 71/610 Letter Town Clerk–Secretary, Ministry of Town and Country Planning 28/3/1950; and T 229/520 Note F. F. Turnbull–W. B. Strath 12/4/1950).
118 HC 16/2/1950; *Standard* 19/5/1950.
119 See Statistical Appendix, Tables G and H.
120 This pressure came from both the Board of Trade and local employers: see CRO Sec/CF/1/9872 Correspondence Town Clerk–A. W. Weekes 23/9/1950 and 26/9/1950.
121 CRC 10/1/1951.

122 HC 13/7/1950 and 7/12/1950.
123 HC 18/7/1950, CRC 13/9/1950, CCC 3/10/1950.
124 HC 1/6/1950, 13/9/1951.
125 T 229/521 Letter H. Macmillan–R. Butler 22/8/1952 and enclosures.
126 In fact, these difficulties meant that there was a considerable 'undershoot' in 1951: see ibid.
127 HLG 71/1287 Letter P. G. Burnett–Chief Estates Officer 20/4/1951: 'the contractors have at times been acting like recruiting agents for the motor industry as no sooner do they secure labour than it disappears to more lucrative forms of employment in the Borough'.
128 Negotiations with Wimpey over the erection of houses had been going on since early 1949 – see, for example, HC 28/4/1949 and 21/6/1949 – and it is by no means clear why the green light was finally given to go ahead with the contract only in the autumn of 1950 (HC 18/7/1950, 21/9/1950, etc.).
129 The 'no fines' system involved pouring a special mix into prefabricated and re-usable shuttering to form the walls of the house. The system's advantages were that it allowed speedy completion, and required the employment of very little skilled labour: *Builder* 31/8/1945 and *Architects' Journal* 27/3/1952. Coventry's contract with Wimpey was for an abnormally large number of houses (over 1,500, a big jump over the usually accepted limit of 500 units per contract) and this allowed further economies of scale: *Architects' Journal* 8/10/1953.
130 Statistical Appendix, Table G.
131 The recommended size for a three bedroom house was 800–900 sq. ft. in the 1944 *Manual* and 900–950 sq. ft. in the 1949 *Manual*. Coventry B.I.S.F. units measured 982 sq. ft., while the A.55 brick-built type used, for example, at Stonebridge Highway, measured 1,100 sq. ft. (Ministry of Health *Housing Manual 1944* (1944) p. 92 and *Housing Manual 1949* (1949) p. 12; CRO Sec/CF/1/9736 Letter City Architect–Town Clerk 5/7/1946; and *Architect and Building News* 31/1/1947).
132 *Architects' Journal* 2/12/1948 and 8/10/1953.
133 See Statistical Appendix, Table F.
134 The figures in this table are not always exactly compatible, and should therefore be treated with some caution. They have been assembled from material in PAC 19/2/1946, 11/3/1947 and 2/10/1951 and HC 19/6/1952.
135 *Standard* 25/1/1952.
136 G. C. Firth *75 Years of Service to Education* (Coventry, 1977) Chapter 8 passim.
137 See Statistical Appendix, Table G.
138 *Report of the Medical Officer of Health for 1948* (Coventry, 1948) p. 57 and the same *for 1950* (Coventry, 1950) pp. 52–3.
139 *Standard* 22/8/1952.
140 *Report of the Medical Officer of Health for 1952* (Coventry, 1952) pp. 140–1.
141 CRO Sec/CF/1/9872 Note City Architect–Town Clerk 21/6/1951.
142 Coventry City Council *Abstract of Accounts for 1950–1* p. 5.
143 Note, for example, an unnamed civil servant's characterisation of Gibson's housing survey as being 'an exhaustive and scientific analysis': HLG 71/914 'Notes on the Housing Problems of the Seven Cities Visited by the Advisory Panel' [n.d. but 1944?].
144 For example, Councillors were familiar with the Peckham experiment, and

intended to include preventive facilities in the proposed health centres for the neighbourhood units: HC 15/2/1945, PHC 25/6/1948.

5 Social reconstruction? Politics and culture in Coventry, 1945–51

1 *Standard* 16/5/1951. The *Standard* commented a year earlier, re the General Election, in rather similar terms: Labour had won because there existed in Coventry 'a hard core of inflexible opinion' in support of its policies (ibid. 4/3/1950).

2 See the election issues of the party's *Coventry Searchlight* 1/11/1937 and 1/11/1938.

3 For which see A. Calder *The People's War* (paperback edn, London, 1971) passim.

4 A favourite device of local politicians during the war, for example, was to link the past (engineering achievement), present (heroic resistance) and future (model, planned city) of Coventry together, to stress an unbroken thread of local accomplishment. The city's self-image was also boosted by the number of dignitaries who visited it over this period.

5 Thus Hodgkinson to the Freemen of Coventry, reported in the *Standard* 3/3/1945: 'The proposal submitted to the Ministry [for a Declaratory Order] . . . was not a party one.'

6 *Standard* 7/11/1945.

7 The Council was prepared to meet the unions if there was a specific matter, like housing progress, to be discussed. But it turned down approaches over more general questions, as when the Trades Council and Confederation suggested meetings on planning and future industrial development in 1945 (PAC 9/1/1945 and CCC 6/2/1945).

8 The Family Health Club, set up in 1944, was heavily influenced by the Peckham experiment, and aimed to create a democratically run model community around flats, a health centre and farm on a 450 acre site just outside Coventry. The Club received some support in the city (it was said to have 650 families enrolled in 1947) and from individual Councillors. But a majority on the Corporation (and in the local trade unions) could not be won over, partly because there was a feeling that the fairest way forward for all was through the implementation of local authority plans. In the end, the Ministry of Town and Country Planning refused the Club planning permission after protests from local residents, and the project fizzled out. (See K. E. Barlow *A Home of Their Own* (London, 1946) pp. 85–7; K. E. Barlow 'The Idea of a Family Health Club' in A. Massey ed. *Modern Trends in Public Health* (London, 1949) pp. 1–14; *Builder* 8/4/1949; CCC 1/7/1947; MRC MSS 5/1/3 Coventry Trades Council Minute Book, E. C. resolution 2/1/1947; *Standard* 16/8/1947, 8/11/1947 and 4/2/1950; and material in CRO Sec/CF/1/8866 and (PRO) HLG 71/13.)

9 *Standard* 31/7/1948, *CET* 11/2/1953.

10 See comments made to Edgar Snow, reported in *Saturday Evening Post* (Philadelphia, U. S. A.) 6/3/1948.

11 *Standard* editorial 31/1/1948.

12 Hodgkinson quoted in the *Standard* 5/3/1949.

13 E. g. editorial in the *Standard* 24/11/1950.

14 In fact, the papers generally supported most of the Council's projects: see,

for example, the *Standard* 16/8/1947 (on neighbourhood units), 16/7/1949 (on housing) and 7/1/1950 (on the investment programme).

15 See Statistical Appendix, Table I.

16 Local Labour party membership in Coventry over the period was as follows:

Year	Numbers	Year	Numbers	Year	Numbers
1936	1,036	1942	247	1948	(no figure available)
1937	730	1943	400		
1938	726	1944	677	1949	3,784
1939	1,017	1945	3,017	1950	4,714
1940	450	1946	3,432	1951	4,557
1941	240	1947	2,449		

(Labour party annual *Conference Reports* 1937–52.)

17 It should be noted that Labour was the only significant left-leaning party in Coventry during these years. The Communist party had some strength in the trade unions but it polled very few votes at elections – about 1 per cent in the 1945 municipal contest, and 0.5 per cent two years later (*Standard* 21/8/1948; 20/10/1945 and 3/11/1945, and 8/11/1947).

18 See, for example, ward profiles in the *Coventry Tribune* 12/4/1947, 10/5/1947 and 24/5/1947; and MRC MSS 11/3/2/58 Minutes of the Fourth Annual Meeting of the Coventry Borough Labour Party 10/3/1948, MSS 11/3/2/77 Coventry North Divisional Labour Party. Minutes of G.M.C. 20/10/1948, and MSS 11/3/70 25i–vii Report by R. B. Ritchie (Agent) 19/8/1949.

19 MRC MSS 11/3/2/53 C.B.L.P. Annual Report 1946 p. 1, and MSS 11/3/70/44i–iii Minutes of the Annual Meeting of the Women's Central Committee 30/1/1951.

20 MRC MSS 11/3/2/53 C.B.L.P. Annual Report 1946 p. 1, and MSS 11/3/2/92 Memo. of a Meeting on the Functions of the Proposed Industrial Committee to be set up by the C.B.L.P. 25/11/1948.

21 *Standard* 8/5/1948.

22 See Statistical Appendix, Table I.

23 See Statistical Appendix, Table J.

24 See, for example, the *Standard* 21/4/1945 (where at a meeting called to discuss the reorganisation of the Coventry Unionist Association, one speaker likened the project to 'an attempt to revive a corpse'; 'Elections were approaching', he went on, 'and they realised they had no secretary or agent and no money') and MRC MSS 12/1/1 Coventry Progressive Party Minute Book, entries for 31/1/1944, 30/7/1945 and 20/5/1946. (The Progressive party was a Tory–Liberal alliance formed in the inter-war years.)

25 MRC MSS 12/1/1 Coventry Progressive Party Minute Book, entries for 1/7/1946, 30/7/1947, 1/3/1948 and 24/5/1948; and *Standard* 16/5/1951.

26 *Standard* 13/8/1949.

27 See, for example, the fairly coherent critique issued to the *Standard* 4/5/1951 and compare to the rather general and vague statements made in various opposition manifestos of earlier elections collected in MRC MSS 11/3/45.

28 This streak of environmental determinism in Labour thinking was rarely explicitly discussed (but see the interview with Coventry's Mayor in the *Standard* 31/8/1946) although certainly pervasive. It was, no doubt, encouraged by the local planners – as Leo Kuper put it, 'Implicit in all Town Planning is some theory of the influence of physical structures on the behaviour of residents' (L. Kuper 'Blueprint for Living Together' in L. Kuper ed. *Living in Towns* (London, 1953) p. 8) – while some of Bevan's speeches (e.g. that reported in *Architects' Journal* 24/6/1948) may have legitimised it, too.

29 J. Alldridge 'The City that Knows Where it's Going', originally published in the *Manchester Evening News*, reprinted in *Camera Principis* Vol. 16 No. 138 Dec. 1947 8–9; L. Thompson *Portrait of England* (London, 1952) p. 79; and P. Thompson 'Playing at Being Skilled Men' *Social History* Vol. 13 No. 1 Jan. 1988 53–5.

30 *People* 10/9/1950.

31 The following figures for 1950, taken from the Board of Trade's *Census of Distribution Vol. 1* (London, 1953), allow a comparative perspective:

	Coventry	*Leicester*	*Nottingham*	*Plymouth*
Head of population per retail outlet	92	68	66	116
Sales per head of population (£)	99	137	144	97

32 *Standard* 9/8/1947.

33 *Standard* 13/6/1952.

34 *Standard* 23/8/1947 and 30/8/1947.

35 In the immediate post-war years, Coventry had 18 cinemas (12 with a capacity of over 1,000). It was estimated that, at the peak, *weekly* admissions were running at about one and a half times the number of the city's population (*Standard* 14/5/1949 and *CET* 2/1/1947). It should be noted, too, that in 1946 the local variety theatre – the Hippodrome – was attracting about 14,000 admissions per week (*Standard* 12/10/1946).

36 The local speedway team was popular enough to draw 18,000 to a meet against Tamworth in 1948, even though at the time it was bottom but one of Division Three in the National League (*Standard* 21/8/1948).

37 *Standard* 27/7/1946.

38 *Standard* 23/7/1949.

39 *CET* 5/4/1947.

40 E.g. the *Standard* 6/11/1948 (which reported the Principal of the Municipal School of Art as considering Coventry 'to be a "get rich quick" city with ugly features too numerous to mention', reminding him of the saying 'where there's muck there's money') and the exchange of letters in the *CET* 5,8 and 9/4/1947 (including one from an actress living in Chelsea, who felt that Coventry had 'lost touch with spiritual values, and, from that, with intellectual pursuits, and might be on the way to losing its soul').

41 J. A. Yates *Pioneers to Power* (Coventry, 1950) p. 122.

42 Thompson *Portrait* op. cit. 81–2.

43 *Standard* 8/3/1947.

44 *Standard* 28/8/1948.
45 *Standard* 28/3/1952.
46 *Standard* 6/12/1947.
47 See, for example, the successful appeal brought by private residents against a proposal for a Council estate in their area: *Standard* 11/9/1948 and 15/1/1949.
48 *Standard* 3/8/1951 and 28/3/1952.
49 HC 8/7/1948, 7/7/1949 and 15/9/1949.
50 *Civic Affairs* Vol. 1 No. 4 April 1948 1.
51 Further information on this project can be found on p. 57.
52 B. Davidson, writing in the *New Statesman* 16/2/1952.

6 Planning the 1950s: the construction of the 1951 Development Plan

1 B. J. Collins *Development Plans Explained* (London, 1951) p. 14.
2 Some background to the exercise may be found in Cmd. 8204 Ministry of Local Government and Planning *Town and Country Planning 1943–1951* (April 1951) pp. 60–1.
3 The authors of the Plan do not appear to have believed that people should have been moved from the Black Country to Coventry, but rather that Coventry could be used – by giving it extra housing and jobs – to attract migrants from other areas who might *otherwise* have gone to the West Midlands. See CRO Sec/CF/1/9928 Letter E. H. Ford–C. Barratt 1/12/1948.
4 HLG 71/1265 West Midlands Plan, Section IV, Chapter 3, Table 1 and (3); and Section V, Chapter 3 (8).
5 CRO Sec/CF/1/9928 Letters by D. H. Gibson (27/11/1948), Ford (op. cit.) and A. H. Marshall (2/12/1948) to the Town Clerk (C. Barratt).
6 HLG 79/126 Letter E. A. Sharp–Sir J. Maude 28/4/1949.
7 CRO Sec/CF/1/9928 Memo. by the Ministry of Town and Country Planning 'West Midlands Plan' November 1950 p. 3 and Appendix A.
8 CRO Sec/CF/1/11178 Planning and Redevelopment (Industry) Sub-committee 'Notes on Discussion with Regional Representatives of Government Departments' 28/7/1948; and CRO Sec/CF/1/9493 Memo. by D. H. Gibson 'Industrial Analysis', enclosed with his 'Summary' of 29/8/1950 to the Planning and Redevelopment Committee.
9 CRO Sec/CF/1/9929 Verbatim Report 'Discussion on Industry in Coventry 16/2/1950' p. 1.
10 CRO Sec/CF/1/9929 Board of Trade Memo. 'Industrial Development in Coventry' April 1950 p. 2.
11 CRO Sec/CF/1/9929 Verbatim Report 'Discussion 16/2/1950' pp. 2–4.
12 ibid. 7.
13 ibid. 4.
14 ibid. 2.
15 ibid. 6.
16 ibid. 3.
17 CRO Sec/CF/1/9929 Verbatim Report of Discussion on 'Industry in Coventry' 31/1/1950.
18 CRO Sec/CF/1/11178 Memo. 'Meeting between Representatives of Trade and Industry in Coventry and Planning and Redevelopment Industrial Sub-committee' 31/10/1950 p. 2.

19 CRO AP/CF/1/209 'Minutes of the 52nd Meeting of the Coventry and District Advisory Committee 14/11/1950' p. 2.
20 CRO Sec/CF/1/9929 BoT Memo. April 1950 p. 3.
21 CRO Sec/CF/1/9929 Verbatim Report 'Discussion 16/2/1950' pp. 2 and 6.
22 HC 8/12/1949 and 16/2/1950, and PAC 5/9/1950.
23 HC 13/4/1950 and 15/6/1950, and PAC 5/9/1950.
24 HLG 71/610 [Unsigned] Memo. to W. B. Vince June 1950.
25 PAC 29/11/1949.
26 CRC 12/7/1950.
27 E.g. L. Silkin 'Creating Communities' *Social Service* Vol. XXI No. 3 Dec. 1947 101–2.
28 CRO AP/CF/1/209 'Minutes 14/11/1950' p. 2.
29 CRC 15-20/2/1950 and 11/10/1950.
30 CRO Sec/CF/1/9929 Verbatim Report 'Industry' 31/1/1950 p. 4.
31 L. Kuper 'Blueprint for Living Together' in L. Kuper ed. *Living in Towns* (London, 1953) pp. 181–4 and CRO Sec/CF/1/9874 P. Sargant Florence 'Third Report to the Planning Officer' 20/1/1950.
32 Kuper op. cit. 179.
33 ibid. 167.
34 Coventry City Council *The Development Plan* (Coventry, 1952).
35 ibid. 52–3.
36 ibid. 61–2.
37 ibid. 72 and 75.
38 ibid. 118–9, 98, 102 and 103.
39 ibid. 94.
40 ibid. 113.
41 The following paragraph is based on material in ibid 82.
42 ibid. 141–54.
43 Calculated from figures in ibid. 124–5.
44 See, for example, the *Standard* 6/2/1953 and *Journal of the Town Planning Institute* Vol. XXXVIII No. 5 March 1952 124.
45 On this point, see especially L. Kuper 'Social Science Research and the Planning of Urban Neighbourhoods' *Social Forces* Vol. 29 No. 3 March 1951 237–43.
46 At least this was the inference drawn in the Coventry planning department: see W. Burns 'The Coventry Sociological Survey: Results and Interpretation' Town Planning Review Vol. 25 No. 2 July 1954 128–48.
47 D. Chapman, review of *Living in Towns*, *Town Planning Review* Vol. 25 No. 4 Jan. 1955 186.

7 Sustainable growth? Coventry's local Economy in the 1950s

1 *Financial Times* 17/11/1951.
2 *The Economist* 15/3/1952.
3 See, for example, SUPP 14/332 Letter A. E. Hunt–Sir A. Rowlands 7/2/1952 on Singer's predicament.
4 *The Economist* 2/2/1952, 9/2/1952; *Standard* 1/2/1952.
5 *The Economist* 15/11/1952 noted that 'short-time working is now the rule rather than the exception'.
6 See, for example, opinions expressed by one of the Rootes brothers,

reported in LAB 8/1740 Note Dame M. Smieton–the Secretary 18/2/1952.

7 T 229/583 Min. by W. Strath 31/1/1952.

8 CAB 134/512 Note by D. H. Lyall 5/11/1952.

9 T 229/583 Letter D. Sandys–R. A. Butler 20/2/1952.

10 CAB 134/847 Cabinet Economic Policy Committee E.A. (53)13 23/1/1953 Note by the Chancellor of the Exchequer 'Special Restrictions' covering Report by the Manpower and Production Committee 'Special Restrictions' [n.d.] Annex p. 2.

11 T 229/584 M.P.C. (52)38 Note by Ministry of Supply 24/11/1952; and material in AVIA 53/432.

12 CAB 134/842 C.E.P.C. E.A. (52)14 14/5/1952 Min. 3.

13 BT 177/388 Note by Lyall 5/11/1952; CAB 134/846 C.E.P.C. E.A. (53)2 28/1/1953.

14 Between Jan. 1953 and Dec. 1955 I.D.C.s were granted for 18 new projects in Coventry, covering 348,711 sq. ft. Over the same period, 73 replacements or extensions were sanctioned, relating to an area of 1,863,178 sq. ft. (Calculated from material in BT 177/1806–1809.)

15 See, for example, the *Financial Times* 29/4/1953.

16 *Standard* 5/8/1955, and MRC MSS 11/3/75 29/1 Minutes of Meeting Held on 28/3/1957.

17 *Standard* 4/3/1955.

18 The order for Avons from Standard was cut quite substantially in the rearmaments programme review, but the Government was keen to keep some of the work going at the company, to maintain flexibility in terms of overall aero-engine production: see MRC MSS 226/ST/1/5/1 18/2/1953 200(c) and 27/2/1953 231; and material in T 225/377.

19 *The Economist* 14/1/1956.

20 See, for example, for Jaguar, SUPP 14/395 Min. by N. Statham 12/11/1954.

21 Calculated from figures in BT 117/621 H.Q. Research Memo. No. 54 Notes on the Location of Manufacturing Industries No. 10 Motor Vehicles, Oct. 1956 Appendices.

22 A. T. Mallier and M. J. Rosser 'Industrial Decline in Perspective' Lanchester Polytechnic Department of Economics Staff Seminar Discussion Paper No. 47, Jan. 1982 Appendix Three.

23 LAB 8/2188 Note by Ministry of Labour 'Employment and Earnings in the Motor Car Industry in Great Britain and Abroad' 10/8/1956 p. 1; and K. G. J. C. Knowles and D. Robinson 'Wage Movements in Coventry' *Bulletin of the Oxford University Institute of Economics and Statistics* Vol. 31 No. 1 Feb. 1969 especially 2–5.

24 MRC MSS 226/ST/1/1/11 13/11/1951 1271 and MSS 226/ST/1/1/12 17/10/1955 1872.

25 *Standard* 4/6/1954.

26 In 1955, Rootes and Standard between them employed 25,300 in Coventry, about half the total in the local motor vehicle sector: see data in BT 117/621 H.Q. Research Memo. No. 54.

27 Standard's approach over wages is dealt with at length in S. Melman *Decision-Making and Productivity* (Oxford, 1958); note especially the information presented on p. 169.

28 Rootes were producing from over eight different locations – in Coventry, Luton, Dunstable and London – at this time: see SUPP 14/366 Memo. by D.

Caplan 'Existing Plans of the Rootes Group' 8/11/1954 and Draft Note on the 'Rootes Group' [n.d.].

29 Note, for example, *The Economist*'s characterisation of the home market as 'something of an enigma': *The Economist* 15/8/1953.

30 For which see W. Plowden *The Motor Car and Politics in Britain* (Pelican edn, Harmondsworth, 1973) pp. 309–58.

31 See, for example, *The Economist* 15/11/1952 and 24/7/1954.

32 See, for example, the *Standard* 16/12/1955.

33 *Motor Business* No. 5 Dec. 1955 29 puts Standard and Rootes's profit margins in a relative light.

34 This table has been assembled from data in MRC MSS 226/ST/1/5/1 (entries for 7/11/1951 109; 18/4/1952 143 (g); 2/7/1952 151; 10/12/1952 184; 17/6/1953 237–8) and *The Economist* 23/5/1953, 13/3/1954 and 17/6/1954.

35 This was particularly so for Standard. Its equity was, in *The Economist*'s characterisation, relatively 'friendless' throughout this period, which made it important that the company maintain a high dividends policy; in fact, the sum covering dividends in 1952–3 was nearly twice that ploughed back into the business (*The Economist* 14/11/1953).

36 The table below presents data for 1952–60 on Standard's prices in relation to those charged for roughly competing products by Ford:

Year	*1952*	*1953*	*1954*	*1955*	*1956*	*1957*	*1958*	*1959*	*1960*
Standard Vanguard:									
Price (£)	590	590	555	599	599	ncf	675	ncf	695
Price per lb weight (d.)	52.2	50.6	47.6	51.3	53.5	ncf	60.3	ncf	60.2
Ford Zephyr:									
Price (£)	532	532	532	532	ncf	ncf	610	ncf	610
Price per lb. weight (d.)	50.2	50.1	50.1	50.1	ncf	ncf	54.5	ncf	54.5
Standard Eight:									
Price (£)	—	339	ncf	359	379	ncf	425	ncf	ncf
Price per lb weight (d.)	—	54.3	ncf	59.1	56.1	ncf	61.7	ncf	ncf
Ford Anglia:									
Price (£)	—	360	360	360	360	ncf	416	ncf	415
Price per lb weight (d.)	—	53.3	50.6	50.6	50.5	ncf	56.6	ncf	61.3

(*Source*: *The Economist* 25/10/1952, 24/10/1953, 23/10/1954, 22/10/1955, 20/10/1956, 25/10/1958, 2/10/1960.) (ncf = no comparative figure available)

37 According to Turner, tractors were responsible for 60 per cent of Standard's net profit in 1951, and perhaps 70 per cent plus in 1953: G. Turner *The Leyland Papers* (Pan edn, London, 1973) p. 27.

38 In 1953, commercial vehicles made up 23 per cent of the 99,025 units produced by Rootes: SUPP 14/366 Draft Note [n.d.].

39 MRC MSS 226/ST/1/1/11 7/5/1953 and 8/3/1954; MSS 226/ST/1/1/12 28/3/1955; and Turner op. cit. 30–4.

40 *The Economist* 17/1/1959.
41 For which see *Motor Business* No. 5 Dec. 1955 31.
42 See BT 117/1479 Memo. 'The Rootes Group Meeting to Discuss the Expansion Project for Dunstable, 11/11/1954' 12/11/1954.
43 *Motor Business* No. 5 Dec. 1955 32.
44 The Rootes brothers had been particularly struck by this aspect of the new technology on a visit to the U.S.A.:

> Sir William referred to his recent visits to the United States in the course of which he had seen . . . a remarkable example of automatic control of machine operation; two similar machine shops had been set up in one of which on the ordinary semi-automatic operation there were some 150 people while in the other, an automatically-controlled shop, there were only 4 people.

(BT 117/1479 Memo. 'The Rootes Group Meeting' p. 4.)
45 There was plenty of scope for developments here, with one estimate being that, of the operations of all the large car manufacturers, only 6 per cent were automated: L. Landon Goodman *Man and Automation* (Harmondsworth, 1957) p. 107.
46 See, for example, MRC MSS 226/ST/1/5/1 10/12/1952 184.
47 MRC MSS 208B TBN 14 Transport and General Workers Union District Committee Annual Report for Feb. 1951 – Jan. 1952 p. 1, and T. and G. District Committee Minutes 7/7/1953; and TBN 15 File on 'Membership Figures' 1955.
48 Note, for example, Coventry attitudes to the Confederation claim of 1952, as reported in the *Standard* 12/9/1952 and 26/9/1952.
49 See, for example, MRC MSS 208B TBN 14 T. and G. District Committee Minutes 1/4/1952 and TBN 15 File on BMC, Confed. Coventry D. C. Minutes 13/1/1953.
50 MRC MSS 208B TBN 10 File on SMC, Letter District Secretary [J. Jones]–G. Martin (Gen. Sec. Confed.) 29/4/1955.
51 Compiled from material in LAB 34/60–71.
52 BT 117/1479 Memo, 'The Rootes Group Meeting' p. 5.
53 *Motor Business* No. 20 Sept. 1959 5–6 and 10.
54 *Standard* 2/3/1956.
55 The following account of the difficulties at Standard in 1956 has been written, unless otherwise stated, from material in LAB 10/1445, especially the diary of events, I.R. 266/3/56 'Motor Car Manufacturing' [n.d.].
56 For a repetition of allegations about C. P. manipulation, see G. Turner *The Car Makers* (London, 1963) pp. 82–3.
57 *Financial Times* 11/6/1956. Interestingly, the *Daily Worker* agreed on the strike's significance, calling it 'a decisive battle and . . . [maybe] the decisive battle of the period into which capitalism is now entering in Britain' (2/5/1956).
58 See reports in the *Standard* 31/12/1954, 7/1/1955 and 14/1/1955, and *The Economist* 18/2/1956.
59 Standard was, at any rate, negotiating at this time for re-entry into the local Engineering Employers' Federation: note Lanchester Tapes No. 51 Interview with A. Dick (Coventry Polytechnic).
60 *Daily Telegraph* 1/5/1956.

61 Lanchester Tapes No. 51. Dick told his interviewer (K. Richardson): 'We fired on the basis of service to the company. . . . I'd hate to admit that any political thoughts came into it, but I think they probably did too.'
62 *The Economist* 25/8/1956 and 24/11/1956.
63 *The Economist* 25/8/1956, 24/11/1956, 12/1/1957 and 23/2/1957.
64 *The Economist* 29/9/1956 and 23/2/1957; and the *Standard* 7/12/1956 and 4/1/1957.
65 BT 177/634 Regional Controller's Report for January 1957 (6/2/1957) p. 2.
66 MRC MSS 208B TBN 16 Local Employment Committee Agendas for 28/6/1956 and 27/6/1957.
67 *The Economist* 27/7/1957.
68 *Motor Business* No. 18 March 1959 4.
69 *The Economist* 23/11/1957.
70 *The Economist* 24/11/1956 and 23/11/1957; and MRC MSS 226 ST/1/1/12 17/10/1955 1872 and 5/11/1956 2159 and MSS 226 ST/1/1/13 4/11/1957.
71 *Motor Business* No. 20 Sept. 1959 5 gives some of Coventry's specialist firms' output figures.
72 For which see R. Fletcher *£60 a Second on Defence* (London, 1963) pp. 44–7.
73 The following paragraph is based on material in AVIA 49/214 C. (57) Memo. by Ministry of Supply 'Industrial Effects of Cuts in the Defence Programme' 27/6/1957.
74 The following paragraph rests largely on material in MRC MSS 208B TBN Machine Tools Industry File.
75 Note, for example, the statement by the Chairman of A. Herbert Ltd. in late 1958 that 'New types of machines are needed': CRO Acc 926/1/1/1 2/12/1958.
76 CRO Acc 926/1/1/1 18/2/1959.
77 Some background material on this enquiry, plus parts of the evidence submitted to it, may be found in MRC MSS 11/3/75.
78 CRO Sec/CF/1/14677 Coventry Borough Labour Party 'Report of the Working Party on Redundancy and the Motor Industry' [n.d.]. If the enquiry had received considerable help from trade unionists and Volkswagen, amongst others, it had been largely snubbed by management in Coventry: ibid. 4.
79 ibid. 5–6.
80 See material in CRO Sec/CF/1/14677.
81 CRO Sec/CF/1/14677 'Note from W. Burns on Town Planning in relation to Industry' [n.d.] p. 1.
82 CRO AP/CF/1/143 'Notes of Meeting at the Board of Trade . . . Birmingham on 17/2/1958' 21/2/1958.
83 CRO Sec/CF/1/14677 Notes of Lord Mayor's First Industrial Conference on 'Town Planning in Relation to Industry' 5/12/1958 and 23/1/1959.
84 CRO Sec/CF/1/14677 Notes 5/12/1958 pp. 2–3.
85 *The Economist* 30/11/1957.
86 *The Economist* 17/1/1959 and *Motor Business* No. 25 Jan. 1961 48.
87 *The Economist* 29/11/1958.
88 Knowles and Robinson op. cit.; and *Motor Business* No. 24 Oct. 1960 especially 29 (where earnings from Coventry firms are presented in a relative light).

89 *The Economist* 28/11/1959 and Turner (1973) op. cit. 34–43.
90 *The Economist* 8/3/1958, 27/6/1959; and *Motor Business* No. 24 Oct. 1960 23–7.
91 See, for example, CRO Acc 926/1/1/1 14/12/1959.
92 A. Ling *Work* (Report No. D.P.R. 3, Coventry City Council Review of the Development Plan, July 1963) p. 19.
93 CRO AP/CF/1/209 Letter V. N. Brailsford–Bryant 2/9/1960.
94 See the careful analysis in the *Standard* 26/6/1959 and D. Butt 'Men and Motors – 1' *New Left Review* No. 3 May–June 1960 10–18.
95 Ling op. cit. 17.

8 City reconstruction: building a new Coventry, 1952–60

1 See Statistical Appendix, Table A.
2 T 229/521 Letter H. Macmillan–R. Butler 22/8/1952.
3 For which note M. Pinto–Duschinsky 'Bread and Circuses? The Conservatives in Office 1951–1964' in V. Bogdanor and R. Skidelsky eds. *The Age of Affluence 1951–1964* (London, 1970) pp. 60–1.
4 HC 6/12/1951, 15/1/1953.
5 HC 6/12/1951; CRO Sec/CF/1/12282 Ministry of Housing and Local Government Circular No. 28/52, 6/3/1952.
6 HC 10/7/1952 and correspondence in CRO Sec/CF/1/12282 (especially Town Clerk–Macmillan 25/7/1952, and E. Burton–Town Clerk 1/9/1952.
7 PAC 19/10/1953.
8 HC 6/12/1951.
9 HC 3/4/1952, 15/1/1953.
10 F. B. Pooley 'Through the Doldrums' *British Housing and Planning Review* Vol. 8 No. 5 Sept.–Oct. 1953 16–18 and 21; and HC 24/4/1953 etc.
11 HC 18/6/1953.
12 *Standard* 25/4/1952; HC 19/6/1952 and 12/11/1953.
13 HLG 102/186 Min. by E. A. Sharp 17/6/1952.
14 HLG 102/86 [unsigned] Memo. 'Coventry. Visit of Minister' [n.d.] p. 2.
15 ibid. 6.
16 HLG 102/186 Note [?] – Sir J. Wrigley etc. 7/6/1952.
17 HLG 102/186 Min. by Sharp 17/6/1952.
18 ibid.
19 HLG 102/186 'Note of a Meeting in Mr. Seal's Room' 9/9/1952.
20 Statistical Appendix, Table H.
21 HLG 102/186 [unsigned] Memo. 'Coventry. Visit' p. 5; HC 13/7/1953.
22 CRC 10/12/1952.
23 HC 11/9/1952.
24 CRC 30/4/1953.
25 HLG 79/877 Report of Inspector 14/12/1953 p. 228.
26 *Standard* 1/5/1953, 7/8/1953, 2/4/1954, 1/10/1954, 6/5/1955. The dates quoted refer in some cases to the opening of trading rather than the ending of building.
27 *Standard* 4/3/1955.
28 PAC 6/1/1953, 3/3/1953, 21/4/1954; *Standard* 17/12/1954.
29 G. C. Firth *75 Years of Service to Education* (Coventry, 1977) pp. 114 and 118.

30 HC 11/12/1952, 26/10/1953, 25/11/1954.
31 Statistical Appendix, Table H.
32 HC 16/11/1955.
33 Statistical Appendix, Table G.
34 Statistical Appendix, Table H.
35 See material in CRO Sec/CF/1/13839, especially Letter Secretary Ministry of Health–Town Clerk 26/5/1952.
36 *Standard* 23/10/1953; CRC 11/11/1953.
37 CRC 11/11/1953, 9/12/1953, 13/1/1954, 29/1/1954; *Standard* 4/12/1953; and material in CRO AP/CF/1/2a.
38 *Standard* 26/2/1954; CCC 2/2/1954; HLG 79/878 Letter D. Eccles–H. Macmillan 17/2/1954 and Note by E. A. S. 12/7/1954.
39 See, for example, FC 23/1/1952, 19/1/1953.
40 See Coventry City Council *Abstract of Accounts for 1954–5* p. 4.
41 ibid. 7.
42 Coventry City Council *Abstract of Accounts for 1953–4* p. 5.
43 ibid.
44 A. H. Marshall 'The Finances of Comprehensive Redevelopment under the Planning Acts' *Journal of the Town Planning Institute* Vol. XLI No. 8 July–August 1955 207.
45 ibid. and HLG 79/879 Note by W. J. Reynolds 11/8/1950.
46 See, for example, CRC 5/3/1952.
47 CRC 13/1/1954 and 10/2/1954.
48 Gibson's resignation is discussed in the *Architects' Journal* 21/10/1954.
49 For details of Ling's career before he came to Coventry see material in CRO Sec/CF/1/11026a and the profile in the *Standard* 29/5/1959.
50 *Architects' Journal* 5/5/1949.
51 See, for example, *Architect and Building News* 24/6/1954, where it was reported that the Council had received a Housing Medal award for Tile Hill (North).
52 See, for example, HLG 79/877 Letter L. F. Boden–Town Clerk 10/7/1956.
53 *The Economist* 23/1/1954, *Listener* 22/9/1955.
54 See, for example, comments by, respectively, D. Rigby Childs, J. M. Richards and 'Astragal' in the *Architects' Journal* 8/7/1954, 20/1/1955 and 3/5/1956.
55 The points made in what follows of this and the next three paragraphs, unless otherwise credited, may be found in the *Standard* 20/5/1955 (Ling's first impressions) and A. Ling 'Coventry Looks Ahead', *Architectural Association Journal* Vol. LXXII No. 803 June 1956 4–14.
56 CRO AP/CF/1/32 Letter V. Brailsford–Town Clerk 1/10/1955; HC 13/1/1955.
57 *Report of the Chief Constable of Coventry for the Year Ended 31/12/1956* p. 18. (Traffic levels at the later date were, of course, very much greater than at the earlier.)
58 Material on negotiations over the ring road is voluminous, if unfocused: see inter alia HLG 71/13, HLG 71/1287 and CRO AP/CF/1/30 and 32.
59 A. Ling 'Housing in Coventry', *Housing Review* Vol. 6 No. 2 March–April 1957 50.
60 ibid. and *Standard* 2/8/1957.
61 CRC 12/10/1955, 20/8/1956, 5/9/1956.

62 CRC 9/12/1954, 9/2/1955, 9/3/1955 and CRO AP/CF/1/2b Letter City Estates Surveyor–A. J. M. Currell 4/12/1959.
63 CRC 28/9/1955 and the *Manchester Guardian* 14/10/1955. Background information on this change may be found in CRO AP/CF/1/5 and 6.
64 This political crisis is examined in more detail below, pp. 92–4.
65 For an overview of this episode, see A. Schonfield *British Economic Policy Since the War* (Harmondsworth, 1958) pp. 196–250.
66 PAC 2/11/1955, 28/2/1956; CRO AP/CF/1/50 'Notes Prepared in Connection with the Visit by Dame Evelyn Sharp . . . on the 27th November, 1956' p. 1.
67 A. W. Cleeve Barr *Public Authority Housing* (London, 1958) p. 130.
68 ibid. 140–2.
69 Coventry City Council *Abstract of Accounts for 1955–56* p. 4; *Standard* 20/1/1956 and 27/1/1956.
70 CRO AP/CF/1/50 'Notes' p. 1 and HC 24/4/1956.
71 CRO AP/CF/1/50 'Notes' p. 2. The Council's argument here was based on the recognition, amongst other things, that full ground rent for any property in the precinct could not be obtained while access ways and neighbouring blocks were still incomplete.
72 CRO AP/CF/1/50 'Notes of Meeting with Dame Evelyn Sharp on 27th November, 1956'.
73 'Unfit' houses in Coventry constituted about 2.2 per cent of the total stock, while the national figure was 6. 6 per cent: Cmd. 9593 *Slum Clearance* (P.P. 1955–56 XXXVI).
74 HC 5/7/1956.
75 HC 20/9/1956, 24/10/1956, 30/10/1956 and 6/12/1956; and – for popular reactions to the Tile Hill blocks – the *Standard* 23/12/1955.
76 *Stage* 27/3/1958, *Standard* 21/3/1958 and *CET* 30/8/1960.
77 Firth op. cit. e.g. 118 and T. Morrison Clayton 'Conjoint Clinics and a New Health Centre at Coventry' *Medical Officer* 29/5/1959.
78 CRO AP/CF/1/32 passim.
79 CRC 6/2/1957 and *CET* 18/10/1957.
80 CRC 12/6/1957 and material in CRO Sec/CF/1/14069 (especially Correspondence Town Clerk and Ministries 27/9/1957, 13/12/1957 and 27/3/1958).
81 Note, for example, the abortive negotiations with John Lewis Properties Ltd. (who wanted 'some very favourable compensating terms' for opening in a city dominated by the car industry and where 'trade of our own pattern is poorly presented') in CRO AP/CF/1/8.
82 *Standard* 13/9/1957, 10/1/1958, 12/9/1959 etc.
83 For some information on interest rates for housing loans, and illustrations on how variation here affected costs, see *Labour Research* Vol. XLVIII No. 1 Jan. 1959 13.
84 Coventry City Council *Abstract of Accounts for 1960–61* p. 4.
85 MRC MSS 11/3/12/86 Letter G. Hodgkinson–G. Reynolds 23/1/1957 and the *Standard* 1/2/1957.
86 From 1/4/1959 industrialists began to pay rates on half the annual rateable value of their properties, not one-quarter. This added a considerable amount to the Coventry total – in 1955–6, for example, the concession had apparently removed half a million pounds worth of rateable value from the

register: Coventry City Council *Abstract of Accounts for 1958–9* p. 4 and *Abstract of Accounts for 1955–6* p. 4.

87 MRC MSS 11/3/12/200 Letter Hodgkinson–F. Williams 27/3/1957.

88 *Standard* 28/2/1958, 3/10/1958, 23/1/1959; PAC 5/2/1959 etc.

89 Statistical Appendix, Table H.

90 The 3,000th 'no fines' dwelling was completed in February 1955, the 6,000th in late 1957: HC 10/2/1955, 5/12/1957.

91 See, for example, HC 26/11/1957.

92 ibid.

93 See, for example, *Standard* 29/11/1957, 28/2/1958; and HC 18/11/1958, 1/1/1959.

94 Statistical Appendix, Table H.

95 Only one block of flats was completed in Hillfields, for example, over this period, and this not until mid-1960: *Standard* 27/5/1960.

96 Statistical Appendix, Table G.

97 Coventry City Council *Abstract of Accounts for 1959–60* p. 6.

98 *Daily Herald* 8/7/1960.

99 *CET* 11/8/1959, 1/2/1962.

100 Broadgate House, for example, went into the black during 1961–2 (*CET* 9/2/1962), while the western link blocks also seem to have been a financial success (see, for example, CRO AP/CF/1/2b Letter City Estates Surveyor–A. J. M. Currell 4/12/1959).

101 Firth op. cit. 118; Statistical Appendix, Table H.

102 *Observer* 30/3/1958.

103 Statistical Appendix, Table F.

104 See, for example, E. Beazley 'Coventry' in the *Architects' Journal* 11/7/1962; G. Logie 'The Lessons of Coventry' *Architect and Building News* 11/7/1962; and Lewis Mumford's piece for the *New Yorker* of the same year, reprinted in his *The Highway and The City* (London, 1964) pp. 130–9.

105 Coventry Corporation's performance on housing was good if crude completion rates are the instrument of comparison, as the figures below (calculated from the annual *Housing Returns*) demonstrate:

City	*Municipal completions 1952–9*	*Municipal completions 1945–59*
Coventry	10,862	13,848
Hull	7,577	10,419
Plymouth	6,887	11,957
Portsmouth	9,672	13,100
Southampton	7,995	10,261

But it is by no means certain that a more rigorous comparison – encompassing factors like quality and the proportion of temporary dwellings to brick houses – would yield such a favourable picture. The situation on cultural provision is more clear cut, in that Coventry's achievements were certainly not unsurpassed: see the Arts Council of Great Britain *Housing the Arts in Great Britain* Pt. 2 (London, 1961).

106 HC 9/12/1954 and the *Standard* 27/1/1956.

107 *Oxford Mail* 8/10/1956 and *CET* 1/2/1962.

108 Logie op. cit. 46.

109 Compare, for example, the following rents charged at 31/3/1960 for a three bedroom, post-war house: Coventry 27s. 6d.; Hull 18s. 8d.; Leicester 22s. 10d.; Nottingham 22s. 9d.; Plymouth 31s. 5d.; Portsmouth 33s. 2d. and Southampton 30s. 10d. (The Institute of Municipal Treasurers and Accountants *Housing Statistics 1959–60* (London, November 1960) pp. 7–10).

110 Again, compare the following figures, taken from ibid. (housing account: analysis of revenue account):

City	*Income as percentage of total income*			
	Rents	*Exchequer subsidy*	*Rate subsidy*	*Other*
Coventry	69.9	22.2	7.8	0.1
Hull	58.9	21.0	18.1	2.0
Leicester	70.6	22.7	6.7	–
Nottingham	72.0	20.2	7.1	0.7
Plymouth	77.6	19.4	–	3.0
Portsmouth	81.0	19.8	(1.8)	1.0
Southampton	76.4	18.5	4.8	0.3
All County Boroughs	69.6	21.6	8.2	0.6)

111 CRO AP/CF/1/136 Letter Ling–A. Goss 11/2/1959.

112 T. Gregory *People and Housing* (Report No. DPR 49, Coventry City Council First Review of the Development Plan, April 1966) p. 48.

113 *Report of the Medical Officer of Health for 1960* (Coventry, 1960) p. 163.

9 An 'affluent society'? Politics and culture in Coventry, 1952–60

1 See, for example, the *Standard* 29/10/1954.

2 See, for example, the *Standard* 1/7/1955.

3 See, for example, the *Standard* 28/11/1952.

4 *Standard* 18/12/1953.

5 See, for example, the *Standard* 6/11/1953, and Canon George Bennett in *The Coventry Watchman* Vol. 6 No. 3 June 1955 42–3.

6 *CET* 4/2/1955.

7 *Standard* 9/7/1954.

8 *Standard* 28/3/1952, 12/2/1954 and 4/3/1955.

9 See, for example, *CET* 2/2/1955, and MRC MSS 11/3/7/528 Letter G. Hodgkinson–J. Latham 12/8/1955.

10 See, particularly, MRC MSS 5/4/1/6 Coventry Trades Council. Secretary's Annual Report for 1952; MSS 5/4/4 C. T. C. Secretary's Annual Report for 1954; and MSS 5/4/5 C. T. C. Secretary's Annual Report for 1955.

11 MRC MSS 11/3/6/112 Letter F. Allaun–R. B. Ritchie 3/3/1955 and MSS 11/3/6/125 Letter Asst. Ed.–L. Flint 10/3/1955.

12 This dispute is fully documented in B. R. Bentley 'Conventions in Local Government: A Study of the Party System in Coventry' (unpublished B. Sc. (Econ.) dissertation, University of Birmingham, 1960) Appendix Three.

13 *Standard* 15/10/1954.
14 MRC MSS 11/3/8/4 Handbill by D. Byrne 30/9/1954 and MSS 11/3/8/5 Letter from J. Jones [?] 1/10/1954; and *Standard* 9/5/1952 and *CET* 3/2/1955.
15 See material in CRO Sec/CF/1/14716 A, a file that contains numerous protests from Coventry ratepayers' associations.
16 *Standard* 9/1/1953 and 26/6/1953 and MRC MSS 11/3/7/387 Letter Secretary–R. Underhill 1/6/1955.
17 *Standard* 27/3/1953.
18 *Standard* 4/3/1955.
19 See, for example, the *Standard* 25/4/1952.
20 *CET* 2/2/1955.
21 *Standard* 27/8/1954.
22 *Standard* 25/4/1952, and MRC MSS 11/3/54/61 *Coventry Citizen* (Election Special) 1955.
23 HC 10/9/1953.
24 *Standard* 2/1/1953.
25 *The Economist* 20/2/1954 and *The Municipal Review* Vol. 25 No. 293 May 1954 84–5.
26 MRC MSS 11/3/7/417 Letter Secretary–A. Waugh 17/6/1955.
27 This episode is discussed in a number of places, but see especially M. Jenkins *Bevanism. Labour's High Tide* (Nottingham, 1979) and P. M. Williams *Hugh Gaitskell* (Oxford, paperback edn, 1982) especially pp. 198–237.
28 MRC MSS 11/3/7/164 Letter Secretary [?]–P. Noel-Baker 12/3/1955.
29 MRC MSS 11/3/6/27 R. B. Ritchie 'Half Yearly Report Ending 31st December 1954'; Bentley op. cit. 134; *CET* 26/3/1955.
30 MRC MSS 11/3/7/165 Letter Secretary–M. Phillips 12/3/1954 [1955?].
31 Bentley op. cit. 134.
32 The national membership figure fell by 17 per cent, compared to a 37.5 per cent decline in Coventry: *Labour Party Conference Reports* for 1953 and 1956.
33 MRC MSS 11/3/6/27 Ritchie 'Half Yearly Report' op. cit. and MSS 11/3/71/6–21 (report on wards, Sept. 1955).
34 See pp. 77–8 above.
35 In April 1954, Coventry Council decided to suspend its Civil Defence Committee until such time as the Government began action and negotiations aimed at ending Britain's status as a nuclear power. This gesture brought the city considerable publicity, but in the end the Council was forced to back down, because of pressure not only from Whitehall but also from the Labour N. E. C. Bentley op. cit. Appendix Four provides a full summary of events.
36 Coventry had 'twinned' with Stalingrad as a result of the two cities' experiences in the war. Controversy arising out of the Soviet delegation's visit to Coventry was as much about cost as about politics: see, for example, the *Standard* 29/10/1954, 19/11/1954 and 10/12/1954.
37 See, for example, the *Standard* 15/10/1954.
38 A useful chart showing Labour's local election performance 1945–58 appears in *The Economist* 17/5/1958.
39 This table is assembled from material appearing in the Registrar General's *Statistical Review of England and Wales*, various editions; and MRC MSS 11/3/54 (e.g. 13i, 14, 18, 23i and 26i).

40 *Standard* 9/1/1953.
41 *Standard* 7/4/1955.
42 *CET* 5/4/1955 and 30/4/1955.
43 Labour escaped the loss of a third seat because the intervention of an 'Independent Liberal' candidate split the opposition vote there: *Civic Affairs* Vol. 8 Nos. 5 and 6 May and June 1955 1.
44 MRC MSS 11/3/7/299 Letter Agent (Cov. E)–G. W. Sheridan 13/5/1955.
45 *CET* 5/4/1955 and 21/4/1955.
46 D. E. Butler and R. Rose *The British General Election of 1959* (London, 1960) pp. 205 and 218; F. W. S. Craig *British Parliamentary Election Results 1950–1970* (Chichester, 1971) pp. 114–16.
47 Crossman later remembered that 'the result [in 1955] was indeed a humiliation which brought to a close an epoch of socialist expansion in the City': see his introduction to G. Hodgkinson *Sent to Coventry* (London, 1970) pp. xxvi–xxvii, and J. Morgan ed. *The Backbench Diaries of Richard Crossman* (London, 1981) p. 421.
48 *CET* 28/5/1955.
49 MRC MSS 11/3/6/318 Letter G. R. Roberts–Editor, *Coventry Labour Voice* 13/5/1955.
50 MRC MSS 11/3/7/387 Letter Secretary–R. Underhill 1/6/1955.
51 MRC MSS 11/3/10/106 Letter Ritchie–L. Williams 17/2/1956 and enclosure.
52 MRC MSS 11/3/7/535 Letter Secretary–F. Chater 17/8/1955.
53 MRC MSS 11/3/4/109 Letter Hodgkinson–W. H. Smith 10/10/1955.
54 For which see MRC MSS 11/3/70 and 71.
55 HC 1/3/1956.
56 *Standard* 27/1/1956.
57 *Standard* 5/4/1957.
58 *Architectural Design* Dec. 1958 474.
59 CRC 10/9/1958.
60 *Standard* 28/10/1955.
61 See, for example, *Standard* 17/5/1957, 10/1/1958 and 22/7/1960.
62 See, for example, *Standard* 13/8/1954, 25/10/1955, 17/5/1957 and 29/5/1959.
63 *Standard* 9/11/1956.
64 In 1961, 53 per cent of dwellings in Coventry were owner-occupied (T. Gregory *People and Housing* (Report No. DPR 49, Coventry City Council First Review of the Development Plan, April 1966) p. 46). The city had, of course, always had a high proportion of owner-occupiers (indeed Swenarton and Taylor suggest that about 38 per cent of dwellings in 1939 were of this type – M. Swenarton and S. Taylor 'The Scale and Nature of the Growth of Owner Occupation in Britain between the Wars' *Economic History Review* 2nd Ser. Vol. XXXVIII No. 3 Aug. 1985 387). But it is doubtful if the numbers involved in this sector had ever increased as fast as they were doing in the late 1950s.
65 See, for example, MRC MSS 11/3/17/115 Letter Ritchie–E. Burton 19/2/1950.
66 See, for example, the description of speedway enthusiasts in the *Standard* 9/6/1950.
67 For an idea of the number and size of the different youth cultures in Coventry at the end of the 1950s, see the series in the *Standard* 29/5/1959, 5/

6/1959 and 12/6/1959.

68 *Standard* 13/8/1954 and 15/2/1957.

69 *Standard* 8/4/1960.

70 *Standard* 29/5/1959.

71 *Standard* 6/9/1957.

72 *Standard* 22/8/1958.

73 Some increase was inevitable in 1957–8 because of, amongst other things, rising costs and a bulge in the number of school-age children, but subsequently the rate remained stable at 20s. 6d. until 1960–1 (see Statistical Appendix, Table F).

74 For one example of this trend, see the remarks on half-day educational schools, in MRC MSS 11/4/3/1 Report of the E. C. to the 13th Annual Meeting of the Coventry Borough Labour Party, 29/10/1958.

75 See above pp. 68–9.

76 MRC MSS 11/3/16/531 Coventry Borough Labour Party. Report of a Working Party on Some Aspects of Housing Policy Pt. 1 Jan. 1959 p. 5; and HC 20/7/1959.

77 MRC MSS 11/3/16/256 Memo. by Ritchie on 'Housing' June 1959; and the *Standard* 24/7/1959.

78 See, for example, Hodgkinson's remark of mid-1954 that there was a need to give some consideration 'to the problem of coloured folks': MRC MSS 11/3/4/28 Letter Hodgkinson–W. H. Smith 16/6/1954.

79 *Standard* 5/9/1958 and 10/10/1958.

80 See the account in P. Woodhall's piece 'Artistically Awake', *Education* 9/12/1960.

81 See material in CRO Sec/CF/1/14973.

82 This table is assembled from material appearing in the Registrar General's *Statistical Review of England and Wales*, various editions; and MRC MSS 11/3/54/30 and 11/3/20/21 i–ii.

83 For a justification of this point, see the *Standard* 18/5/1956.

84 MRC MSS 11/3/17/115 Letter Ritchie–Burton 19/2/1958; MSS 11/3/18/66 Letter Ritchie–G. Casey 21/1/1959; and MSS 11/3/18/78 Letter Ritchie–Burton 20/3/1959.

85 The national swing to the Conservatives at the election of 1959 was 1.1 per cent, while in Coventry it averaged 1.4 per cent and ranged from −0.5 per cent (Cov. East) to 3.2 per cent (Cov. South): Butler and Rose op. cit. 205, 218 and 220.

86 *Standard* 20/5/1960.

87 MRC MSS 11/3/66/51, 147 and 151 Correspondence Ritchie–R. Underhill 20/3/1959, 15/10/1959 and 26/11/1959; H. R. Underhill 'West Midlands Loses Seven', *Labour Organiser* Vol. 38 No. 449 Oct./Nov. 1959 191–2; and *Standard* 4/12/1959.

88 D. Butt 'Men and Motors – 1' *New Left Review* No. 3 May–June 1960 10–18.

89 *CET* 13/5/1955.

90 *Standard* 29/8/1958. See also the article on Coventry in *The Times* 31/3/1959.

91 The manuscript of Wiles's play, and various press cuttings on it, can be found in a bound volume referenced q. JN 822–914, in Coventry City Library's Local Studies Section.

92 Interestingly, many Coventrians seem to have found the play much funnier than the author intended, often laughing at what seemed to be the wrong

places. See the reviews in bound volume cited in n.91, particularly the piece in the *CET* 1/3/1960.

93 *Daily Mail* 1/3/1960.

94 See, for example, G. Turner *The Car Makers* (London, 1963) especially p. 109.

10 Some conclusions

1 The cities' populations in 1939 were as follows:

Coventry	229,500
Hull	317,800
Plymouth	200,900
Portsmouth	259,000
Southampton	181,250

See D. Rigby Childs 'A Comparison of Progress in Rebuilding Bombed Cities' *Architects' Journal* 8/7/1954 41.

2 See A. Ravetz *Remaking Cities* (London, 1980) pp. 19–41 and passim. for a discussion of this period in town planning.

3 M. Lock 'The Revolution in Town Planning' in F. J. Osborn ed. *Planning and Reconstruction 1944–45* (London, 1944) p.95.

4 S. D. Adshead and H. T. Cook *The Replanning of Southampton* (Southampton, 1942); Osborn op. cit. 349 (on Portsmouth); J. Paton Watson and P. Abercrombie *A Plan for Plymouth* (Plymouth, 1943); E. Lutyens and P. Abercrombie *A Plan for the City and County of Kingston-upon-Hull* (Hull, 1946).

5 Useful contemporary reviews of some of the various plans are R. L. Reiss 'Plan for Kingston upon Hull' *Town and Country Planning* Vol. XIV No. 56 Winter 1946–7 170–5; D. Plumstead 'The Plymouth Plan' *New Statesman* 17/6/1944; and H. M. Medland 'Plymouth's Plans' in B. Bliss ed. *The New Planning* (London, 1945) pp. 76–81. Very little, if anything, appears to have been written in the war, or just after, about either Portsmouth or Southampton.

6 J. Hasegawa 'The Replanning of the Blitzed City Centres in Britain: A Comparative Study of Bristol, Coventry and Southampton 1941–1950' (unpublished Ph.D. dissertation, University of Warwick 1989) pp. 100–3.

7 ibid. and HLG 79/267 Letter Hon. Sec. Hull and District Chamber of Trade–Ministry of Town and Country Planning 8/5/1946.

8 HLG 71/914 'Notes on the Housing Problems of the Seven Cities Visited by the Advisory Panel' [n.d.] pp .3 and 4.

9 According to Childs, the populations of Hull, Plymouth, Portsmouth and Southampton were still below their 1939 levels in 1949: Childs op. cit. 41.

10 See Statistical Appendix, Table D.

11 See, for example, on Hull, BT 177/185 Board of Trade Memo. 'Kingston-upon-Hull. A Survey of the Industrial Structure and Post-War Employment Prospects' (Sept. 1948); and, on Southampton, Hasegawa op. cit. 119–22.

12 D. Rigby Childs 'Portsmouth. A Survey' *Architects' Journal* 30/10/1952; HLG 79/593 Letter Town Clerk–W. C. Kirk 30/5/1946 and Note J. H. Waddell–[?] Wiltshire 14/2/1947.

13 Hasegawa op. cit. 119–22.

14 *Western Morning News* 17/10/1945, 1/11/1945 and 2/11/1945; *Hull and Yorkshire Times* 10/11/1945.

15 See, for example, for the Board's very interventionist stance on Hull, HLG 71/600 [unsigned] 'Notes for the Minister on the Present Position' 3/12/1945 and HLG 79/269 (P.L.J.[?]) 'Kingston-upon-Hull C.B. Case History' (?/5/1947) passim.

16 HLG 71/15 Memo. by M. G. Kirk 'Portsmouth C.B. Reconstruction and Redevelopment' 31/12/1946 and voluminous material in HLG 79/593.

17 Silkin, anyway, felt this was so, telling representatives from the blitzed towns on one occasion:

> The Treasury – with whom we are perhaps if I may say so within these four walls, rather too closely tied up in the 1944 Act – have perhaps too big a say in these [reconstruction] matters. Their interest was naturally to cut down.

(HLG 71/601 'Verbatim Report of Conference on Reconstruction Problems, 30th October 1947' p. 3.)

18 *The Times* 19/2/1946; and HLG 79/266 Note by H. Gatliff [Assist. Sec., MTCP] 'Hull. A Personal Impression' 14/2/1946.

19 See, for example, contributions from local authority representatives at the conferences with Silkin during the autumn of 1947 (HLG 71/601 Verbatim Reports 23/10/1947 and 30/10/1947, etc.).

20 Hasegawa op. cit. 215–16.

21 H. Myles Wright 'The First Ten Years' *Town Planning Review* Vol. 26 No. 2 July 1955 75.

22 ibid.; see also L. Silkin 'Planning and the Public' *Journal of the Town Planning Institute* Vol.XXXIX No. 2 Jan. 1953 26–8.

23 *Southampton Daily Echo* 21/4/1950, 27/4/1950 and 12/5/1950.

24 J. R. Atkinson, review of Portsmouth's Development Plan *Journal of the Town Planning Institute* Vol. XL No. 2 Jan. 1954 45.

25 The Labour majority on the Council had declined from 16 (50–34) to 8 (46–38) between 1945 and 1947. In 1951, Labour finally lost its majority in terms of Councillors altogether, but was kept in power by its Aldermen (*Hull and Yorkshire Times* 3/11/1945, 8/11/1947 and 12/5/1951).

26 Hull's waiting list was said to be 11,000 in December 1946 (*Hull and Yorkshire Times* 18/1/1947), but it had grown to 15,000 by the beginning of the 1950s (see, for example, the *Builder* 19/3/1954).

27 Hull Corporation were particularly troubled by 'terrific' opposition from the local Chamber of Trade, who employed a full-time organiser in their efforts to keep the shopping centre in its pre-war form: see HLG 79/267 Memo. by E. R. Voyce 'Interview at Hull on 8/7/1946' 12/7/1946, and material in HLG 79/260.

28 D. Rigby Childs 'A Survey . . . of Hull' *Architects' Journal* 2/7/1953 6.

29 HLG 79/536 Memo. by H. W. J. Heck 'Meeting at Board of Trade Offices, Plymouth, 3/7/1947' [n.d.]; and HLG 71/1283 [unsigned] Memo. 'Planning Technique. Appreciation of State of Central Area Planning as at 1st January, 1949' [n.d.].

30 HLG 71/2229 Letter R. A. Butler–H. Macmillan [n.d., but Sept. 1952] and Note 'Minister's Conference with Labour Members' 11/12/1952.

31 Some scattered figures appear in HLG 2223–9 (files on steel and capital

allocations, 1949–53). Otherwise, there are only fairly impressionistic surveys, such as that carried out by *The Times* in September and October 1952, together with D. Rigby Childs's work for the *Architects' Journal* between 1952 and 1954 (i.e. his pieces on Hull (2/7/1953), Plymouth (12/6/1952), Portsmouth (30/10/1952), Southampton (16/4/1953) and the comparative progress of all the blitzed towns (8/7/1954)).

32 It should be noted, however, that much of the data collected in these tables must be treated with caution. Figures on 'houses destroyed' and specific capital allocations, to take two examples, often differ in the various official files. The global estimates on factory destruction and re-building are also rather unreliable. Finally, it is by no means certain that the comparisons that are presented are really contrasting like with like. It would be important to know, for example, in any definitive statement on reconstruction, much more about house size, in order to make sense of the crude figures on numbers destroyed and numbers rebuilt.

33 This table is based on material in: HLG 71/915 W.(S.N.)(45) (Final) 'Report of the Inter-departmental Committee on Special Needs of Particular Areas in Relation to the Post-war Building Programme' 23/5/1945 Appendix One; HLG 71/914 'Notes on the Housing Problems' op. cit.; and Childs 'A comparison' op. cit. 46.

34 This table is based on material in Statistical Appendix Table C; and Childs 'A comparison' op. cit. 48.

35 This table is based on material in HLG 71/1571 Memo. [unsigned] 'Blitz Reconstruction' [n.d.].

36 This table is based on material in Childs 'A comparison' op. cit. 44.

37 HLG 71/2222 Correspondence and enclosures between F. E. Budd and E. F. Muir, 10/2/1949 and 15/2/1949.

38 See, for example, on Plymouth, *The Times* 20/9/1952, and more generally, J. H. Nicholson *New Communities in Britain* (London, 1961) pp. 17–33.

39 *The Economist* 23/1/1954.

40 L. Grebler *Europe's Reborn Cities* (Washington DC, 1956) p.70.

41 *Standard* 15/11/1957; and W. Millinship 'Coventry: Is This Our Future?' *Observer Magazine* 14/11/1965 23.

42 Millinship op. cit. 23.

43 See, for example, the *Standard* 18/5/1956.

44 See Janet Morgan ed. *The Backbench Diaries of Richard Crossman* (London, 1981) p. 716 where Labour support in the late 1950s is described as 'growing squashier and squashier and less and less solid'.

45 The electorate in Coventry was 176,539 in 1950 and 193,497 in 1960 (Registrar General's *Statistical Review of England and Wales* for 1950 and 1960).

46 See inter alia P. Corrigan et al. *Socialism, Merit and Efficiency* (Fabian Tract No. 530, Sept. 1988); D. Eversley *The Planner in Society* (London, 1973) especially pp. 158–68; J. Gyford *The Politics of Local Socialism* (London, 1985) especially p. 10; and J. Hinton 'Self-help and Socialism' *History Workshop Journal* Issue 25 Spring 1988, especially 100 and 117.

47 P. B. Bart and M. C. Cummings 'Resurgence of Coventry' *National Municipal Review* [U.S.A.] Vol. XLV No. 5 May 1956 227.

48 Hodgkinson in *CET* 12/6/1945.

49 Hodgkinson, transcribed interview, CRO (OH 11/1) p. 8.

50 See, for example, the *Standard* 4/1/1952.
51 Bart and Cummings op. cit. 227.
52 *Town and Country Planning* Vol. XXX No. 3 March 1962 118.
53 The following figures for percentage turn-out allow some sort of comparative perspective on participation in municipal elections:

Area	*Election and per cent turn-out*							
	1945	*1947*	*1949*	*1951*	*1953*	*1955*	*1957*	*1959*
All County Boroughs in England and Wales	45.6	52.6	52.2	44.4	45.2	43.8	40.0	41.0
Coventry	44.4	54.2	57.3	50.2	44.7	51.0	45.7	47.4

(Source: Registrar General's *Statistical Review of England and Wales*, various editions.)
54 See, for example, the *Standard* 15/12/1945.
55 See the tabulated listing at JN 711 in the Local Studies Section, Coventry City Library.
56 CRO AP/CF/1/209L (ii) 'Frequency of Comments – Ward Meetings' 15/5/1962.
57 See, for example, the *Standard* 14/6/57 on Bell Green: 'The most striking fact is that most of the new residents are well satisfied with their homes and there is a general atmosphere of contentment on the estate.'
58 See, for example, MRC MSS 11/3/6/429 Letter R. B. Ritchie–J. Latham 8/7/1955.
59 The newly appointed Vicar of Binley, quoted in the *Standard* 1/2/1952.
60 *Standard* 22/2/1952.
61 *Standard* 21/8/1959.
62 MRC MSS 11/3/4/109 G. Hodgkinson–W. H. Smith 10/10/1955.
63 MRC MSS 11/3/6/27 R. B. Ritchie 'Half Yearly Report' 3/12/1954 p. 1.
64 See F. Carr 'Engineering Workers and the Rise of Labour in Coventry 1914–1939' (unpublished Ph.D. dissertation, University of Warwick, 1978) p. 367
65 Quoted in the booklet 'Welcome to Citizenship. Coventry 13–14/10/1960', CRO Sec/CF/1/14973.
66 The following two paragraphs are based on a reading of the *Coventry Tribune*, Labour's paper which was published between 1946 and 1948. See especially the issue of 10/1/1948.
67 See, for example, the *Coventry Tribune* 29/3/1947: 'The electorate contains thousands who show no intelligence when it comes to paying extra rates.'
68 This table is assembled from information in CRO Sec/CF/1/14817.
69 This table is assembled from information in CRO Sec/CF/1/14817.
70 See Crossman's introduction to G. Hodgkinson *Sent to Coventry* (1970) pp. xvii and xxvii; and Morgan op. cit. 580 and 622.
71 This table relates to the 61 candidates whose trade union affiliations are clear, out of the total of 86 people who appear one or two times on the candidates' listings of 1949, 1952, 1953, 1955, 1956, 1958 and 1959. See MRC MSS 11/3/42.
72 MRC MSS 11/3/6/566 Letter Ritchie–F. Allaun: 'we have always had very close relations as a Labour Party with the shop stewards' movement.

Indeed our relations with the shop stewards' movement have been much closer than our relations with the full-time trade union officials, although those, of course, are quite cordial'.

73 For more information on Hodgkinson, see his autobiography, cited in note 68 (above). Stringer left few records, and biographical information on him is scarce; but see the brief profile in MRC MSS 11/3/28/301.

Index